Taking Out
Your
Mental Trash

Taking Out Your Mental Trash

A Consumer's Guide to Cognitive Restructuring Therapy

Rian E. McMullin

W. W. Norton & Company

New York · London

Copyright ©2005 by Rian McMullin

For information about permission to reproduce selections from this book,
write to Permissions, W. W. Norton & Company, Inc., 500 Fifth Avenue,
New York, NY 10110.

Manufacturing by Hamilton Printing
Book design and composition by Charlotte Staub
Production manager: Leeann Graham

Library of Congress Cataloging-in-Publication Data

McMullin, Rian E.
        Taking out your mental trash : a consumer's guide to cognitive
restructuring therapy / Rian McMullin
                p. cm.
        "A Norton professional book"
        Includes bibliographical references and index.
        ISBN 0-393-70487-4
            1. Cognitive therapy. 2. Behavior therapy. I. Title
RC489.C63M365 2005
616.89'142—dc22   2005048829

ISBN 0-393-70487-4 (PBK.)

W. W. Norton & Company, Inc., 500 Fifth Avenue, New York, NY 10110
www.wwnorton.com

W. W. Norton & Company, Ltd., Castle House, 75/76 Wells St., London W1T 3QT

    2   3   4   5   6   7   8   9   0

An ounce of blood is worth more than a pound of friendship. SPANISH PROVERB

I dedicate this book to all my families:

To my wife Robyn Strike McMullin and her Australian relatives:
 her mother, Marie Strike
 her brother and sister-in-law, Peter and Gai Strike and their children,
   Katelyn and Mitchell
 her sister and brother-in-law, Leanne and Peter Boss, and
   Nathan, Daniel, and Matthew
 her sister and brother-in-law, Jenny and Richard Burns and
   James, Joshua, and Amelia

To my daughter and son-in-law, Linda and Rick Bobbitt and my grandsons,
 Danny and Chris

To my daughter Michele Ryan

To my sister and brother-in-law, Anne and Jim Barilla

To my brother and sister-in-law, Tom and Ruth McMullin and their son and
 daughter-in-law, David and Ming Ming McMullin

To my sister and brother-in-law, Kathy and Tom McCann and their children
 and grandchildren:
   Tom and Lisa McCann—T. J., Tyler, and Annelies
   Peggy and Tim Kelly—Keegan, Kathryn Grace, and Brendan
   Mike and Mary McCann—Michael, Mary Kate, Kayla, and Bob
   Katie and Jack Tawney—Sarah and Matthew
   Kristin and Chris Cuomo—Megan, Christopher, and Katelyn
   Mariryan and Brandon Starr

Contents

Preface

Prefaces wear many disguises, call themselves by various names, and pretend to come on various businesses . . . but their errand is always the same; they are there to apologize for the book; in other words, furnish reasons for its publication. MARK TWAIN

My excuse for writing this book is to offer the consumer what has previously been available only to professional audiences. This book is a layperson's guide for my professional works, particularly *The New Handbook of Cognitive Restructuring Therapy Techniques* (McMullin, 2000).

You can use this book as a guide to counseling or as an introduction to Cognitive Restructuring Therapy (CRT). It provides a straightforward explanation of my approach.

I present 48 short chapters, each with similar sections. To aid the reader I sprinkle icons throughout the text. Chapters begin with a discussion of the key concept, followed by an illustration of the concept in the form of a brief story, an analogy, or a composite case example from some of my clients. I then move to the key section of the chapter—the exercise. I provide 52 exercises in this book, offered in a step-by-step fashion with examples and illustrations. If you want to get the true feel for CRT, it is important to do the exercises, not just read about them. Worksheets are given for about half of the exercises. Feel free to make copies so you can use them again. For a few chapters, I provide a footnote or reference, but I have tried to keep these to an absolute minimum. If you are interested in more details, or your wish to find the sources for my ideas, I recommend that you look at one of my textbooks, especially the *New Handbook*.

How This Book Is Organized

The book is divided into six parts, and each part presents a key area of CRT. Because much of the later chapters are based on the earlier material, exercises, and worksheets, it is important that you read all of part I first.

Part I: ABCs

The first part consists of seven chapters, and the basic foundation of CRT is presented. You should read all the chapters, even if you are in therapy or are familiar with cognitive theory. Most important, this section presents the core exercises and worksheets that you will use for the rest of the book.

Part II: Types of Mistaken Beliefs

Here I present the 11 most common categories of beliefs that cause people the most problems. If you are a client in counseling, your therapist may suggest which ones to read. If you are reading this book on your own, you may decide which type of thinking is relevant for you. You should become familiar with all of them in case you find yourself some day thinking in this way.

Part III: Analyzing Your Beliefs

After you have identified your key beliefs, values, and attitudes, you will want to make a decision about which beliefs are damaging and had best be thrown into the trash and which ones are useful and had best be kept. The six chapters in this section will give you some tools to help you make this decision. Everyone should read at least the first and last chapters (Chapters 19 and 24).

Part IV: Changing Beliefs

Most people want to start here with how to correct their problems. The eight chapters in this section give you some core CRT techniques. You should read Chapter 25, "Countering," Chapter 30, "Quantum Leaps," Chapter 31, "Living by Our Core Values," and Chapter 32, "Beyond Payoffs." Read any others that interest you, of course. If you are in counseling, your therapist will select the chapters that will best help you and offer you advanced procedures that are beyond the scope of this introductory guide. The techniques in this part will be helpful only if you have done the preparatory work.

Part V: Seven Beliefs To Be Trashed

In this part I picked seven specific beliefs that have caused trouble for many people. I provide some of the strongest counterarguments against these damaging thoughts. Read those that you believe may be relevant to you.

Part VI: Specific Problems

Most people are aware that they have a problem, but they are unaware of the cause. Here I present some common problems such as anxiety, difficulties getting along with others, depression, and problems with intimate relationships. I don't cover the problems completely; my only purpose here is to give you a new way of looking at them that may help you cope with them. Read those that have been assigned to you, or that you believe may be relevant.

Appendices

For those readers who want to know more about my background, I have provided some information in Appendix A, "About the Author." For those professional therapists or counselors who may wish to use this book as a client manual, I offer guidelines in Appendix B, "To the Professional Therapist."

What This Book Can't Do

As the subtitle suggests, this book is a consumer's guide to CRT. It is meant to accompany counseling. However, I am fully aware that many people will read it independently. I wish to remind these readers that this is an introductory guide and includes only a very small percentage of the procedures and techniques a counselor could provide. This book may still help people who read it on their own, but it cannot begin to replace the individual attention, feedback, and human contact that can only be provided in face-to-face counseling.

I hope you find this Guide helpful.

Rian McMullin, Ph.D.
Kaneohe, Hawaii

Part I

ABCs

Painting Our Own Pictures

No man lives in the external truth among salts and acids, but in the warm, phantasmagoric chamber of his brain, with the painted windows and the storied wall.
ROBERT LOUIS STEVENSON

IN THIS CHAPTER
- An overview of the essential outlook of Cognitive Restructuring Therapy (CRT)
- An analogy about the human brain showing how CRT is different from many other therapeutic approaches
- Focusing on a reversible image

Some people use the analogy of a computer to explain how the human brain operates. They believe that the brain is a computerlike machine. Moreover, they assume that the brain is like an exceedingly elaborate computer, and suppose that it processes information, gathers and analyzes data, and stores information in gigabytes of memory. This is not the case.

The brain is radically different from a computer. It changes, develops, and secretes chemicals. It isn't a mechanism that clicks, buzzes, and whirrs. It isn't a machine at all. It's alive.

The brain is a marvelous living thing. It accepts, stores, and retrieves data, but it also does much more. What's marvelous about it is that it dramatically transforms data. It reaches far beyond the information available and creates a whole new world. It consumes raw bits of information and transforms them into intricate patterns, themes, and stories.

Our brain functions far more like an artist painting a picture than like a computer running a program. Through its pictures we see, feel, and touch the world. Like the artist, our brain collects various materials to paint. It grabs magenta memories, mixes them with cyan emotions, and gathers some green from instincts, and some brown, yellow, and white from our senses. It doesn't just throw these colors randomly on the palette of our mind. It composes panoramic scenes, portraits, dramas, triumphs, and tragedies with its brush strokes.

Sometimes the pictures it paints are masterpieces of creativity and imagination. The theories of Albert Einstein, Thomas Jefferson, and John Stuart Mill are as much works of art as the paintings of Nicolas Poussin, Claude Monet, and Vincent van Gogh. The creations of these brains can enrich and ennoble our lives, giving us new ways to perceive the world we live in.

Other brains can paint bizarre disturbing portraits of the upsetting sides of life. The philosopher Frederick Nietzsche and the artist William Blake generate the same feeling of horror in some people, but we need to see these views also, because life's disturbing aspects may also be enriching.

We are all artists. Our paintings determine whether we will feel happy or sad, enraged or broken-hearted, or enraptured. The world doesn't create our emotions; our brain does. Sometimes our paintings are so disturbing that they give us pain. They can hurt us so badly that we can have trouble functioning effectively.

It's not so much that some of us don't know how to draw, or that we paint bungled and botched pictures; it's more that some of us have never learned to draw our own pictures. We grew up trying to copy other people's paintings; or worse, we learned to paint by the numbers. As adults we try to pass off these forgeries as our own. We have never learned to paint our own visions based on our own life experiences.

Homework

I have found that the best way to explain CRT is to show you rather than just tell you. All the exercises in this book are carefully chosen to give you an experience about the concepts being presented. They are all designed to help you gain insight and understanding of the key concept in each chapter. To develop this insight, it is important that you do them.

There is only one exercise for this chapter. Its purpose is to show you how your own brain works. It consists of a reversible drawing—a picture that contains two images, depending on how you perceive the drawing. It is a famous picture that has been published many times—you may have seen it before (Hill, 1915). A British magazine, *Puck*, originally published it in 1915 and called it, "My Wife and My Mother-in-Law" (those were more chauvinistic times). It has also been called "The Old Woman and the Young Woman."

The exercise isn't just a silly little puzzle; it illustrates how we transform all that we see. We view the universe based on these transformations. What we think of ourselves, how we experience others, what we deem as good or bad, beautiful or ugly; what makes us laugh or cry, what makes us hate, what makes us love; all are based on the pictures we create.

What brains we have! Linguistics professor George Lakoff (1987) has noted that "the mind is more than a mere mirror of nature or a processor of symbols, . . . the capacity for understanding and meaningful thought goes beyond what any machine can do" (p. xvii).

 EXERCISE **1.1 Reversible Image**

Step 1. Look at Figure 1.1 and try to see both the young woman and the old woman.[1]

Step 2. Practice switching from one image to the other until you can do this easily and quickly. Now see if you can discover how you were able to switch the image. What were you doing in your brain that enabled you to transform this drawing?

Step 3. Write down your answers to the following ideas.

How were you able to switch? _____

Figure 1.1 The old woman and the young woman

If you think it was where you looked on the picture, see if you can shift the images by looking at the same spot. _____

_____

_____

If you think it was the image you pictured in your mind's eye, try to shift the image without thinking of any prototype. _____

_____

_____

What other things did you do to make the images shift? _____

_____

_____

Taking Out Your Mental Trash

Review of Exercise

We perceive one image or the other, not because of the picture but because of our brains. The brain isn't just a computer; it doesn't just add up the raw data in the picture; it transforms the picture. I don't think any computer could interpret this picture so, but our brain can, instantaneously and automatically. Our brain takes the lines and shadows in the drawing and combines them with our memories of similar drawings. It is we who create the theme, young woman or old woman.

 The most important thing to realize is that neither the old woman nor the young woman is actually in the picture. The picture is really just a series of ink spots on a piece of paper, nothing more. We may see the young woman or we may see the old, but it is not a sign that we are sick if we see one thing or that we're stupid if we see another. We create the image based on the tapestry of our own visual memories. The ink spots are the canvas; we are the artist.[2]

---

[1] If you had difficulty seeing both images, some hints may help. The tip of the nose of the old woman is the tip of the chin of the young woman. The ear of the young woman is the eye of the old. The mouth of the old woman is the neck band of the young. The young woman is looking away while the old woman is looking toward you.

[2] There may be some hidden images in the trash can on the book cover. Can you find any?

chapter **2**

The ABCs of Cognitive Restructuring Therapy

We all do no end of feeling and we mistake it for thinking.   MARK TWAIN

To solve a problem we try to find the cause of it. If our car doesn't run, we check to see if it has gas, the battery works, or the wires are connected. If we flip the light switch but the bulb doesn't light, we check the bulb or the fuse. We correct problems based on the causes that we find.

This sounds so obvious that it doesn't even seem worth mentioning; but when it comes to our emotional problems, many of us ignore the obvious. We recognize that we all get upset at times. We know we all occasionally feel anxious, scared, angry, or depressed. We accept that everyone some-times depreciates his or her self, damns other people, or feels that certain life conditions have become intolerable. So, what do most of us do when we have one of these emotional outbursts? Do we carefully go out and look for the causes?

Not usually. Many of us try to discover the causes of our feelings in a hel-ter-skelter way until by luck we stumble across an answer, or more likely, we collapse from exhaustion and conclude that the problem is unsolvable. Because emotional problems are the same as any other kind, if we don't identify the correct cause, we won't solve the problem, and we will still feel the painful emotion. But how do we find the causes of emotional problems?

The fields of psychology and psychiatry have so many different theories about causes that it is easy to get confused. It may be helpful to start with two simple formulas. Learning and memorizing them now will save you much time and effort later on.

Old Formula

$$A \xrightarrow{\hspace{4cm}} C$$

- *A* stands for an activating event: the situation we are in, a trigger in the environment, a stimulus, anything that starts the whole process of reacting.
- *C* stands for our reactions—our emotions and our behavior. *C*s appear to be the consequences of *A*s.

The old theory asserts that *A*s cause *C*s, that situations in our environment cause our emotions. So, when we get upset about something, we immediately look outside ourselves to see what might be causing the feeling. Consider the following example:

Unknown Anxiety

EXAMPLE

Imagine one Sunday afternoon you are sitting in your chair reading the paper when suddenly you start feeling anxious. The fear is strong, seems real, and it bothers you. You know the *C* immediately. You feel it. Your heart is beating faster, your breathing is rapid and forced, and you feel hot and are perspiring. You have a desire to get up and move around, or even better, to run. It's hard to just sit there in the chair but there's no place to run and nothing to run from. This is the *C* in our formula—fear. Of course, *C*s can be any emotion—anger, sadness, panic, and frustration—but for our example, let us say you are feeling anxious.

The question that would probably leap into your mind this Sunday afternoon is, "Why? Why am I suddenly feeling scared about something, and what am I scared about?"

The old formula offers an answer. It is your *A*—the situation you are in. It's what a videocamera would record if it were viewing your situation with no interpretation and no feeling. The camera would only record the sights and sounds that were occurring while you were sitting in your chair. Was the television or radio on? What program was being shown? Were you reading the paper? What were you reading? Were other people in the room and, if so, were they talking or looking at you? Where you eating or drinking something? What were the sounds outside? Were you looking at something or staring off into space? All these and more are the *As*.

Now according to this old formula, you would look at your *As* to see what is causing your fear. The old theory suggests that some *A* caused your fear, and that if you look very carefully you may be able to find it. Once you do, you only need to remove the offending *A* and your fear should dissolve.

This *A*-causes-*C* theory is so popular that we hear it all the time. Do you still think that the old woman/young woman was really in the picture? How many times have you heard people say, "You really made me angry," "He got me upset," or "The news really depressed me"? All these statements imply that some outside *As* caused us to feel some inside *Cs*. The idea is so universal that it seems like common sense. But is it true?

No! Outside things exert little power over us. Our senses make us aware of the outside world. If we close our eyes or cover our ears, the external world disappears and its effect on us is minimal. If we can't detect an object with one of our senses, the object can't make us laugh or cry, run away, or sing or dance. Outside things have no magical powers—they can't sneak inside our heads and create our feelings. They simply sit in sensory darkness waiting to be observed by us.

The correct formula is what follows. It is simple and has been stated many times before, but it is so essential to our understanding of ourselves that it is worth memorizing. It was created by one of the world's most famous psychologists—Albert Ellis, the author of over 77 books and the father of modern cognitive therapy (Ellis, 2004a). Others have tried to improve upon this formula, but it is still one of the best ways to explain the cause of our emotions.

New Formula

$$A \longrightarrow B \longrightarrow C$$

B represents cognitions, beliefs, and attitudes

As you can see, we have added an additional letter—B. It represents several things: our beliefs about the situation, our thoughts, imaginations, perceptions, conclusions, and interpretations or seeing an old/young woman in a reversible drawing. But mostly, *B* stands for our brain, how our brain takes the raw information about the *As* and molds this raw data into patterns, schemata, themes, stories, or images.

Almost all of your emotions and behavior can be understood by using this new formula. So, instead of simply looking at our *A*s, we had best look at the *B*s (the cognitions we had about the *A*s) that created our reactions.

The following example illustrates this principle.

THE OLD WOMAN AND THE YOUNG WOMAN

EXAMPLE

When we looked at Figure 1.1 in the first exercise, some of us may not have noticed all the *B*s that fed into our final perception There were many. Some of them were:

- figure and ground
- assumption
- memory
- instructions (from self or others)
- expectations
- self-efficacy
- trial and error

First, we looked at the ink spots on the paper to determine what was *figure and ground*. We are used to reading black letters on white paper so we probably looked for a pattern within the black spots. (This *assumption* can sometimes be mistaken, as demonstrated by the example in Figure 2.1 below.)

WHAT IS THIS?

EXAMPLE

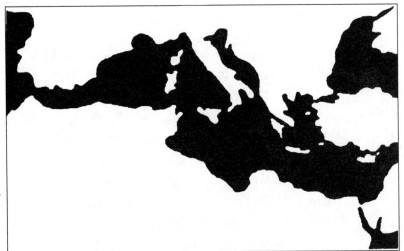

Figure 2.1
What is this?
(Block & Yuker, 1989)

Next, we searched though our *memory* to recall if we had ever seen a similar pattern before. Because we were *instructed* to try to find an old or young woman, we had a certain *expectation* about what to look for, so we reviewed our memory of drawings of an old and a young woman to find a match. If we are good at visual puzzles, we had high *self-efficacy* that we would be able to find the image and this encouraged us to keep on looking. Finally, through *trial and error* we kept changing the way we looked at the drawing until we were able to see both images. All these *B*s could have happened in less than a second.

Homework

The following exercise should help you distinguish among *A*s (situations), *B*s (beliefs), and *C*s (emotions and behaviors). It is a necessary precursor for all the other exercises in the book.

 EXERCISE ### 2.1 List of Daily Beliefs

Use Worksheet 2.1, Daily List of ABCs

Step 1. Identify the strongest negative emotion you have had during the last 24 hours. You may have had many, but choose the strongest. Look for emotions such as fear, sadness, or anger. Allow yourself to recapture enough of the emotion to be able to identify it.

Strongest Emotion (C): _____

Step 2. Next, recall what was happening in your environment at the time. What was occurring right before you felt the emotion? Be sure not to include any of your thoughts at this point. Your environment is what a stationary TV camera would pick up if it were observing the scene. The camera wouldn't interpret what it saw; it would simply record it.

To find the precise environment, you may need to pinpoint the exact time that you felt the emotion. If the time is not readily apparent, review your activities for the last 24 hours. Begin when you woke up and visualize in detail what you did. Keep reviewing the day, until you first notice the emotion. When you find the correct time, review everything going on around you while you were feeling the emotion. What were you looking at? What sounds did you hear? Were there any smells or tastes present? Were there any internal sensations you were having right before the emotion occurred, such as an upset stomach, arm pain, a feeling of dizziness?

Situation (A): _____

_____

_____

_____

Step 3. Finally, find your belief. What did you tell yourself in the situation that may have caused you to feel the emotion? In most cases, you will have told yourself many things. Try to find the key sentence that passed through your mind.

If you are not sure, go ahead and guess. You will know that you've found the right belief if it serves as a bridge between the environment and your feeling. If you can imagine everyone who holds that belief feeling the same emotion, then you probably found the correct one. If someone else could have had the same thought but wouldn't feel the emotion, then you haven't found the correct belief and need to keep on searching. (The next few chapters will help identify the type of *B*s to look for).

Belief (B): _____

_____

_____

_____

2.1 Daily List of ABCs

Date:

MONDAY *Strongest Emotion (C):* _____

Situation (A): _____

Belief (B): _____

TUESDAY *Strongest Emotion (C):* _____

Situation (A): _____

Belief (B): _____

WEDNESDAY *Strongest Emotion (C):* _____

Situation (A): _____

Belief (B): _____

THURSDAY *Strongest Emotion (C):* _____

Situation (A): _____

Belief (B): _____

FRIDAY *Strongest Emotion (C):* _____

Situation (A): _____

Belief (B): _____

SATURDAY *Strongest Emotion (C):* _____

Situation (A): _____

Belief (B): _____

SUNDAY *Strongest Emotion (C):* _____

Situation (A): _____

Belief (B): _____

Examples of Homework

Example 1. Bill is a 34-year-old junior executive

Strongest Emotion (C): Anger

Situation (A): At 3:15 in the afternoon, Bill's boss called him into his office and criticized him for turning in a report late.

Belief (B): "It is unfair that he criticized me. My secretary didn't have it done on time. He is always trying to catch me making mistakes."

You may think that the boss's criticism caused Bill's anger, but in truth, it's what Bill believed about the criticism that counts. Had he thought the criticism valid, he might have felt guilty or worried, but anger was felt only when his brain created the belief that the criticism was "unfair." His core thought was the belief that the world should be fair, and that it is terrible if people are unfair. If he keeps expecting and demanding the world to be fair, he will be angry most of the time.

Example 2. Barbara is an attractive, thin, 25-year-old single woman

Strongest Emotion (C): Depression

Situation (A): Barbara was looking at her body in the mirror after she got out of the shower.

Belief (B): "Look how fat I am! It's horrible!"

Some would think that the visual impact of seeing a fat body is responsible for Barbara's response. Who wouldn't be upset? The answer is, many people.

Barbara had to believe many things in order to get upset. First, she had to tell herself that there is an ideal female weight (a cultural standard that constantly changes) and that she has an obligation to be this weight. The origin of this sense of obligation is a mystery.

More importantly, Barbara had to conclude that she had crossed an imaginary line into what she believes is an unacceptable weight, and she had to have told herself that it's terrible to be over this line. The effect of her reflection in the mirror pales in comparison to all the thoughts required to get her upset. The weight of her thoughts, not her body, caused her depression.

Example 3. John is a married, middle-aged man who worries constantly about his health

Strongest Emotion (C): Fear

Situation (A): John felt a pain in his stomach.

Belief (B): "It must be stomach cancer, just like my uncle."

Even something as basic as pain is interpreted by our brain. If our muscles are sore after a heavy workout, we may judge the pain as a sign that our workout was successful. The pain of childbirth may be far greater than the pain of disease, but the latter is far more onerous because the brain interprets the two pains in quite different ways—one brings forth life, the other may destroy it. John became afraid not because he felt pain, but because he interpreted the pain as the worst thing he could imagine—cancer. If John keeps looking for the worst consequences of everything he can imagine, he will be in a constant state of fear.

 Our thoughts are the cause of our emotions. When we feel scared, depressed, or frustrated and want to know what causes these feelings, we can use the above exercise to find out. The exercise and its extensions can ultimately help us change the upsetting emotions that cause ongoing disruptions in our lives.

chapter 3

Our Mighty Thoughts
The Royal Road to Self-improvement

Men are disturbed not by things, but by the views which they take of them.
EPICTETUS

IN THIS CHAPTER
- Three exercises show how beliefs and attitudes can cause emotions and feelings

Most people aren't persuaded that their beliefs (*Bs*) alone can cause their upset feelings. They still think the view expressed in the above quote is counterintuitive. They believe that other people, places, or things, *make* them upset, that the problem is outside their thoughts, in their environment, their surroundings, or in their inherited nature.

Many people think so. They may blame their genes, how their parents treated them, traumatic events that happened when they were young, rotten luck, their unconscious, living in a dysfunctional society, or that they are just a rotten person. They think that almost anything—except their own thinking—causes their emotional upset.

This truth has been recognized for centuries, even though many people have stumbled over it, picked themselves up, and brushed themselves off pretending nothing had happened. It's not primarily the world, our environment, our biochemistry, or any other external force that causes us to feel things; it's our own brains. It's the way we have learned to look at things; what we tell ourselves, our perceptions, conclusions, and judgments. It's the organ in our head that takes in data, a big stew of raw information, puts it all together in a pattern, and gives the whole world meaning. Sometimes the patterns we create make us feel worthwhile. Sometimes the patterns cause us to feel pain or act meanly toward others. Whatever it is that we feel, it's always the way our brain puts things together, not the things themselves, that cause our emotions.

 The reason some of us miss this truth is evident. Our thoughts occur so rapidly and seem so fleeting that most of us don't notice that we are thinking anything at all. All we perceive is that something objective, concrete, and easy to see is happening in the environment; then we feel an emotion which is palpable and intense. We ignore transient thoughts in the process.

So, the fault lies not in our stars, but in our brains. The major reason we feel inappropriately upset is that some of our beliefs are flawed, especially our attitude about the world. The world is fine just the way it is. We need to convince ourselves that the faint little voice we hear inside our head is the culprit. This is necessary if we are to manage our lives effectively.

Homework

If you are still not convinced that your beliefs are all that powerful, the following exercises present further evidence for you to consider.

 ### 3.1 A Day at the Beach

Imagine for a moment that you are walking alone on a tropical beach. It is midsummer and very warm. It is late in the afternoon. The sun has not yet begun to set, but it is getting low on the horizon. You feel the cool, hard-packed sand beneath your feet. You hear the cry of seagulls and the roar of ocean waves in the distance. You can smell and taste the salt in the air. As you continue to walk, the sky turns crimson, gold, and amber. There is an afterglow of rainbow colors glistening around the palm trees. The sun is beginning to set into the ocean. The sky turns blue, then turquoise; soon you are enveloped in a deep purple twilight. A cool breeze comes off the ocean. You lie down on a sand dune and look up at the night sky. It's a brilliant starry night. You feel surrounded by the cosmos. A deep sense of calm and peace overtakes you. You feel at one with the universe.

While reading this, how did you feel? _____

If you felt calm, it is because your imagination created the calm. Your biochemistry, unconscious, present environment, or early experiences were the same when reading this as before. What changed were your thoughts.

If you didn't feel calm at all, it's your imagination just the same.

To prove it, imagine this: Suppose you had this type of internal dialogue when reading the passage, "I am walking on a tropical beach," But instead of thinking about the beach, you thought, "No I'm not! I am really sitting at home in a chair."

Or when reading, "It's in the middle of summer and very warm," you told yourself, "Nonsense, it's freezing cold outside."

You read, "I hear the cry of sea gulls and the roar of ocean waves in the distance," but you thought, "That's silly. All I hear are my kids fighting in the next room."

You read, "The sun is beginning to set in the ocean," but imagined instead, "Idiot! The sun doesn't set in the ocean; besides I live in Kansas."

It doesn't matter what you read, it only matters what you thought. If you thought these things to yourself, there is no way you would have felt calm.

While reading the scene, you can create any emotion you want. For instance, you will create anger if you think, "Last time I walked on a beach I was with Bruno before he left me for that idiot Fifi." You can create fear if while reading, "A cool breeze comes off the ocean," you imagine, "Poisonous jelly fish are creeping onto the shore, dragging their slimy bodies behind. They encircle me, waving their rancid tentacles at my legs, grabbing, grasping for me. I run but can't escape."

You can create any emotion you wish. All you have to do is think it. So, it's not the words on the page, your present environment, or your past that creates these feelings. It's what your brain does with the scene; it's what you choose to think; it's what you wish to imagine.

EXERCISE

3.2 Lunch at Work

Imagine you are sitting in a cafeteria at work and you see two colleagues talking in whispers and occasionally glancing in your direction.

What are you feeling? _____

What you feel is dependent on what you tell yourself. If you think, "How terribly rude they are talking about me behind my back," you may feel angry. If you think, "They must have found out about the mistake I made yesterday on the Hutchinson account," you may feel guilty. If you believe they are planning a surprise party for your birthday next week, you may feel happy. The environment is the same in all cases. Your different beliefs alone produce the different emotions.

EXERCISE 3.3 Seeing a Snake

Imagine that you are sitting on a playground swing. You suddenly look down and see a snake coiled around your legs.

What do you feel? _____

Unless you like snakes, you will probably be upset. Impulses from your brain send neural–chemical messages to your endocrine glands. These release hormones into your bloodstream that produce metabolic changes. They signal your muscles and limbs and cause you to have a startle response. If someone asks you why you are upset, you may breathlessly point to the snake.

It looks like a clear environmental cause. You see the snake (*A*, the trigger) that causes you to become afraid (*C*, the feeling). But if a small boy came over, picked up the snake, and showed you that it was a rubber snake, would you still be afraid? In most cases, probably not.

What's the difference? The trigger is the same; you still see the snake lying at your feet, but you feel differently. What changes is what you think (your *B*). In the first case, you probably instantaneously thought several things: "It is a snake. It is real. It may be poisonous. It could harm me." Remember, although it can take several seconds to read these thoughts, you could have thought them all in a millisecond. In the second situation you probably thought, "It's a toy snake. Toy snakes can't hurt me. I have no reason to be upset."

Seeing the snake didn't make you feel anything at all; it's what you said to yourself about what you saw that made the difference.

chapter 4

Emotions
How to Discover Our Feelings

Cherish your own emotions and never undervalue them. ROBERT HENRI

IN THIS CHAPTER
- Understanding the importance of emotions in CRT
- Using an analogy of colors
- Assessing the strength of emotions

People unfamiliar with cognitive therapy often have the misconception that it deemphasizes the importance of emotions in favor of cognitions. It is an understandable mistake because of the word *cognitive* in CRT. But CRT fully recognizes the importance of emotions and accepts that feelings are the starting point for all of us. We do not get upset because we are worried about our irrational thoughts or because we are unsure whether our beliefs are true or false. Instead, we get distressed because we feel anxious, fearful, panicky, depressed, or some other unpleasant emotion.

Therefore, your starting point of CRT is not to focus on your thinking, but rather on your feelings. The first step for you is to discover exactly what you are feeling and to give it precisely the right name. You might legitimately ask, "So what if I don't know the correct word for my emotions? What does it matter?" My feelings are still the same, they still hurt, and whatever causes them is still there, so it really doesn't matter if I call an emotion by one name or another.

Surprisingly, it does matter. In fact, it matters a great deal. What we call an emotion is important, because the label we give it tells us how to handle the feeling and what action to take. For example, if we label an emotion as fear, we will look hurriedly around to find out what may be dangerous, and because we call it fear we will look for a way to protect ourselves or run away. On the other hand, if we label an emotion as anger our whole temperament will change. We will look out sternly to see who it is that has caused our anger. Instead of running away, we will angrily approach the person and demand that they stop. If we label an emotion as a higher state of emotional arousal caused by the fact that we drank 10 cups of coffee, we won't do anything about it; we won't run away or attack. Instead, we will stop drinking coffee, take time to relax, and wait for the stimulant to wear off.

 Therefore, it is very important that we label an emotion correctly, because the name we bestow upon it tells us precisely what to do about it. It tells us whether we should stop everything else we are doing to try to remove the feeling or whether we should ignore it and go on about our daily activities.

In this way our emotions are like another sense, like seeing, hearing, smelling, or tasting, all of which tell us about the world. The other senses tell us about the outside environment. Our emotions are an inner sense that tells us what is happening inside of us. It can be a very useful sense. It can tell us about things that we have no knowledge of otherwise. Fear can tell us of a danger that has snuck in underneath our radar that we haven't seen or heard. Grief can remind us of the severity of a loss that we have not allowed ourselves to be aware of. Anger can show us that someone is trying to attack us even though this attack cannot be seen, heard, or directly observed.

Understanding Emotions

It may seem difficult to understand emotions because they seem so vague and wispy. They are not concrete objects that we can see, hear, taste, or smell. Instead, they are vague feelings inside of us that get stronger or weaker and may change from one to the other. They can be very difficult to label.

It may help us to look at emotions in the way that we look at colors. You may know that all colors are made up of three primary colors—red, yellow, and blue. The great variety of other colors (the hundreds of other shades and hues we have), come from blending these basic three. It is a highly complex process, but to greatly simplify it: if we mix yellow with blue, we get green. If we mix red and blue, we get purple. Another way of getting more colors is by increasing the intensity of the color. For instance, a light hue of red would give us pink, while a dark intensity gives us scarlet. We could have a light sky

Taking Out Your Mental Trash

blue, but if we increase its intensity and go up the strength scale, we would create dark navy blue.

 Emotions are like colors. Our culture and our language even recognize this fact. For instance, we associate anger with the color red, "He was red with rage." For fear we think of yellow, "He is a yellow-bellied coward!" We connect depression or sadness with the color blue, "Martha has the blues." So there's a correlation, a correspondence between the three basic colors and the three basic negative emotions: red equals anger; sadness equals blue; and fear equals yellow.

Like colors, mixing our primary feelings of anger, fear, and sadness can make all the various nuances and shades of emotions. We get secondary emotions by mixing two primary ones; for example, we get envy if we mix sorrow (blue) with fear (yellow). Our language also recognizes this when it says, "George was green with envy."

We can also get different emotions by varying their strength. Some of the words we use for emotions show different strengths as demonstrated by the following scales.

FEAR

low		medium		high
concern	worry	fear	panic	terror

ANGER

low		medium		high
irritation	annoyance	anger	hate	rage

SADNESS

low		medium		high
boredom	discouragement	depression	dejection	despair

Figure 4.1 Different emotional strengths

If you wish to know what you are feeling, you can use colors as a guide. To find your negative emotions, you first need to identify the mix of your primary colors—fear, anger, and sadness. Next, you need to determine each color's strength.

Homework

The following exercise has been designed to take you step by step through the process. It is based on the work of Eugene Gendlin (1996).

EXERCISE ### 4.1 Focus on the Colors of Your Feelings

Read the complete exercise before you start.

Step 1. Relax and close your eyes. Be silent with yourself. Take a moment just to relax. Pay close attention to a very special part of you, that part where you usually feel emotions like fear, or anger, or sadness. See what comes when you ask yourself, "How am I now? How do I feel? What is the main feeling for me right now?" Let the emotion come, whatever way it comes to you, and see how it is. Take about a minute to do this.

What did you feel? _____

Step 2. Keep focusing on that place inside yourself, where you feel things, but this time focus on each of your primary emotions. Do them one at a time. Ask yourself if there is an element of fear (yellow) in what you feel. Now, try the right word that accurately describes what you sensed. Use the scales to find exactly the right word. Don't just make up a word, let the word come naturally as you focus on your feeling. Look for a click between the feeling and the words. Keep switching back and forth between the words you come up with and your felt sense. Keep doing it until you feel, "Yes, that's it; that is what I am feeling."

What did you feel? _____

Step 3. Focus on your other primary negative emotions in the same way: anger (red), sadness (blue). Is there an element of anger or sadness in what you are feeling? Try to find the right words to indicate the amount and strength of each emotion.

What did you feel? _____

Step 4. Now, using the scales on the next page, rate how strongly you felt the emotions.

If you felt fear, how much fear? (Put an "X" on the spot.)

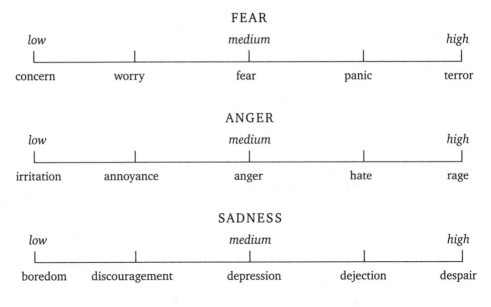

FEAR

low		medium		high
concern	worry	fear	panic	terror

ANGER

low		medium		high
irritation	annoyance	anger	hate	rage

SADNESS

low		medium		high
boredom	discouragement	depression	dejection	despair

Figure 4.2 Rating your emotions

There are many variations to this exercise. You have been given only the basic procedure. Some extensions are:

- Focus on the positive as well as negative emotions (happiness, joy, peacefulness, contentment, excitement, or pleasure).
- You can describe what you're feeling in terms of phrases and sentences. ("This feeling that I have inside of me is like a string tightening.")
- You can focus on another aspect of the emotion rather than its strength, like does it feel hard or soft, sticky or loose, vague or solid, hot or cold?
- Does the emotion change or merge into other emotions as you continue to focus on it?
- Does it become stronger or weaker after you name it?

 Heed this note of caution. This exercise can uncover some deep feelings. At such times, you should talk to your therapist or if you are not in counseling, you may find it useful to have an empathetic listener to help you get through some of the tougher parts. You need to repeat the basic exercise many times until you can do it smoothly before moving on to the extensions. Do the exercise only when you feel ready and only if you feel comfortable doing so.

EXAMPLE

THE STORY OF LESTER

Lester was a single businessman in his 40s who was having a great deal of difficulty with his romantic relationships. His past was littered with a succession of botched and bungled romances. When he thought about them he was unable to identify exactly what had happened. He described them in a very confused, discordant manner.

He did the focusing exercise and went through all the extensions. He then described what he found.

> I feel this inner conflict of wanting to be very close to a woman but at the same time feeling "trapped" if I get too close. I have a love/hate; fear/joy; acceptance/anger conflict with a woman I have fallen in love with. These are bad feelings. If I don't care for the woman, I don't feel this conflict.
>
> It is a feeling of sadness and loneliness. It feels very empty. It also feels twisted—like all these emotions don't belong, like they come from somewhere else and have just attached themselves to my relationship. They are very old feelings, like they started long before I dated. Mostly though, I feel regret that they are there. They seem to be muddling up what would otherwise be a clear pool of good feelings.
>
> The twisted part comes a day or two after I am with a woman. I remember feeling this many years ago when I fell in love for the first time. My feelings for her didn't seem quite real; they seemed kind of strange.
>
> There are times when I am with a woman I love when I can see things clearly. These times only occur occasionally, maybe for a day or so, and then I slip back into the old murky pool of feelings. At these times it feels like I can see her as a separate individual with her own struggles, triumphs, and tragedies. I don't think she exists only for me. It's like I lose myself during these times and see her as independent from me.

Lester did not know it at the time, but he was exactly right. By doing the exercise, he found out what his problem was. It turned out that his twisted feeling was not love but emotional dependency. When he fell in love with a woman, he became so emotionally dependent on her that she would feel smothered. He inwardly demanded that she provide him with everything to keep him from feeling totally alone in the world. He would use her as his sole meaningful contact with the rest of humanity. Without her, he would be very alone. Of course, such feelings strangled love and the woman would soon leave just to keep herself from being smothered and to save whatever was left of her individuality. Lester then felt devastated and thought, "Alone again, naturally."

There is a good end to the story. Lester finally learned the difference between love and dependency. It wasn't easy; it took him a long time. But he discovered that mature love is based on two people giving and sharing, not based on one person being subsumed by the other. He has been happily married for many years now.

The focusing exercise does not solve problems; it is only a first step. It's like opening a door to see what's inside. We still have to find out why we feel as we do; and most importantly, we still have to discover how to cope with what we feel. But it's a powerful and necessary first step. If we don't know what we are feeling, we won't have a clue as to what to work on. If we are not prepared for what we might find inside the door, we had probably best not use this technique. We should wait until we feel more comfortable looking at our emotions, or, if necessary, get help from someone who can guide us through our journey.

chapter 5

Critical Life Events
Keep Track of the Little Things

Experience is not what happens to a man; it is what a man does with what happens to him.
ALDOUS HUXLEY

IN THIS CHAPTER
- Understanding what makes an event critical
- List of critical events: childhood, adolescence, and adulthood

The most powerful *A*s are those critical experiences that happen to all of us, and we judge them as the most important influences in our lives. Many people think that these big events are more important than little events, and this appears to be obviously true. Aren't the most important influences in our lives those critical events that happen to all of us? Whether it is the death of a grandparent, the time our mom went to the hospital, or the day our brother was born, these events seem crucial in the formation of our personalities.

Surprisingly, these events may not be that important. For many of us it's not the big swirling things that count, it's the little puny things. We can trace back many of our problems to what seem to be, at least on the surface, trivial events. Maybe it is the time we didn't get that special gift we wanted for Christmas; or when we couldn't find our mother in the supermarket; or that Friday night we forgot our lines in the Easter play; or when we went to the party, but nobody asked us to dance.

Trivial experiences can pack so much punch that they can haunt us for years. Some events are critical not because of what happened but because of what we conclude about what happened. We may recover from a traumatic event like the death of our grandmother if we conclude that grandma had a full, rich life and is living with God in heaven. But we may never get over the death of our pet turtle if we conclude that God shouldn't let turtles die because He didn't create a turtle heaven for them to go to.

It's not the strength of our experiences that makes events critical; it's the brute force of our conclusion. Some of our deductions about tiny things can be enormous. It's as if we were walking down one path in life and we tripped over a pebble and suddenly took off and traveled down a totally different path.

Here are some examples.

AVERAGE ALBERT

Albert was a C student in grade school. His average performance was tough on him because his older brother and sisters were the top students in their class. One term he tried as hard as he could in math. He had never received more than a C-, but this time through hard work, he was able to get a B+. When he received his report card, he ran home excitedly to show his dad. After glancing at it, his dad said, "That's OK son. Now, if you just put in a little more effort you can earn an A next time." That was it; it was all his dad said. From this "little" event, Albert formed some big conclusions.

- "If you don't do things perfectly, you might as well not do them at all."
- "To be worthwhile you have to be the best."
- "I can never be the best in everything, so I can never be worthwhile."

When Albert grew up, he hadn't gotten over what his Dad said because despite being a successful, accomplished businessman, he still felt inferior. He thought his father would still not approve.

NEVER ALONE MARTHA

Or consider the case of Martha. She was attractive, 35, single and popular, but for some reason she was afraid to be alone. She felt anxious whenever she was by herself. As a result, she collected friends and tried to get enough of them so that she had an ample supply. She would store the numbers of all her past and present acquaintances on her cell phone and would call them all the time—when she was jogging, waiting in line, playing tennis, driving a car, talking to a person standing in front of her, at a theater, eating in a restaurant—everywhere. She would never have anything particular to say to them; she just wanted to know that they were there and that she was never alone. She stockpiled boyfriends as well and was afraid to end any relationship in case she ran short. So, at parties she would have all her ex-boyfriends line up on the couches and sit there staring at each other. It made her feel more secure, but it put a strain on the festivities.

When Martha thought about the critical events in her life, she could find no instances where a parent had abandoned her as we might suspect. Instead, she only had a few minor experiences that most children have had. What were not minor were her conclusions. She had chicken pox at six and remembered her mother sitting up by her bedside all night for several nights. She lived on a busy street, and her father warned her that she should never cross the street by herself. Her older sister had gotten pregnant before she married, so as a teenager, Martha was told never to go to parties by herself.

From a whole series of incidents like these, Martha developed the following life philosophy—"The world is a big and dangerous place, and I am weak and helpless. I need other people around me to be safe."

Well, you can see that with a philosophy like this she could never allow herself to be alone. She had to surround herself with as many people as she could just for safety. And this is exactly what she did.

Divorced Children

EXAMPLE

A final example. Many people come from divorced homes, but divorces are most damaging when children misinterpret the cause. Unfortunately, many children conclude that they were the cause. From an adult point of view, the child's misinterpretation is astounding, but from the child's view, it is quite natural. One man thought he caused his parents to divorce because he didn't keep his room clean. A woman remembered thinking her mom left because she kept soiling her dresses.

Review of Examples

There are many other incidents that could be listed, but they all have the same source—little events with big conclusions. These conclusions, erroneous or not, can guide the rest of our lives.

The interesting thing about these strange conclusions is that most people don't change them even when they grow up. Apparently once we conclude

Taking Out Your Mental Trash

something when we are quite young, we tuck it away in the back of our brains and consider it to be just one of those basic truths of life not subject to further review. So, as we get older and learn about the world and ourselves, we still have this old conclusion sitting there in the closet of our mind churning away. The result is that mature, intelligent adults can be walking around running corporations and raising their families, but still thinking in the dark recesses of their brains that they were rotten kids because their cluttered rooms caused their parents to get a divorce.

Homework

You may find that "little things" have been very important in your own life.

It can be painful to look into your past. Old raw memories can be brought up again. Only do the exercise if you feel ready. If you are in counseling, your therapist will be a big help. If not, it is important to reach out for help if you need it.

EXERCISE

5.1 List of Critical Events

Use Worksheet 5.1, "Childhood List of Critical Events"
Use Worksheet 5.2, "Adolescence List of Critical Events"
Use Worksheet 5.3, "Adult List of Critical Events"

Step 1. Construct a list of some critical events in your life. Don't only choose negative events or big events (like the death of a loved one); pick your small turning points. They could be positive or negative and they may not seem significant to an outside observer. But if they are important to you, include them. Try to pick events from three periods of your life: your childhood, your adolescence, and your adult years (use worksheets).

Step 2. Go though each event and remember what happened (*A*) and how you felt (*C*). But more importantly, try to remember what you thought (*B*). What did you tell yourself at the time that got you so upset? What did you conclude about yourself because of the event? Try to pinpoint exactly how you changed your view of the world.

Though early erroneous conclusions have a tendency to last, you are not stuck with them. You once learned them, so you can unlearn them.

5.1 Childhood List of Critical Events

1. What happened (A & C)?

_____

_____

What did you conclude (B)?

_____

2. What happened (A & C)?

_____

_____

What did you conclude (B)?

_____

3. What happened (A & C)?

_____

_____

What did you conclude (B)?

_____

4. What happened (A & C)?

_____

_____

What did you conclude (B)?

_____

5. What happened (A & C)?

_____

_____

What did you conclude (B)?

_____

5.2 Adolescence List of Critical Events

1. What happened (*A* & *C*)?

   What did you conclude (*B*)?

2. What happened (*A* & *C*)?

   What did you conclude (*B*)?

3. What happened (*A* & *C*)?

   What did you conclude (*B*)?

4. What happened (*A* & *C*)?

   What did you conclude (*B*)?

5. What happened (*A* & *C*)?

   What did you conclude (*B*)?

5.3 Adult List of Critical Events

1. What happened (*A & C*)?

_____

_____

What did you conclude (*B*)?

_____

_____

2. What happened (*A & C*)?

_____

_____

What did you conclude (*B*)?

_____

_____

3. What happened (*A & C*)?

_____

_____

What did you conclude (*B*)?

_____

_____

4. What happened (*A & C*)?

_____

_____

What did you conclude (*B*)?

_____

_____

5. What happened (*A & C*)?

_____

_____

What did you conclude (*B*)?

_____

_____

chapter 6

Find All Your Cognitions
Worn Glasses

It is hard to let old beliefs go. They are familiar. . . . Like a man who has worn eyeglasses so long that he forgets he has them on, we forget that the world looks to us the way it does because we have become used to seeing it that way through a particular set of lenses. Today, however, we need new lenses.
KENICHI OHMAE

IN THIS CHAPTER
- Understanding the variety of cognitions that may be connected to our emotions
- Surveying a checklist of beliefs

You may accept the *A, B, C* theory. You may understand that the emotions you feel at *C* are not caused by critical events at *A*, but are caused by your beliefs at *B*. You may know your beliefs are mighty when you read about the concept and keep it in the abstract. You also may generally see its truth when looking at other people's thoughts and emotions.

But when our own powerful emotions get aroused, our acceptance of the principle often vanishes. When a critical event happens, like losing our job, or getting an illness, or having our boyfriend or girlfriend leave us, the last place we will look to find the cause of our pain is our beliefs. We will insist that losing our job, getting ill, or losing our lover is causing our upsetness and nothing else.

 The reason we may think this way is that we are not aware of the great variety of thoughts that are running around in our heads. Like worn glasses, we may have had them on for so long that we forgot we were wearing them.

EXAMPLE

STEVE—A WORRIED FATHER

Steve was a successful self-employed businessman in his mid-30s who was married and had three children—two daughters and a son. One day his wife called him and said his son was complaining of severe intestinal cramps and had been rushed to the hospital. After Steve got to the hospital, he heard that his son had a severe obstruction in his intestines and would need a tricky operation to clear it.

As we would expect, Steve was fearful and worried that the operation wouldn't go well. He later told me it was the worst fear he had ever felt in his whole life, and this fear lasted for several days. Fortunately, the operation was a success, and his son completely recovered. But what he had difficulty recovering from was the power of the emotion he had felt. He had been in the military and found this fear was far greater than what he had felt in combat. He didn't understand why.

Steve understood the principle that his beliefs were mighty and could cause his emotions—in the abstract. But when it came to his emotions about his son, he rejected the principle. He said, "You mean to tell me that it's only my beliefs about by son which caused me to worry so much and not the fact that he was injured and needed surgery? " He was upset about the whole idea that just his thoughts had caused such a great mountain of fear, not the reality of the pending operation. "You think I made the whole thing up in my head?"

But I persisted. I told him it was indeed his beliefs about his son and the operation—not the fact of it—that got him upset, but many of his thoughts were realistic and to be expected from a caring parent. But there may be others he had that were not so useful.

The difficulty was that he had not bothered to look at his own thinking at all, so he had not discovered most of his thoughts. Therefore, he was unable to understand why he was more afraid of his son's surgery than fighting in combat. After we went through all the thoughts (included in the examples below) he then understood and accepted that his thought were indeed mighty and had caused his pain.

Homework

EXERCISE

6.1 Find All the Cognitions

Use Worksheet 6.1, "Find All Your Cognitions"

Step 1. Look at the lists of your critical events (Worksheet 5.1, 5.2, and 5.3). From the lists, pick one of your critical events where you had a strong emotion.

Step 2. Using Worksheet 6.1, try to identify all the beliefs you may have had about the event. What were all the things you told yourself in the situation that caused you to feel the emotion? You probably told yourself many things. Like Steve, it is important that you find them all. To help you, use the following list of cognitions.

Some of these cognitions are so important that Part II of this book presents 11 chapters that dig into these beliefs in detail. Be sure to read those chapters that are relevant for you. For now, however, be aware of the great variety of cognitions you may have had during your critical situation.

Expectation
What you expected of yourself in the situation.
(Example from Steve: "As a father I have the absolute obligation to protect my son from pain, injury, and harm, to the utmost of my ability.")

Self-efficacy (see Chapter 8, "Self-concept")
What you thought the chances were of you fulfilling your expectations.
(Steve: "I am not in control of the situation. I am not the surgeon or the anesthesiologist. I am forced to put my son's life in the care of strangers.")

Self-esteem (see Chapter 12, "Self-esteem")
How your overall opinion of yourself influenced the situation.
(Steve: "I guess I haven't been a very good father. I have spent too much time at work and not enough with the kids.")

Selected Memory (see Chapter 14, "Choosing Our Past Carefully")
What you remembered from the past.
(Steve: "I thought of all the times I didn't play catch with him or missed his soccer game because I stayed late at work.")

Images

What pictures popped into your head during the situation.

(Steve: "I pictured my poor little son being bent over in agony and lying on the operating table feeling terrified. ")

Selective Forgetting (see Chapter 14, "Choosing Our Past Carefully")

What memory you forgot or ignored.

(Steve: "The surgeon telling me this type of operation is done all the time and there is very little chance of something going wrong.")

Self-instruction (see Chapter 9, "Our Secret Teachers")

How you thought you should have behaved in the situation.

(Steve: "To help my son, I have to be cool, calm, and collected, but I don't feel this way.")

Words (see Chapter 11, "What's in a Name?")

The words you used to describe the situation.

(Steve: "It's terrible, horrible, and catastrophic, and I can't stand it!")

Attribution (see Chapter 17, "Who's to Blame?")

What did you guess was the cause of the problem.

(Steve: "I should have watched my son's diet better and had him visit the doctor more.")

6.1 Find All Your Cognitions

Pick one of the events (*A*) on your Critical Event Sheets (Worksheets 5.1, 5.2, and 5.3).

_____

What emotions you felt. How strong? (*C*)

anger ?   _____

fear?   _____

depression?   _____

others?   _____

Find all your cognitions (*B*)

Expectation
What you expected of yourself in the situation.

_____

_____

_____

Self-efficacy
What you thought the chances were of you fulfilling your expectations.

_____

_____

_____

Self-esteem
How your overall opinion of yourself affected the situation.

_____

_____

_____

Selected Memory
What you remembered from the past.

_____

_____

_____

Images
What pictures popped into your head during the situation.

_____

_____

_____

Selective Forgetting
What memory you forgot or ignored.

_____

_____

_____

Self-instruction
How you thought you should have behaved in the situation.

_____

_____

_____

Words
The words you used to describe the situation.

_____

_____

_____

Attribution
What you guessed was the cause of the problem.

_____

_____

_____

chapter 7

Core Beliefs
How to Find Your Core Assumptions

There is only one good—knowledge, and one evil—ignorance. SOCRATES

IN THIS CHAPTER
- Grasping the importance of our core beliefs
- Digging to find our key assumptions
- Master List of Core Beliefs

Only we can know our own selves from the inside out. Only we are aware of our true emotions, our hidden secrets, and private dreams. Only we have stored in our memory the millions of pictures, feelings, and recollections gathered from the innumerable experiences encountered during our journey through life. But despite all this, despite the fact that we alone have this intimate knowledge of ourselves, there is one thing that we might not know about ourselves. That thing may be patently obvious to everyone around us, but totally unknown to us. It is our *core assumption*, the core belief we have about life.

This key belief lies at the base of all our other attitudes and anchors our values, and if it is false, it can handicap us throughout our lives.

Many of us know that our beliefs are multilayered. We are aware that we have surface beliefs and underlying ones. The following reverse pyramid (Figure 7.1) may best illustrate the multilayered principle.

At the top of the pyramid lie our surface thoughts, the beliefs that we are aware of and that we usually share with others. When we are asked what are we thinking, we usually pick out one of these surface beliefs. At

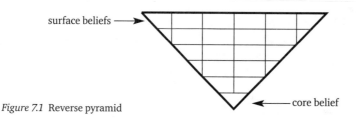

surface beliefs →

← core belief

Figure 7.1 Reverse pyramid

the bottom of the pyramid are our core assumptions. They are not readily apparent to us or to others, and some work is required to uncover them. It's not necessarily true that these key beliefs are unconscious or that we fear uncovering them (this is probably true of only a small percentage of our beliefs), but our core assumptions are so basic and so fundamental to us that we may not be aware that we have them. It is analogous to a fish not being aware of water because it has lived in water all of its life; it was born in water, breathes it, reproduces in it, and finally dies in it. It does not know water exists because it is not aware that there is a waterless place in the universe. Likewise, many of us have lived with our core beliefs for so long that we are not aware of their existence.

We cannot rightly claim to have complete knowledge of ourselves unless at some point in our lives we discover what our core assumptions are. Our surface beliefs, attitudes, values, biases, and prejudices are all based on these key beliefs, and true enlightenment can only come with a firm knowledge of these keystone thoughts.

The following story about Mary may help show how important our core assumptions can be, particularly when they are false.

DIAMOND IN THE ROUGH

When Mary was young, she was different from the other girls. She amused herself by reading philosophy books while her peers played with Barbie dolls. Her grades in school were not good, and although her teachers thought she had potential, she answered questions in odd ways that the teachers judged as aberrant. Her friends of choice were older people until her parents pressed her to associate with people closer to her own age.

Mary didn't think like most people. She tried to explain why she believed certain things or why she thought so differently, but when she tried to explain her ideas, nobody really understood what she meant. She concluded that she

Taking Out Your Mental Trash

was too vapid to explain things well. Most of the other girls rejected her and were embarrassed to be seen with her, so she spent much of her early life alone. Her parents worried and sent her to therapists who never found anything specifically wrong with her. She just didn't seem to fit in with her peers.

Mary was quite young when she realized that she was being rejected. She was sure it was because she was a "birdbrain." She didn't understand why others believed the way they did, and she hadn't met anyone who thought like her, so she concluded that she was a "real idiot." She developed the core assumption that she must be "retarded" in some way and that other people were simply smarter. This was the only explanation she could find that fit into the puzzle of her life.

Mary acted out this theme throughout much of her middle years. She didn't attend college because she felt that college was only for bright people, and she didn't want to embarrass herself. Her family didn't press her. They encouraged college for her brothers, but believed that girls only went to college to meet husbands, and since she preferred reading philosophy to meeting boys, they saw no reason to spend their money. She took odd jobs but they bored her very quickly, so she kept looking for other work that might be more interesting. She never found a job she liked, and concluded that she was too dull-witted to enjoy work. She occasionally took some adult education classes at the local university but received only average grades—she didn't seem able to give the answers the professors wanted; she answered essay questions in strange ways.

Her relationships with men followed a similar pattern. She didn't act like other women; she didn't try to flatter men or boost their egos or wear seductive clothing. Most of the time she just wanted to talk, to find out what they thought about things. Most men just tried to get her into bed, and when she wouldn't play the seduction game, they thought she was strange, so they usually left her for someone more traditionally feminine. Mary concluded that she was too "lame-brained" to attract men.

As she got older, things didn't get any better for Mary. She never went to college. "Too "harebrained" she thought to herself, but she continued to enroll in noncredit courses as a nondegree student. She would sneak into graduate-school lectures on philosophy when she could. She would hang around with the students after class and try to open a conversation, but she found most students were disinterested in discussing what had been covered in class; they were only concerned with the grade they would receive on the next test. Those few who would talk about the subject would ignore Mary when they discovered she wasn't a real student and hadn't even earned an undergraduate degree.

Because of a series of critical events early in her life, Mary had come to an incredibly erroneous assumption about herself. She'd noticed that she was different from others, and had concluded (as many children do) that this difference meant that she was inferior in some way. Her peers and teachers treated her this way, so she believed it herself. Because of all these experiences, Mary's core assumption became her overriding philosophy, the glasses through which she perceived the world. At the base of her philosophy was one simple theme: "I am stupid." Since she held this belief over many years, it took on the strength of religious dogma.

In reality, what made Mary so different was that she was a genius—one of those rare people who come along only infrequently. She could see things in a clearer and more comprehensive way than the vast majority of people. While she was brilliant about most things, she couldn't read herself at all. It may sound strange for someone to be so aware in some areas but totally blind in others, but this is often true of geniuses, and it was true of Mary.

Mary's story has a positive ending. She kept talking to people about her ideas, but no one paid much attention. One day, in an informal setting, Mary met a famous professor who immediately recognized her as a genius. The people she'd met before hadn't recognized her ability because it takes talent to recognize genius; it takes a Haydn to recognize a Mozart. The professor who met Mary had the knowledge and understanding to recognize the extent of her ability.

She directed Mary to a college where she could pass classes by challenging the courses, enabling her to complete her undergraduate degree very quickly. (She took the final exams and when she answered the questions satisfactorily, she was given credit for the class.) Later the professor got her into a good graduate school and helped her receive an assistantship so that she could afford to attend.

Mary has done very well since then. She completed her Ph.D. in record time, has published many articles in professional journals, and wrote a book. Her most recent work was reviewed as one of the most innovative in her field. For the first time in her life, Mary is content and happy.

The following exercise may help you find your core assumptions. Before you do the exercise please read all the steps and the two examples.

Homework

EXERCISE

7.1 Master List of Core Beliefs

Use Worksheet 7.1, "Master List of Core Beliefs"

Step 1. Gather together the Worksheets that list your beliefs.
- Worksheet 2.1, Daily List of ABCs (may be several sheets; p. 14)
- Worksheet 5.1, Childhood List of Critical Events (p. 32)
- Worksheet 5.2, Adolescence List of Critical Events (p. 33)
- Worksheet 5.3, Adult List of Critical Events (p. 34)
- Worksheet 6.1, Find All Your Cognitions (p. 39)

Step 2. Read over all the beliefs on your lists. Be aware of the situations that preceded them and the emotions that followed them.

Step 3. What Is the Underlying Belief?
When you find a belief, ask yourself the following questions concerning the belief.
"So what if . . .?"

Or

"Why does it matter if . . .?"

Keep asking questions until you find a core answer (the two examples below will help you understand how to do this). It is important to mentally ask the questions, and then wait for your brain to create the answers. It takes lots of practice to do this right. It may be very difficult to be so ruthlessly honest with yourself. When you ask yourself, "So what?" or "So what if?", don't allow yourself to make up an easy answer. Keep looking for the honest answer. After you find it, ask yourself the same question again to get to the next layer of your beliefs. Wait for the next answer, and when you know you've discovered the right one, ask again. Keep asking and answering the question until you can answer no further. At this point, you have found your core thought and are at the bottom of your reverse pyramid.

Step 4. How Are Your Beliefs Related?

Search for the relationship between your beliefs. When you find several beliefs that look similar, look for a common element that ties them together.

This procedure is similar to the analogy questions in some intelligence tests. For instance:

How are these two items alike?

 cats and dogs. Answer—household pets

 pen and pencil. Answer—writing instruments

 lake and pond. Answer—bodies of freshwater

The aim of this mental exercise is to find the best relationship between the two items. "Best" means neither too abstract (such as cats and dogs are both animals), nor too concrete (both words have four letters).

For example, suppose you found the following beliefs on your lists:

Childhood list   A: "I lost a fistfight."

        B: "I am not a very good fighter."

Adolescent list   A: "My girlfriend left me for another boy."

        B: "Girls don't like me."

Daily list   A: "A younger colleague got promoted ahead of me."

        B: "I don't have the get-up-and-go that he has."

A core underlying belief that may tie the thoughts together is, "I am inferior as a male."

Step 5. Put the core beliefs you find from Steps 3 and 4 on your Master List of Core Beliefs (Worksheet 7.1).

You will know that you've found the core belief if the thought serves as a bridge between the situation (*A*) and your feeling (*C*). If you can imagine everyone who holds this belief feeling the same emotions that you did, then you are probably correct. If someone could have had the thought but wouldn't feel the emotion, then you haven't yet found the key cognition.

Don't be too concerned if you haven't found exactly the right core belief or found exactly the right wording. If you are in counseling, your therapist will be your most valuable help. If you are not in counseling, understand that the only mistake you can make in building your master list is that you have too few items not too many. So, if you doubt that you have found a core belief include it on your master sheet just the same. You can always refine it later.

These exercises are just a start. We all have a series of core beliefs connected to a series of inverted pyramids. There may be hundreds. In one particular situation, several pyramids may be activated, causing different thoughts and feelings. But underlying them all may be a few key beliefs, a few core assumption that ties them all together.

7.1 Master List of Core Beliefs

1. _____
2. _____
3. _____
4. _____
5. _____
6. _____
7. _____
8. _____
9. _____
10. _____
11. _____
12. _____
13. _____
14. _____
15. _____
16. _____
17. _____
18. _____
19. _____
20. _____

Public Speaking Anxiety

A middle-aged executive was very successful at his work, yet he always worried about giving talks to large professional business audiences. He followed these steps to find his core belief.

Belief: "They may not like my talk."

He engaged in the following self-dialogue:

QUESTION: "So what if they don't like my speech. What would that mean?"
ANSWER: (He waited for the answer to come.) "They won't respect me."

QUESTION: "Why would it matter if they didn't respect me?"
ANSWER: "Then I guess it would be true that I'm not worthy of their respect."

QUESTION: "Why would it be true?"
ANSWER: "I tend to believe what other people think of me."

QUESTION: "More than what you think of yourself?"
ANSWER: "Yes!"

QUESTION: "Why?"
ANSWER: "I don't like myself very much."

"I don't like myself very much," was his core assumption.

He found that this belief was the common element behind other beliefs. Because he didn't like himself he thought, "I must do everything perfectly well"; "If I make a mistake it is terrible"; "It is easier to avoid than to face certain life difficulties"; "Strong stable individuals should not ask others for help."

To effectively work on his fear of public speaking, he had best work on the full range of his beliefs, starting with his surface thought and ending with his core belief.

The Story of Al

Al was an attractive, single 35-year-old man with a good job who thought he was a rotten person. He couldn't find one positive thing to say about himself, but objectively none of his beliefs were true. He thought he was ugly despite the fact that women were constantly trying to meet him and go out with him. He thought of himself as an uncaring person despite doing charity work on his weekends for Big Brothers. All of his negative self-perceptions were unrealistic.

His attitude about himself was a riddle. Why did he think this way? Looking at how he completed the exercise may help us see the answer.

He engaged in the following self-dialogue:

QUESTION: "So maybe I am inferior in some ways. Why is this a big deal?"
ANSWER: "That would be terrible!"

QUESTION: "Why?"
ANSWER: "Because people wouldn't respect me or like me. They would look down on me."

QUESTION: "So what? They already look down on me, and I don't like myself either."
ANSWER: "Because it would be such a loss, so unfair and unjust."

QUESTION: "Why unfair and unjust?"
ANSWER: "Because I wouldn't be living up to my potential."

QUESTION: "What potential?"
ANSWER: "I'm basically a special person and should perform better than other people."

This was it. The core assumption at the base of his pyramid was that he was an Einstein. It wasn't just a wish but a firmly felt core belief. He felt upset when other people treated him as an ordinary mortal. It bothered him when he had to do mundane things such as balancing his checkbook or taking out the garbage. What bothered him the most was his own discouragement about himself. Every time he made a mistake, he would attack himself unmercifully for making what he believed to be a stupid error. His internal dialogue told him that it's bad enough for a normal person to do this, but for someone who has the potential to be important, it is intolerable. He didn't feel inferior to others, he felt inferior to the expectation created by his core assumption.

The similarities and differences between the two examples, Al and Mary, are important. On the surface, they both seem to have the same belief, "I am inferior." But thoughts exist in layers, and the bases of Mary's and Al's pyramids were quite different. Mary believed herself inferior because of a misattribution. She noticed that she was considerably different from others and concluded that she must be stupid. Al believed he was inferior because of a self-demand. He noticed that his real achievements didn't equal his overblown expectations.

Just knowing these two people's surface beliefs doesn't help us understand them, we need to know what their core assumptions are.

The same is true for you. To deeply know yourself, you had best discover your core assumptions.

Part II

Types of
Mistaken
Beliefs

chapter 8

Self-concept
Whose Mirror Are We Using?

We don't receive wisdom; we must discover it for ourselves after a journey that no one can take us or spare us.
MARCEL PROUST

IN THIS CHAPTER
- Identifying our self-concept
- Discovering the origins of our self-beliefs

One of the most important beliefs we can have is our attitude toward ourselves. We call it our self-concept, and it represents the core view we have of our selves in the world. This powerful cognition determines how we act, how we feel, and whether we will conclude that our lives are happy or miserable.

Where does our self-concept come from, and how do we place value on our own worth? There is one most likely answer. When we are children, we cannot accurately appraise our own merit. At 7 or 8 years old, we are not capable of making a correct judgment. We only learn our value by absorbing the rating of others. We start rating our selves as positive or negative and think aloud, "This is a good self. This is a bad self. This is a flawed self. Others have better selves. This is an evil self. This self has merit. This self is worthless. This self is sick."

 We use other people as our mirrors to judge our own worth. If they accept us, we feel worthwhile and believe we must be OK. If others treat us badly, then we perceive that we must be bad and that this badness is part of us.

And here is where the problem begins. Others don't judge us accurately. The mirrors through which we perceive our own self-worth are distorted. Because of their own insecurities or problems, our significant others may reflect back a perverted or warped image. But we accept this distorted view as the truth about who we are. So we take others portraits of us as factual and tuck them away in our mental cellars and refer back to them for the rest of our lives. These views are the first portraits we draw of ourselves. Later portraits we see are often rejected if they differ too much from the original composition.

The value we have assigned to ourselves can have huge staying power. Our early rating of self-worth can last throughout our lives unless we actively do something to change it. Our value becomes the central structure through which we filter all we feel; all we think; all we do.

THE STORY OF CYNTHIA

EXAMPLE

Cynthia was born into a dysfunctional family, and when she started to form her self-concept at around the age of 7, the family was in a constant state of uproar. Her father drank too much. Her brother was in constant trouble with the law. Her mother was an enabler who kept the family together by minimizing all of the problems and pretending not to notice that the family was in trouble. Her mother clung to only one principle—keep the family together, no matter what.

Cynthia's self-concept formed in this negative environment. She concluded, as most children would, that there was something wrong with her. "I must be a bad person to be treated so poorly," she thought.

As outside observers, we could see that Cynthia was wrong. We would recognize that she was an attractive, pleasant, highly intelligent, creative young lady. We would know it wasn't her fault that she was beaten, abused, and ignored. We would identify that her family was the problem. But Cynthia didn't see it this way. Her only mirror was the reflection her family gave her. Therefore, her self-concept was distorted.

Cynthia didn't know that her family's problems had twisted her view of herself; she didn't know that her family was dysfunctional. Being 7 years old and on the receiving end of a mountain of abuse, Cynthia concluded that she was the cause of it all.

This mistaken self-perception was built on and enhanced over the years.

She survived by turning off her emotional switches and becoming stoical. The family judged her demeanor as strength. Not having any other person with even the appearance of strength, the family turned to her for support. She became the family's hero and head nurse; she was substitute wife for the father, confidante for the mother, parent to her brother—all by the age of 14. She sacrificed her adolescence in a doomed attempt to keep her family together.

Later on in life, it took Cynthia many counseling sessions to finally identify who really had the problem.

Although there are many measures of self-concept, the following simple exercise may be helpful. It will give you an idea of how you view yourself and where this view might have come from.

Homework

 EXERCISE

8.1 Whose Mirror Have You Used?

Step 1. Look at the 11 traits listed below. They are placed on a continuum (e.g., introverted on the left and extroverted on the right). Place an X about where you think you belong. The farther you place the X to the left or right (introverted/extroverted), the more you think you possess that trait. An X in the middle means you judge yourself as evenly split.

average

introverted	extroverted
dull	bright
bad	good
shy	bold
serious	happy-go-lucky
weak	strong
conservative	liberal
suspicious	trusting
tense	relaxed
practical	imaginative
cool	warm

Step 2. Focus on those traits which you judged yourself as different from the average (an "X" toward the left or right). For example, let's say you marked yourself as shy rather than bold.

Step 3. Think back and see if you can remember the first time you thought of yourself in this way. ("The first time I remember thinking that I was shy, I was in grade school.")

Step 4. At this earlier time, can you remember significant people around you who viewed you in the same way? ("Yes, my teachers, family, and friends thought that I was shy and withdrawn.")

Step 5. Is it possible that your view of yourself was just a mirror reflection of others' views of you? ("Yes, I started becoming shyer because I thought that was what people expected of me.")

You can try an important variation of this exercise. Rate yourself throughout different periods of your life (childhood, adolescence, young adult, and adult). Did you continue to use other people's mirrors, or did you start to develop your own self-concept? Many people have found that during different life periods the source of their self-concept changed. They discovered that the older they got, the more their rating came from their own judgment rather than simply being a reflection of others. If this happened to you, this is a positive change. When you shift toward your own internal view based on your own life experiences, you become free to define who you are.

 Our view of our self is at our center; it is what makes us tick. Through our self-image we see the entire world and all the people in it, and it is this view that can make our life happy or turn it into a private concentration camp.

chapter **9**

Our Secret Teachers
Do We Have Good Instructors?

It's easier to give advice than receive it, and a lot less trouble.   MARK TWAIN

IN THIS CHAPTER
- Listening to our inner voice
- Identifying our teachers

 Most of us realize that we have another voice in our head that talks to us and gives us advice. It has been called many things: our inner guide, super-ego, private wisdom, or hidden child. As we read this, we may hear another voice speaking. It may be loud or soft, intrusive or in the background, but if we pay attention to it, we can hear it. This voice is like a teacher. Sometimes it gives us good advice, sometimes bad, and we need to know the difference.

Maybe the voice is suggesting what we should eat for dinner tonight or reminding us to tune up our car on Saturday. It could be chiding us about how we erred on a business project, or telling us to take an exercise class.

Whatever it's telling us, it's not cause for concern. We all have this voice inside us somewhere, a stream-of-conscious dialogue going on all the time. Don't be concerned. It's our own brain talking and teaching us, and it's perfectly normal. Although we can focus our attention on only one task at a time (like reading this book), our brain can still process other undigested thoughts, images, and experiences. It's like having two tape recorders going at once—one reading the book, the other thinking about other things.

Nasty Teachers

EXAMPLE

Some people have voices that are nasty. One woman's inner voice was like Cinderella's stepmother. It kept yelling, "You stupid, lazy slob! You haven't done anything with your life. You haven't had a relationship with a man that's amounted to anything. What a rotten piece of garbage you are and always will be."

Another woman had a teacher so mean that she called it, "The Nazi in My Head." It would cruelly attack her for the slightest mistakes. She finally decided to "fire" it and hire a new teacher.

A millionaire businessman had a voice that would never let him succeed. It kept shouting, "You think you're God's gift to the world because you're rich, don't you? Well, you aren't anything. You can make all the money in the world, but you will always be a classless bum."

Too Nice Teachers

EXAMPLE

Just as some people have nasty teachers, others can have teachers that are too kind. Spike, a heroin addict, had a teacher who was a cross between Pollyanna and a Little Sister of the Poor. It would tell him things like, "Don't worry about those nasty old cops arresting you for holding up a liquor store again. It's not your fault; it's just that you had a bad childhood. Deep down inside you are still a good boy. Poor dear."

What Spike really needed was a teacher with the temperament of a Marine drill sergeant who would say something like,

> You're bull-shitting yourself again. How has your life been going up to now? No wife, no friends, no job, sick all the time, in and out of jails and hospitals, out of control, violent, terrible mood swings, paranoid, no house, no home, no possessions. Enjoying life so far? How do you explain all these problems? It's not normal to have these things happen to you. Most people don't experience these problems in an entire lifetime. There must be some explanation for having these problems. There is. It is because you are a romping, stomping addict. Do something about it and stop, or don't do anything about it and stew in your misery, but stop blaming everybody else. You are the only one that is responsible." (McMullin & Gehlhaar, 2004, p. 79–81)

If he had had a teacher who used this approach, he would have been forced to face his addiction.

Taking Out Your Mental Trash

Origins of Teachers

Where do our teachers come from? How do we pick them? Many of us can identify the source. Often we recognize the voice and can picture the person speaking to us. Sometimes we hear a parent or other relative, or we may picture a real teacher, doctor, or coach we once knew. Possibly, we even imagine hearing someone we never knew: a historical figure like Abraham Lincoln, a literary character like King Arthur, or when young, fantasy figures such as Harry Potter, Super Friends, Wonder Woman, Superman, or Spiderman.

It is still not clear why we choose one teacher over another, but we seem to pick them at an early stage of life, probably late childhood or early adolescence. The teenage years are such a traumatic time for most of us that we feel the need for guidance. So, if it's lacking from the outside, we create our own on the inside. A boy who feels weak often creates a Rambolike teacher to make him strong. It's his mind's way of teaching him what he thinks he needs to learn. Another boy who wishes to please his father but feels he isn't succeeding may bring his father inside his head to give him private instruction. An adolescent girl who feels lonely may create a kindly grandmotherly teacher to give her the emotional chicken soup she wants.

There is nothing wrong with creating these teachers to help us when we are young. But as we get older, we may need to replace them with new teachers to guide us. Things become bungled and botched when we don't know when to retire them. Spike, the heroin addict's soft teacher, may have been helpful when he was little because he grew up in an abusive family. He needed to create a caring person to help him cope with a hostile environment, and his voice helped him then. But when Spike became addicted to heroin, he needed a different voice—a tough, streetwise guide, someone who could help him fight a serious drug addiction. The kindly grandmotherly teacher who had helped him as a child, hurt him as an adult. Unfortunately, he never fired her; she had tenure.

Hiring New Teachers

It is possible to replace our teachers; many people have done so. One sign that therapy is succeeding is when people change their teachers. In most cases, they replace bad voices with good ones. Their new teachers start to say things like, "You didn't succeed, but it was a good try. I know you feel bad, but hold on; it will pass. Keep working on it, you'll make it."

A man replaced his Genghis Khan-type teacher with a group of wise elders. One was a Buddhist monk, another was Albert Einstein, and the third was his kindly old grandfather whom he had hardly known. Whenever he felt sad, he closed his eyes, relaxed, and imagined these three people sitting with him and giving him advice. They would sometimes debate what he should do, and he would sometimes argue back, but he was confident that they cared for him, and he usually found their advice helpful.

We constantly have an internal dialogue with ourselves. We talk to ourselves continuously, giving advice, making evaluations, trying out new strategies, and teaching new principles. But we rarely notice this voice. The following exercise will help you find your own teacher.

Homework

 9.1 Who is Your Teacher?

Use Worksheet 9.1, "Who is Your Teacher?"

Step 1. Take some time and focus on your internal voice. Write down what you are hearing, or record it on a tape recorder. Don't try to make complete sentences or to keep irrelevancies or distractions out; don't censor your thoughts for grammatical or personal reasons. Write down everything exactly as you hear it.

Step 2. Put your writing or tape away for a few days.

Step 3. Bring the material out when you feel like it. Look at what you wrote and see what kind of teacher you have. Does it remind you of anyone? Is it the same teacher you have always had or has your teacher changed? Is the teacher still helpful or is it time for you to retire him or her and hire a new one?

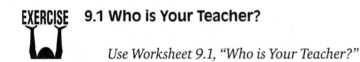Of course, we don't really have a teacher inside us; the voice we hear is our own. It's just us talking to ourselves, and it's always nice to have interesting company along for the ride. If we hear a nasty voice, we had best get rid of it, but if it's a good teacher giving wise advice, we should listen.

Taking Out Your Mental Trash

9.1 Who is Your Teacher?

Write down what you hear when you listen to your inner voice.

_____

_____

_____

_____

_____

_____

Is it positive or negative? _____

Do you recognize the voice? _____

Has it been the same voice you have always heard or has it changed?

_____

Does the voice help you or hurt you? _____

What kind of teacher would you like to have in your head? _____

_____

_____

_____

chapter 10

Cultural Beliefs
Are We Independent Thinkers?

From the moment of his birth the customs into which [an individual] is born shape his experience and behavior. By the time he can talk, he is the little creature of his culture. RUTH BENEDICT

IN THIS CHAPTER
- Understanding the importance of our reference group
- Examining our own reference groups
- Surveying some key cultural beliefs

Some of us maintain a certain self-deception about our beliefs, attitudes, and values. We think they are our own creation. We assume we wove our attitudes out of blank cloth from our own imaginations without copying the patterns from others. We think our beliefs were formed in isolation. We have difficulty recognizing that our culture showed us how to look at the world. It teaches us:

- what to perceive
- what to ignore
- what we must believe
- what we must reject
- what is good behavior
- what is bad behavior
- who are strangers and how should we treat them
- what personal information are we allowed to share with others
- who can we marry and who we must not
- what is our purpose for being on this planet

What's Our Culture?

Our culture can be different things. We can identify with the beliefs of many different types of groups: cultures, races, subcultural groups, geographical regions, language groups, nation states, religious affiliations, and political parties. Because there are so many potential groups, it is hard to determine why some of us adopt the beliefs of one group over another.

 Sociologists offer an explanation. They use the term *reference group* and describe it as not necessarily the group that we are born in, grew up in, or that other people think we are in—but the group we identify with. Thus, you could come from an upper-middle-class, Irish Catholic family from the East Coast, and may have been brought up in a liberal, democratic household, but you may mentally identify with the beliefs of a frontier, cowboy, macho, independent, conservative culture because you spent your childhood watching Westerns and reading cowboy stories. Our reference group is the mental home that we live in, and it is the group that most influences our beliefs.

The following exercise will help you identify your reference groups and enable you to see where some of your beliefs may have come from.

Homework

EXERCISE 10.1 What are Your Cultural or Reference Groups?

Use Worksheet 10.1, "Your Groups of Origin and Reference Groups"

Step 1. Groups of origin. Make a list of the groups others would put you in. Write them in the second column of the worksheet. Use the following list of groups as a guide.

Step 2. Reference groups. Next, list the groups you associate with, identify with, or mentally feel part of. Put them in the third column of the worksheet. Use the following list of groups as a guide.

LIST OF GROUPS

Ethnic Group. These are the cultural groups you come from and the groups you associate with such as Italian American, African American, Native American, British Australian, French Canadian, Maori, Hawaiian, Aboriginal, or Irish.

Religious Group. These are not only the major faiths but the subdivisions such as evangelical, orthodox, fundamental, radical, or agnostic.

Political Group. These are Independents, Democrats, Republicans, the Green Party, Libertarians, Labor, Liberal, Conservative, and subdivisions such as a Kennedy liberal, a Reagan republican, or neocon.

Regional Group. This is the state, province, section (Easterner, Westerner, Islander), also city or town if you identify with the area, such as New York, Greenwich Village, Soho, South Philly.

Occupational Group. These are farmers, teachers, doctors, students, retired, and subcategories such as grade school teacher, cardiologist, high school/university student.

Aficionado Group. Are you a fan of a leisure activity? For instance, sportsfan, stamp saver, birder, hunter, baseball card collector, golfer, surfer, crossword puzzler, New York Yankee fan, video game player, civil war reenactor, bowler, romance novel reader.

Other. Any other group or subgroup that you think you share beliefs with.

Step 3. Think of the reference groups that are most important to you. Focus on the beliefs, attitudes, and values of each group. How are the group's beliefs and values different from those of other groups? For example, if you picked a regional group, you might suppose that Philadelphians value the arts while Denverites like the great outdoors. If you picked an aficionado sports group, you may assume that New York Yankee fans like winning no matter what the cost while Chicago Cub fans like being the underdog. List the distinctive values of your reference groups in the fourth column of the worksheet.

Step 4. Focus on the similarities between your personal beliefs and the beliefs held by the different groups you have listed. Are they the same? Are they different? (e.g., Do you like the arts? Do you believe in the underdog?). Write the differences and similarities in the last two columns.

Most people who did the exercise said they learned their attitudes from their culture. They discovered that they shared many values that derived from their reference groups. Many were surprised about how few beliefs they created on their own.

10.1 Your Groups of Origin and Reference Groups

Groups	Group of origin	Reference group	Group's distinctive attitudes and values	How are your beliefs different from those of the group?	How are your beliefs similar to those of the group?
Ethnic					
Religious					
Political					
Regional					
Occupational					
Aficionado					
Other					

What Beliefs Did Our Culture Teach Us?

We are born and raised in a culture that teaches us various beliefs. As we grow, we are taught these beliefs directly, but we also learn them by unconsciously observing others. It may come as a shock to many of us that so much of what we value has come from our culture. Often, we only become aware of this when we live in another culture and notice that its underlying values are considerably different from our own. We detect that our core assumptions about the world and ourselves are quite at variance to this new culture. Only then, do we realize that we have implicitly learned all kinds of things when we were growing up—things we did not know we were learning, things that gave us our core foundations, and our perceptual ground from which we view the world.

Worksheet 10.2 lists some of the most common assumptions held by people from a variety of cultures. Take the quick survey yourself and see how you score.

10.2 Survey of Some Common Cultural Beliefs

Step 1. Read each belief in the following list.

Step 2. Rate whether you agree, are neutral, or disagree with the following statements.

- Making mistakes is terrible.

  agree   neutral   disagree

- My emotions can't be controlled.

  agree   neutral   disagree

- I should be terribly worried about threatening situations.

  agree   neutral   disagree

- Self discipline is too hard to achieve.

  agree   neutral   disagree

- I must depend on others.

  agree   neutral   disagree

- I can't stand the way others act.

  agree   neutral   disagree

- Every problem has a perfect solution.

  agree   neutral   disagree

- I should be better than others.

  agree   neutral   disagree

- If others criticize me, I must have done something wrong.

  agree   neutral   disagree

- I should do everything perfectly well.

  agree   neutral   disagree

- I have to help everyone who needs it.

  agree   neutral   disagree

- I must never show any weakness.

  agree   neutral   disagree

- Healthy people don't get upset.

  agree   neutral   disagree

- Be wary of strangers. Avoid people who look, act, and think differently from you.

  agree   neutral   disagree

- I should never hurt anyone, even by accident.

  agree   neutral   disagree

- There is a magic cure for my problems.

  agree   neutral   disagree

- Personal problems are private and should not be revealed to anyone outside the family.

  agree   neutral   disagree

- Strong people don't ask for help.

  agree   neutral   disagree

- I can do things only when I'm in the mood.

  agree   neutral   disagree

- I am always in the spotlight.

  agree   neutral   disagree

- It's others' responsibility to solve my problems.

  agree   neutral   disagree

- People ought to do what I wish.

  agree   neutral   disagree

- Giving up is the best policy.

  agree   neutral   disagree

- I need to be sure in order to decide.

  agree   neutral   disagree

- Change is unnatural.

  agree   neutral   disagree

- Knowing how my problems got started when I was young is essential to solving them.

  agree   neutral   disagree

- Everybody should trust me.

  agree   neutral   disagree

- I should be happy all the time.

  agree   neutral   disagree

- There is a secret, terrible part of me that controls me.

  agree   neutral   disagree

- Working on my problems will hurt me.

  agree   neutral   disagree

- The world ought to be fair.

  agree   neutral   disagree

- I am not responsible for my behavior.

  agree   neutral   disagree

- It is always best not to be genuine.

  agree   neutral   disagree

- It is dangerous to feel emotions.

  agree   neutral   disagree

- People shouldn't act the way they do.

  agree   neutral   disagree

Step 3. Score your survey. Give yourself three points for each agree, two points for neutral, and one point for disagree. Add them up for a total.

Step 4. Review the answers you agree with. Where did you learn the belief? You could have learned them from many places—your family, your friends, your colleagues, the media, or from your own life experiences. But some values you may have learned from your reference groups. Try to find the exact cultural source for each belief.

The average score was 45. What does this mean?

A high score (52+) simply shows that you identify more strongly with these cultural beliefs than most other people who took the survey. A low score (37-) means that you identify less with these values.

Most people who took the survey reported that they learned many of the beliefs from their culture. For example, people who thought that "making mistakes is terrible and that they must do everything perfectly" often said they identified with American culture. Many who believed that "self discipline is too hard to achieve" and that "we can only do things when we are in the mood," said they identified with a non-Western culture. People who held the value that "emotions are dangerous," often traced the attitude to what they said were certain aspects of the cultures in Great Britain and British

Commonwealth, and former Commonwealth countries (Canada, Australia, New Zealand). Those who were convinced that "personal problems are private and should not be revealed to anyone outside of the family," often said they identified with Asian cultures. Almost all reported that their cultures taught them to be wary of strangers and to avoid people who looked or acted differently from them.

It is important to understand that these preferences are just cultural tendencies. People all over the world share many of the beliefs listed above. These beliefs are not confined to one country or one culture. You hear these beliefs wherever you travel.

It's not that one culture is rational and the other irrational; one is healthy and one is sick; one enlightened, the other backward. All cultures have some of these beliefs and attitudes. The only difference among them is that different cultures emphasize different ones.

"Most people are other people. Their thoughts are someone's opinions, their lives a mimicry, their passions a quotation." (*Oscar Wilde*)

What's in a Name?
Be Careful What You Call Something

In real life, unlike in Shakespeare, the sweetness of the rose depends upon the name it bears. Things are not only what they are. They are, in very important respects, what they seem to be. HUBERT H. HUMPHREY

IN THIS CHAPTER
- Appreciating the importance of the words we use to describe ourselves and others
- An exercise on switching labels

Shakespeare's famous line "A rose by any other name would smell as sweet," means that we can give something a different name, but it doesn't change what it is. While this is certainly true if you are a rose, a Capulet, or a Montague, it is not true in many other areas.

A name has a connotative as well as denotative meaning, and some names collect powerful emotional responses. Consider the emotions generated by labels such as: *terrorist, pedophile, commie, insane, 9/11*; or *sweetheart, mom, democracy, God, freedom*. Even our fairy-tales emphasize the importance of using the right name.

RUMPELSTILTSKIN

Remember the German fairy-tale collected in the 19th century by the Grimm Brothers. The version below I adapted from one of their traditional tales.

A beautiful and clever miller's daughter became queen of a realm by contracting with a dwarf to spin straw into gold. But in order to get the gold, she had to promise to give the dwarf her first-born child.

A year after she became Queen, she had forgotten all about her promise until she brought a beautiful daughter into the world. Suddenly the dwarf appeared, demanding to take the child. But she grieved so sorely until her tears softened him, and he said, "You can keep your child only if you can tell me my true name. But you only have three days to do it. If you don't I will surely take the child."

The first day the queen guessed all the common names in the kingdom, but the dwarf kept replying, "Your highness, that is not my name."

The second day the queen tried names from other realms, and from lands far away, but the dwarf kept saying, "Madam, that is not my name."

On the third day, the Queen sent her nurse out into the Kingdom to find if they had missed any names. The nurse came back saying she couldn't find any new names, but told her that something interesting had happened. When she was returning to the castle, she took a short cut over a high mountain pass. In a small, hidden, forest valley below, she saw a little cottage with a fire out front. She saw a tiny man jumping, hopping, and dancing around the fire. She could hear him singing in a high squeaky voice,

> Merrily the feast I'll make.
> Today I'll brew, tomorrow bake;
> Merrily I'll dance and sing,
> For next day will a stranger bring.
> Little does my lady dream
> Rumpelstiltskin is my name!

The queen suddenly jumped up and demanded that the dwarf materialize. When he appeared she said,

"I am ready to make my guess."

"This is the third day, the dwarf said. " This is your last chance."

"Is your name George?"

"No, madam."

"Is your name Fred?"

"No, madam!"

"Is your name John?"

"NO, MADAM!"

"Perhaps, then, your name is Rumpelstiltskin?"

The dwarf cried in horror and ran out of the palace screaming. He was never seen again.

As the fable suggests, names can be very powerful, and can have almost a magical quality. In some religious and cultural rituals, they must be spoken in exactly the right way for the magic to take effect. But in most cases, names are quite arbitrary, indicating only a consensus about what something should be called. Often one name can substitute for another quite easily. The exception to this generalization is found in certain names that have a strong emotional component. Changing the name may often switch the emotional connotation.

Some of us consistently choose names with negative connotations to describe ourselves. We could just as easily select neutral or positive words. The names we pick change how we feel about ourselves. Do the following exercise to prove the point.

Homework

 EXERCISE

11.1 What's in a Name?

Use Worksheet 11.1, "What's in a Name?"

Step 1. First read the worksheet example on page 74 and then go to step 2.

Step 2. In the first column of Worksheet 11.1 write the trait you are describing in neutral terms such as "I change my mind a lot," "I accept what other people tell me," or "I don't work real hard." Try to think of the trait neutrally in terms of your objective behavior rather than in terms of what you feel about it.

Step 3. In the second column, list the major negative names you could use to describe the trait such as *wishy-washy, gullible,* and *lazy.*

Step 4. In the last column list positive names that you could use to describe the same traits, or the same behavior, such as *flexible, trusting,* or *easy going.* Use a good thesaurus if you need to.

Step 5. Every time you notice the trait, practice using the positive name to substitute for the negative label.

EXAMPLE OF WORKSHEET 11.1

I am a person who . . .	I could call myself . . .	But, I also could call myself . . .
changes my mind a lot	wishy-washy	flexible
accepts what other people tell me	gullible	trusting
doesn't work real hard	lazy	easy going
takes risks	foolhardy	brave
expresses my own opinion	egotistical	assertive, genuine
helps others in need	an enabler	charitable
talks a lot	a motor-mouth	expressive
is nontraditional	a malcontent	independent
tries to please others	a sycophant	kind, caring
has strong beliefs	conceited	self-confident
is emotional	hysterical	exuberant
looks at life positively	a Pollyanna	optimistic
loves a lot	infatuated, lovesick	loving, affectionate

WORKSHEET

11.1 What's in a Name?

I am a person who . . .	I could call myself . . . NEGATIVE	But, I also could call myself . . . POSITIVE

Some people may argue that a negative word is more logically correct than a positive word. For example, they suggest that wishy-washy people change their minds more often than flexible people; therefore, wishy-washy is a more accurate name. Although there may be some concrete differences between synonyms, many differences are purely reflective of our own value system. We refer to people as wishy-washy because we think they change their minds more than we think they should—not because there is some objective standard of how often people are permitted to switch their opinions and still be called flexible. Likewise, when we call someone "lazy" we may think they are unnecessarily idle. But since everyone is always doing something (e.g., sleeping, resting, thinking, playing), what we really mean is that they aren't doing what *we* think they ought to be doing.

If we change some of the names we use to describe ourselves, or others, we can produce instantaneous and dramatic shifts on how we feel about them.

Taking Out Your Mental Trash

chapter 12

Self-esteem
Too Little or Too Much?

Every act of conscious learning requires the willingness to suffer an injury to one's self-esteem. That is why young children, before they are aware of their own self-importance, learn so easily; and why older persons, especially if vain or important, cannot learn at all.   THOMAS SZASZ

IN THIS CHAPTER
- Probing the ideal amount of self-esteem
- Surveying our own self-esteem

Our movies and TV shows suggest that we can't have enough self-esteem. They teach us an admiration for people with high self-esteem—people brimming over with self-confidence, people who are certain they can accomplish whatever they set their minds to. The picture created is virtually that of a winner—if one can envision a man or woman so pumped up and bulging with virtues above those of the average human capacity. In the movies, their achievements, display their noble, upright, altruistic, and courageous temperaments. They are always succeeding—with negligible effort; succeeding where everyone else fails; succeeding without practice or guidance; even succeeding in rescuing those among us who suffer from the most damnable human condition that exists—low self-esteem.

Most of the psychological literature on self-esteem emphasizes the damage caused by low self-esteem. Many people underrate themselves, think they are less than others, and believe they can't do things as well as others. Certainly there are a great number of these people in the world. They are shy and unassuming, defer to others, and take no credit for their accomplishments, which are often significant. It is sad that these people do not see their inner worth accurately, particularly when others do. In many cases, they are our favorite people; we enjoy their company and find them kind and caring.

What we often ignore is self-esteem that is too high. Our cultural message is that this is impossible. The idea is based on an unforgivable ruse which is also a core misperception of our society—high self-esteem is the Olympian ideal. We prohibit our children from thinking poorly about themselves, and we solemnly inform them that if they neglect our advice, they will mangle their lives. How could this be anticipated to help our children?

 In recent years, many people have been bombarded with the affliction of too high self-esteem. And during all this time, there has been no lack of talk-show counselors, academic professors and scholars, gurus, and lay advisors impatient to cheer this disgrace, uphold the indomitable rightness and sagacity of it, and bless those who practice it.

Few in American society believe that anyone can have too high self-esteem. Maybe it's our strong desire to support the underdog. Or maybe it's the Horatio Alger fiction that anybody can do anything in our democracy, if they simply put their minds to it. But whatever it is, too high self-esteem can cause atrocious problems in our children. Here are some:

- It makes children demand that the universe pay them what they think they are owed. They keep failing to understand why things don't happen the way they should.

- While we wish to show our children that we love them, and we wish to give them our full acceptance and a sense of basic security, we can give them too much security. Yes, hard as it is to believe and roundly condemned as this idea may be, a too secure, too perfect early environment can keep our children from ever learning how to handle conflict or frustration. They never have to deal with failure because we never allow them to fail. They never learn to cope with difficulties and never have to work through problems.

- The results of all this pumping up of egos can be devastating to children. We may turn them into moral cripples. To live with other people our children must see that they aren't better than everyone else. They must perceive that they have the same basic worth. If they think too highly of themselves, the complementary view is that they think too poorly of others. Almost all the dictators and despots of the last century thought this way about the people they oppressed. They believed that they had the right to rule people's lives because they were so superior to the masses.

- High self-esteem people often get enraged, surprisingly, for the simple reason that they expect too much. They expect to accomplish anything they put their minds too. When reality crashes down upon them, they turn against other people for not giving them what they think is owed to them.

- Expecting always to succeed will mean our children will spend too much time in endeavors that they have little talent for, while ignoring those things that they can succeed in. In addition, they will not learn certain principles in life that need to be learned such as:

    We can't have everything we want.
    Others have rights too.
    Bad things happen to good people.
    We can't control everything and everyone.

- People with too high self-esteem attribute failure to forces outside themselves rather than to themselves. Thus, when a goal isn't reached or a major problem occurs, these people attribute this failure to something in the environment not to themselves. They therefore do not attempt to correct any of their own mistakes. Blamers and condemners keep looking in the wrong place to find the solution. They paint a negative portrait of the rest of the world to explain why others have such rotten taste not to recognize that they are a masterpiece.

- Too high self-esteem keeps people from learning. If our children start engaging in hurtful behavior later in life—drugs, crime, harming others—they will have no motivation to change. They need to be taught that they are not good people when they hit others, snort cocaine, cheat on exams, or slander their peers. Discontent breeds change. Complacency breeds stagnation. A person with Olympian self-esteem has no reason to make any changes at all.

Nowadays, there is an affirmation industry that instructs us how to keep any negative experiences from lowering our self-esteem. Modern day gurus teach us positive self-affirmations to prop up our sagging egos when we commit another mistake or botch another job. These can damage us in the following ways.

EXAMPLE

DAMAGING SELF-AFFIRMATIONS

PROBLEM	SELF-AFFIRMATION
Dropped out of school?	"A person should be judged by his basic worth not his accomplishments."
Keep using cocaine?	"I'm not to blame. I had bad potty training."
Beating up your wife?	"Nobody's perfect. We are all fallible human beings."
Cheating your business colleagues?	"It's business, not personal. To get ahead, you have to grab what you can in life."

We should be dismayed when parents praise their children for mediocrity, when they construct a bubble around their child where failure and frustration are screened out, when they scramble over each other to fulfill their child's every craving, whim, or even a hint that their child has an unmet desire? Consider the following example.

Prince in Disguise

EXAMPLE

Mike was a single, good-looking man in his 20s. But he had some major problems. He couldn't maintain good relationships with women and had a history of failed love encounters. He wasn't successful at work because even though he was quite bright and very creative, he didn't like doing the menial tasks concomitant to any job, so he would end up being fired. He had emotional problems, minor to begin with, but he built them into powerful upheavals because he seemed incapable of tolerating even the smallest frustrations.

This happened because it was the way his self-esteem was formed. He was the youngest in a large family. Before he was born, his mother had two miscarriages. The doctor told her she should never have another child, because it might kill her. But she liked motherhood and desperately wanted one more. Finally, Mike, to the surprise of his father, mother, and the medical profession, was born. His mother then had a hysterectomy so for sure Mike was her last.

As one can imagine, the family treated Mike as a prince. He was a cute baby and spoiled by everyone—particularly his mother. When Mike started to form his self-esteem, he looked in the mirror and saw reflected a special child who was adored and treated as royalty by his family, a unique gift from God, not at all like other boys. That's what was reflected, so that's what he saw. He didn't know anything about his mother's miscarriages, her hysterectomy, being the last possible child. He didn't understand that because of the family's own needs, losses, and thankfulness, the mirror was warped and didn't reflect him accurately. Instead, he really thought he was royalty.

Life was wonderful for Mike until he went to school. Then the problems began because the kids didn't treat him as royalty. They had the audacity to treat him like everybody else—a normal human being. His schoolmates didn't need him in the same way that his family did. But, of course, he didn't know this. All he understood was that he wasn't being treated like a prince. So, he got angry with his peers and demanded that they treat him properly. This further enraged his schoolmates so they picked on him and ridiculed him. He became the brunt of all their practical jokes. This just made Mike feel worse; he got angrier; he made more demands; and a vicious cycle developed until Mike had no friends at all. He became a social isolate.

Now, one may expect that when Mike was treated a lot worse at school than at home, he might have concluded that there was something wrong with home. But he didn't. Instead, he concluded there was something wrong with school. He thought his schoolmates were jealous. They attacked him because they saw how special he was and couldn't stand feeling inferior.

He kept thinking this way throughout his life. When he dated he didn't understand why his girlfriends didn't treat him as his mom had. To him it was obvious what was wrong—*wrong girlfriend*! So, he spent most of his adult years searching for a woman who had enough sense to treat him properly. He kept searching, but he never found her. He told people, "With women's liberation, it's really hard to find a good woman nowadays."

When he experienced the normal fears, frustrations, and petty annoyances that we all have, Mike's reaction was one of rage. He thought, "It's unfair that life is so hard on me; something is wrong; it shouldn't be this way!" So, when some frustration occurred, like a sales clerk not giving him immediate attention or some other minor annoyance, he would throw a temper tantrum and walk out. This did not endear him to sales clerks, or anyone else for that matter.

Well, you see Mike's problem. He had what is called "The Prince in Disguise Syndrome"—the belief that one is uniquely special and entitled to extraordinary treatment by the world. His image of his self was so distorted, so unrealistic that it kept him from coping with normal conflicts. So, he didn't cope at all. He just sat there and felt cheated. And all these problems were created because of the warped image he had seen in his family's mirror. His problems continued until the day he finally accepted that he was a fallible human being (FHB) like all the rest of us. When he threw the, "I am a prince in disguise," attitude into the trash, his life improved immeasurably.

 We should try to get our self-esteem as close as possible to what we actually can do. Either way, it is important that our self-esteem fits with our real ability to handle the situation. Ideally, it is neither too low nor too high, but like Goldilocks, just right.

The following exercise may help you take a snapshot of the accuracy of your own self-esteem.

Homework

EXERCISE

12.1 Self-esteem Scale

Step 1. Think back in your history. Imagine some important events you have undertaken, such as enrolling in school, getting married, making the sports team, becoming a parent, finishing a major project, overcoming a personal problem, getting a promotion. Relax and focus on this particular event.

Step 2. Now, think back to one of these events. What did you think were your chances of success at the time? Did you believe you would succeed or fail? Try to find a percentage—50% chance of success, 20% chance. Put an "X" on the following continuum to indicate your prediction.

> *Example:* "I am 80% certain I can handle the new promotion."

```
|_____|_____X_____|
low chance of success      50%        high chance of success
```

Step 3. Now record how well you think you actually did.

> *Example:* "I did a bad job, hated it, and left the company. I would
>   give myself only 20% success."

```
|_____X_____|_____|
unsuccessful            50%           very successful
```

Step 4. Compare the two scales. Was your self-esteem too high, too low, or about right? (e.g., I overestimated my ability by 60%.)

Step 5. Go through a variety of other events to establish your average self-esteem. Mark on the slide rule how well you thought you would do at the time. Record how well you actually did, and notice the difference. Did you keep under- or overestimating yourself? Was your self-esteem generally too low, or was it too high? Possibly, you found it mixed. Did you underestimate your ability in some things, but overestimate your ability in others? If this is the case, look for the reasons why you overestimate or underestimate your performance.

If we look at real self-esteem, the genuine article, we see it is based on our experience with the world. Self-esteem is a side effect of a multitude of successes and failures, good and bad decisions, right and wrong actions we have made. Realistic self-esteem comes from the constant commerce between the world and us. It provides us with feedback about how well we are doing and what we need to work on. Self-esteem is causally associated with our accomplishments and failures, not blindly disconnected from the world's feedback. When we think about real self-esteem, that which is created by our intercourse with the world, not by what we have artificially propped up by saccharine self-affirmations, we cannot relate real self-esteem to anything counterfeit, anything lacking in worth, anything lacking in dignity. The real kind of self-esteem provides us with a great gift—a true portrait of ourselves. This gift can successfully guide us through the rest of our lives.

chapter 13

Prejudice
Our Fear of Strangers

A great many people think they are thinking when they are merely rearranging their prejudices.
WILLIAM JAMES

IN THIS CHAPTER
• Grasping the roots of prejudice
• Facing our own attitudes

 Prejudice has many causes, but the belief that *one group of people is inherently better than another* may be at the heart of it. Those who are prejudiced believe this. They judge people by the group they are in, rather than by the individual; and then they place a negative value on the group (e.g., my group is good, while your group is evil.)

Because of this fallacy, some people develop a strong feeling of fear and hatred toward certain outsiders. They learn this when they are young and can keep this attitude for a lifetime. They reject outsiders as suitable workers, friends, or mates. They place others in a box of stereotypical traits that keep them from seeing others as individuals. Through years of practice, they build higher and higher fences to separate themselves from others until all understanding and communication breaks down.

This fear and hatred of strangers has a name, xenophobia. On the face of it, xenophobia looks like a trivial fear but it is by far the most common fear and certainly the most damaging. You will find it in every country. It can be defined as:

Xenophobia. n. Hatred or distrust of foreigners or strangers. (*Xenon* from the Greek word meaning stranger, and *phobia* from the Greek word meaning fear. Together they signify an exaggerated and persistent dread of, or aversion to, foreigners and strangers.)

The Ugly American

EXAMPLE

René was a charming, attractive, single young man from France and his company had recently transferred him to the United States against his wishes. He was having a terrible time here. He felt deeply homesick, couldn't find any fellow Frenchmen to talk to, and spent his evenings and weekends alone staring at the TV. His isolation was causing a depression, and his office colleagues told him he needed to get out of the house and start meeting people. They encouraged him to join some clubs, but he always refused, insisting that there would be too many Yanks there. A curious attitude since he was now living in the United States and this country has a tendency to be overrun with Yanks.

After exploring why he felt this way, it was discovered that his early experiences with Americans were negative.

He grew up in a small town in the south of France; it was fairly isolated and far off the usual tourist routes. He had heard American music and seen American movies and TV shows, but he had never actually met an American before.

One day he went to town with his father and saw a very fat man standing in the local hotel. The man was dressed in green baggy shorts and was wearing an orange shirt with prints of little yellow fishes all over it. He was shouting at a clerk behind the desk. Apparently, he was complaining about the room not having a colored television or something and was demanding that the clerk find him a TV immediately. He yelled that France had the worst service he had ever seen, and that this kind of thing wouldn't be tolerated back home. While he was brow beating the clerk, his two pudgy children were running up and down the lobby pulling leaves off the potted plants and climbing over the furniture while his obese wife looked on with a bored expression. René's father turned to him and said, "Those are Americans!"

He never forgot this impression. It colored all his subsequent contacts. Later, when he saw other American tourists he remembered only those who looked and acted like the man in the lobby. Those who didn't, he assumed were from Canada or some other place.

His selective perception picked out only those Americans who were egotistical, fat, noisy, and who spent their vacations insulting his country. As a result, he learned to feel a repugnance to anyone and everything American. When his boss told him he had to work in the United States, he adamantly refused; but finally, to keep his job, he reluctantly agreed.

Later, his isolation was broken when his colleagues at work asked him to do things with them. So, he got out of his apartment and went to some clubs. He reported that although he found some ugly Americans, most of the time he met people very similar to his French friends back home. He even became close to a few Americans and spent some of his free time going to baseball games and parties with them. His loneliness was gone and his depression lifted.

But strangely, his fallacy continued. Even though he had met a number of nice Americans, he concluded that they must be those rare exceptions. His attitude probably remains to this day.

Xenophobia is everywhere. It also lives across the United States. Students from the Northeast have heard their parents say, "You won't learn anything if you don't go to an Ivy League School. Your education will be barbaric. There is no culture west of the Allegheny mountains." Out West you hear, "People from the Northeast are intellectual snobs, pompous, stuffy people."

In the South, xenophobia takes the form of, "Damn Yankee carpetbaggers," while up North you are warned that everybody in the South is, "a bigot, a hick, or a dumb redneck."

In Texas xenophobia has appeared as Texas against the other 49 states. "Tex'ns vs. the Feds," as they put it. When Texans drive north into the mountain states they hear, "Flat landers only come up here to buy all our land and ruin our environment."

In Washington and Oregon, there were bumper stickers saying, "Out of staters, go home!" Visiting Californians were warned not to drive with California license plates because, "Californians only come up here to buy all our land and ruin our environment."

Xenophobia exists in other countries. In Australia, xenophobia may be directed toward anybody not Australian. First in line are the Japanese, "The Yellow Peril." In the past, the government had one immigration plan, "The White Australian Policy." This has changed, but some Australians still believe in the old philosophy. Second in line are the Irish. In this land instead of hearing Polish jokes, as you would in America, you hear the same jokes, but about the Irish. When England founded the country two centuries ago, it sent boatloads of Irish political prisoners along with the convicts from British gaols. Despite their mutual suffering at the hands of Britain, they didn't keep good company together. Some Australians, particularly those with English pedigrees, don't like the Irish emotionality; it conflicts with their British reserve. If somebody shows strong emotion, they call it, "Having a Paddy." Read Paddy (a derogatory name for the Irish) for Patty and you understand the meaning behind the statement.

Xenophobia is even alive in paradise, in Hawaii. Some Euro-Americans say Hawaiian natives are stupid, uneducated, and totally without drive or motivation. But some Hawaiians believe a person is either Kamaaina—a native-born islander, a good guy, one of "us"; or Haole—a nonnative, often from the mainland, a bad guy, one of "them." You can understand the feeling for Haoles by learning the original meaning of the word in Hawaiian. The translation is, "Those without souls."

I am not just picking on these countries. Xenophobia is everywhere. No matter what the country or culture, somebody, somewhere hates them, even where you would least expect it. For example, in several countries people from Great Britain (the Poms) are often considered too stuffy and snobbish; Americans too arrogant, aggressive, and egotistical; the French (the Frogs) effetes who have loose morals; New Zealanders, inferior people from a little country. The Canadians? Too much like Americans. (This seems really strange. As a U.S. expatriate living overseas once told me, "Can you imagine anybody hating Canadians. Who goes around saying, 'Those rotten, no good, lousy Canadians'?" But some people do.) No country is exempt.

Homework

EXERCISE 13.1 What Do You Feel About These Groups of People?

The following exercise won't take long. Be as honest with yourself as you can.

Step 1. Look at the list on the following page. Pick the groups that interest you, and focus on your overall feeling about people in the group. Try to recognize your true feelings.

Americans	French	Australians
Russians	English	Irish
Israelis	Palestinians	African Americans
Latin Americans	Irish Americans	Asians
WASPs	Mormons	Catholics
Muslims	Liberals	Conservatives
Rich people	Poor people	Men
Women	Adolescents	Elderly
Arabs	add your own	

Step 2. Next, for the items that you select, try to remember the first time you ever heard of the group, learned about them, or met someone in the group. Remember the situation as exactly as you can (i.e., The first time I met a Mormon was when a young man in a white shirt and dark suit knocked on my dorm door in college.)

Step 3. What overall feeling did you have about them at the time?

Step 4. How might your first feelings have been mistaken?

Step 5. How have your feelings changed over time?

If your feelings about the group came from a single powerful emotion—based either on your own or on a significant other's traumatic experiences (like René's)—your overall feeling is likely to be one of prejudice. True knowledge doesn't come from traumatic experiences; it comes from long-term contact and acquaintance with multiple members of a group. Most people probably agree with the following general impression.

Universally, most of us who have had a sufficient number of contacts with members of another group conclude the same thing. Ignoring the differences in customs, we judge most people in the other group to be similar in essentials to people in our own. There are always some negative examples, but we have found most of them are good decent people.

 We could discount xenophobia as just normal pride in people like ourselves, a natural nonpathological rooting for the home team. But inside this self-pride may lurk ugly damage. The "others," the "strangers," the "foreigners," are perceived as evil, sinister, and malevolent. This produces an almost spiritual rejection of people who act and appear different from us. And from this contempt, spring the psychological roots of prejudice, bigotry, and discrimination, which have caused a lion's share of misery on our planet.

If we are indeed to become a global village, we must conquer our own xenophobia to create a more fair-minded and calmer world. But our first task in this endeavor is to change our attitudes, a difficult but not impossible task. It is best we get started right away. And a good way to do this is by recognizing the core fear deep inside all of us of those strange people who are different.

chapter 14

Choosing Our Past Carefully
Keeping Our Memories from Fooling Us

The palest ink is better than the best memory. CHINESE PROVERB

IN THIS CHAPTER
- Recognizing how our memories can fool us
- Remembering the past more accurately

 Many of us believe we have a good memory. Because the impression in our mind is clear and concise, we think our recollection must be correct, but we are often wrong. We fail to recognize that we don't accurately recall our past, we choose selectively, and we often make a poor choice.

At first appearance, it may seem that "choosing our past" is a meaningless phrase. What possible sense could be behind it? Is it like one of those wise Zen sayings full of contradictions? Isn't our past our past? What happened, happened? How can we change something that happened before and doesn't exist anymore? Isn't our past total and complete just the way it is?

This idea is true in rational terms, the past is unalterable; the actual past, that is. But what can be changed and is quite alterable is our memory of the past. Our view of the past is incomplete. No one remembers things exactly the way they were—our memories are too poor for this. We selectively remember some things, and we selectively forget others.

Our memories can be so bad that we can recall events that never occurred. One man distinctly remembered being abused by an uncle when he was 10. When he checked he found the uncle had died before he was 8.

He had never been abused at all, but his best friend had, and he had empathized so completely that he imagined it had happened to him.

Other people remember an event that they read in a book, or saw in the movies, but later they forgot the source and thought it had happened to them. There is a famous instance of this type—the case of Bridey Murphy. Under hypnosis, a woman named Virginia Tighe recalled living in Ireland in a previous lifetime under the name of Bridey Murphy. Some people checked her description of the Irish village and found her reports to be amazingly accurate. Her case was used as evidence for reincarnation. But later, a Chicago newspaper reporter discovered that she had learned these stories from an elderly woman, the real Bridey Murphy, who had lived in Chicago across the street from her when she was 5. As a child she used to sit on the old woman's porch and listen to stories about the old Irish village.

We call up from our memories those events that fit with our current mood. Many people who feel unhappy about the present, preconsciously choose to remember positive things from their past. In their brains, they make their childhood appear rosy. They remember the happy times: the birthday presents, the romances, the achievements. But they selectively forget the sicknesses, the disappointments, the broken hearts, and the pain.

VIVIAN'S HUSBAND

EXAMPLE

Vivian remembered her first marriage with great fondness. She was a stunningly attractive woman in her early 40s who had been a fashion model, but she had also been married four times. She spoke about how wonderful her first husband was, how kind, handsome, and strong. She spent years regretting the loss of the relationship and kept trying to find him. This regret had only started after her fourth marriage was failing; before this, she hadn't thought of him at all. This made her memory suspect and in need of confirmation. Reluctantly she checked with some friends and found out that her first husband had been a horror. He drank much of the time, cheated on her constantly, couldn't hold down a job for more than a few months, wouldn't come home for days on end, and sometimes physically abused her. How could she have forgotten all this?

As we have said, we remember things based on our present needs, not based on the reality of the past. When her fourth marriage was failing, she tried to comfort herself by recalling at least one good relationship in her life. She didn't have one, so she created one in her memory. She only recalled the few good things about her first husband and totally forgot the many bad things.

Whenever we start reminiscing about the past, whether about the great experiences we had in high school, our first love, or the wonderful time we had living in Commerce, Ohio, we had best be careful. Our memories may be fooling us. We may have created a fantasy that never existed because we selectively screened out all the contrary themes, emotions, and experiences that did not fit with the mood we were trying to strike. Fooled by this distortion and taking it as truth, we then live as if this fabricated memory was real.

The following homework exercise may help you test some of your memories so that you may recall your past more accurately.

Homework

EXERCISE

14.1 Remembering Carefully

Use Worksheet 14.1, "What Do You Remember?"

Step 1. Pick some experience in the past that you have a strong memory of but that may not actually be true. It can be anything—the great job you think you once had; a wonderful early romance; how gloriously happy you were when you lived in ———.

Step 2. Vague remembering. Review this past event generally. Don't try to recall all the details. Simply allow the overall memory of the event to emerge. Write down what you recall.

Step 3. Relax. Listen to a relaxation tape, a nature tape, or relaxing music.

Step 4. Meticulous remembering. Imagine traveling back in time to the early event. Pick a specific scene to focus on. Use all of your senses to fill in the scene. For example:

- *Vision*—What colors, lighting, objects, movements, and point of view do you see?
- *Sounds*—Do you hear background sounds, music, people talking in the next room, traffic outside?
- *Smells*—What odors do you notice?

- *Kinesthetic*—Are you moving or standing or lying down?
- *Emotional*—Are you feeling happy? Sad? Angry? Scared?

In what combination and strength do your senses mix? Go through each step; don't jump ahead or generalize. Use as much detail as possible. Stimulate your memory by using aids such as photos, diaries, or letters. Remind yourself of what other events were happening at the time. Use any cues that help you recall the earlier event.

Step 5. Record. On the worksheet, jot down what you remembered.

Step 6. Contrast. Compare the first remembrance (vague remembering) with the last (meticulous remembering). What did you fail to remember? What did you forget? What did you make up?

14.1 What Do You Remember?

Early memory _____

I vaguely remember _____

Meticulous remembering

    The specific scene _____

    What did I see? _____

    What did I hear? _____

    What did I smell? _____

    Other senses? _____

    What did I feel? _____

Contrasting vague remembering with meticulous remembering.

    What did I fail to remember? _____

    _____

    _____

    _____

    What did I forget? _____

    _____

    _____

    _____

    What did I make up? _____

    _____

    _____

    _____

Most people discover that they forgot some important features from the earlier time. Their meticulous remembering recalled some events and feelings that they had totally forgotten. For some people, these newly remembered aspects of the past dramatically changed their overall feelings about what had happened.

 Sometimes unhappiness in our present life is due to the distorted past we have created in our memory. In such cases, the only way to become content in the present is to force our self to remember the past more accurately. For life to guide us, we should remember our history in as unbiased, unprejudiced, dispassionate a manner as possible. It is best to choose our past carefully.

chapter 15

Dream Interpretation
What They Mean and
What They Don't Mean

In dreams we are true poets; we create the persons of the drama . . . and we listen with surprise to what they say.   RALPH WALDO EMERSON

IN THIS CHAPTER
- Investigating the significance of dreams
- Finding the meaning behind our own dreams

Many people believe that all our dreams have deep significance. Nowadays, some specialists who study these matters don't think so.

Our pop culture tells us that all our night dreams are bursting with great significance. For example, have you ever stood in line at a checkout counter in a supermarket and noticed those little pamphlets they have on the racks? Most of the pamphlets reveal secrets about relationships like, "How to know if your husband is having an affair," or, "What 10 things you must avoid to keep your marriage alive," or, "Astrological signs of your pet." Some of us also may have occasionally noticed books like *Dream Interpretation*, which give us advice about the underlying meaning of our dreams. These books describe different kinds of dreams and explain what they mean. For instance, if we dream of sharp objects such as knives or razor blades, it means we are angry; if we dream of traveling, we are bored. But according to the book, many of the dreams show that we are sexually aroused. If we dream we are falling that means we are attracted to a stranger; if we dream about fruit like oranges and bananas we are thinking of sexual organs; if we dream of objects and furniture as chairs and tables standing upside down it means we must have oral sex on our minds—obviously.

One has to admire books like these, the authors have courage. Most of the writers don't offer any explanation about how they know what our dreams mean. They just say it. They quote no research. They imply there is no reason to question their conclusions, hinting that if you were smart and in the know like them, you would realize their interpretations are obvious. That's a clear giveaway. Most times when someone says, "It's obvious that . . . " or "Obviously one can be certain that . . ." The one thing you can be sure of is that whatever follows is anything but obvious.

Dream interpretation is not new. Dreams have been big things in the history of psychology and psychiatry for a long time. They were central to Freud's theory. He thought they were the royal road to the unconscious. By understanding one's dreams, Freud believed, one could chart the hidden impulses lying deep inside one's personality. So, for years professionals would spend countless sessions with their clients listening to their dreams and asking probing questions about their meaning so that the patients' underlying conflicts could be revealed.

But nowadays many of the public have misunderstood dreams. Many recent sleep and dream researchers have found that dreaming is as much physical as psychological. They have concluded that dreams usually do not provide dramatic insights into the core nasties inside our personalities. They have found that dreams are very individualistic and full of private associations that make it very difficult to interpret unless one knows the dreamer extremely well.

To give you an idea of how many present-day professionals look at dreams, consider the following example.

WATERY DREAMING

EXAMPLE Imagine that the day you dreamed, you woke up late for work and almost had an accident when pulling into the parking lot. You felt anxious. Your short-term memory recorded this information as raw data number 1. When you returned home that evening you felt bored and watched an old rerun of *The Love Boat*. Your visual memory recorded this as raw data number 2. At night as you are sleeping, the water faucet in your bathroom is dripping and this information from your preconscious is recorded in your brain as raw data number 3. In addition, your right leg is crooked under your left. This information is sent up your spinal cord and processed in the sensory motor area of your brain as raw data number 4.

So, you have four bits of raw data recorded in your brain. How does your brain combine the data to form a dream?

We know that the brain isn't just a calculator that totals up raw data; it is far more creative than this. The brain takes the data from the different sources and combines them into patterns, themes, and stories. It creates the best story it can considering the data available. It searches through its long-term memory to find a story that best combines the four bits of data.

When we are awake, we call these stories *thoughts, conceptions,* or *beliefs.* But when we are asleep, we call them dreams. Dreams are bizarre because they have so much less input from our senses and so much more input from other areas, like our emotions, drives, long- and short-term memory, or physical state at the time of dreaming. Without our senses guiding our dreams, they have a strong tendency to float around a lot.

So what kind of dream might your brain create from these four bits of raw data? Here is one possibility.

> You dreamed you were on a South Pacific cruise (the Love Boat data); you hit a coral reef (the near accident); you broke your leg on the side of the ship as you jumped overboard (the crooked leg); and you fell into the water (the dripping faucet).

Of course, our dreams are never based on just four bits of data. They are based on thousands of bits coming from our memory, our emotions, our senses, and our physical state. Our brain takes all this data and combines it into the most sensible story it can.

If there is some emotion that keeps recurring in our dreams that we haven't noticed much when awake, it can be useful to focus on dreams. If we dream violent stories we may be angry; if we dream of running away from things we may be scared; if we dream of being chased by others we may be feeling guilty. But most times these themes are not a big surprise to us. We might very well be aware that we are angry with our boss, so it shouldn't be a big surprise that we have a dream of violence. Or if we are on our umpteenth diet, it is hardly remarkable that we dream of food.

One thing is clear, though, books that tell us exactly what our dreams mean, or that pretend to unlock the secrets of our unconscious are drivel.

The authors haven't the foggiest idea of who we are or what our private symbols may mean, so they are just making the whole thing up.

So mostly, dreams show us how our brains work, and don't uncover evil things buried in our depths. But there is one type of dream that has more meaning—pleonastic dreams.

Pleonastic Dreams

Some of us, maybe most of us, have pleonastic dreams. They are recurring dreams that we experience repeatedly. We find ourselves in the same place or involved in the same conflict over and over again. We may have a recurring dream for years or even throughout our life.

In the past, many theorists attributed great importance to pleonastic dreams. They viewed them as messages from the deepest layer of our unconscious. They thought these dreams reccurred because they were archetypes of our lifelong unfulfilled wishes and hopes, or that they meant people were repressing some deep, dark sexual or aggressive conflict.

Nowadays, most researchers conclude that pleonastic dreams simply reveal that we find ourselves in the same type of situation that we have been in before. Our brain is accessing the same type of data available to it and arbitrarily comes up with the same theme.

But occasionally pleonastic dreams can tell us something more interesting. They may reveal a core theme or core philosophy we have about life. They reiterate our favorite stories or our preferred themes.

Most people are probably aware of the theme anyway, because our brains take our thoughts, impulses, and emotions and form them into patterns when we are awake. When asleep, these patterns transform into dreams. Over the years, recurring dreams may change slightly as our view of the world changes, but the story remains the same because the theme is the same. The following dream is a good example of a pleonastic dream.

THE PUZZLE OF THE WOLVES

EXAMPLE

Mark was a 45-year-old, hard working, divorced, professional man who complained of no major emotional problems. But he was bothered about one particular pleonastic dream. He explained it in detail.

> I am in a log cabin in the middle of winter. It's midnight. The cabin sits all by
> itself in the center of an empty meadow in a huge Alaskan valley. There are

no towns, villages, or people around for hundreds of miles. I am alone in this wilderness. Heavy crystallized snow coats the ground. The air is sharp with the clear coldness one feels in the middle of a long winter's night.

I hear sounds in the distance. They come from a dark woods surrounding the meadow. I can't see into the woods, but I hear the sounds getting louder. I look out from a frosted window and see darken shadows running across the meadow. Initially, only an occasional shadow darts past, but soon I see more and more streaks. The howling gets louder. As the shadows move closer, I can make out their form; they are huge gray wolves. There are at least 20 of them. The wolves surround the cabin as the moon reflects off their shining eyes. I bar the door and block the windows, but the wolves try to get in. I can hear them scratching at the door. I hide away in the closet as the howling gets louder and louder. Some wolves have gotten into the cabin and are trying to find me. They smell me in the closet and try to get to me. Right before they are about to break in . . . Stop! . . . the dream ends.

This was the earliest version of Mark's dream. He had dreamt it about once a year since he was a boy. He said the dream scared him, but he wasn't so much afraid of it as he was perplexed by it. His major feeling was puzzlement. He had to try to figure out a way to fend off the wolves. He had to solve the puzzle.

As he got older the dream changed. It always started the same, but over the years, he tried to protect himself against the wolves in different ways. As an adolescent, he tried to jump from the cabin and run into the Arctic woods. But the wolves would always chase him down and trap him in a ravine. The dream would end as before, with the wolves closing in on him. As a young adult, he tried fighting the wolves. From the window he would shoot at them with a rifle, chase them with a Bowie knife, or grab them by their tails. But something would always go wrong: the gun wouldn't shoot, the knife would disappear, or his hands wouldn't work, and he would end up grabbing empty air.

The last time Mark had the dream it ended differently. He remembers this last dream very well. It started in the usual way. The wolves got closer and closer; he was feeling more and more puzzled. But this time he remembers not only being in the dream but at the same time observing himself in the dream. He recalled that this was the same dream he had throughout his life and that none of his previous solutions had worked. He remembers that in the dream he heard himself talking out loud and saying something like:

Oh boy, same old dream. Nothing I do ever works. I can't protect the cabin because the wolves always break in; I can't run away because the wolves always chase me; I can't attack because my weapons never work. I am tired of all this, tired of dreaming about these damn wolves. I'm not going to hide away in this cabin anymore. I'm not going to try to run away again. I'm not going to spend my time trying to fight them with weapons that don't work. What I am going to do is get my cross-country skis, go out in the soft powder snow, and ski in the moonlight. I'm not going to run or hurry; I'm just going to take a nice little midnight stroll. If the wolves want to eat me up, so be it. I'm not going to keep running from the wolves. I'm going to do exactly what I feel like doing and the wolves can be damned.

In his dream, he quietly thought this over and over to himself. It became almost like his mantra, his chant. He waxed his cross-country skis, put them on, and started to ski in the moonlight meadow. He skied straight ahead and continued to do so as the wolves ran around him howling and snapping and jumping. He didn't change his pace or turn back; he just kept on skiing, schussing along in the fresh powder looking at the moonlight and feeling the clear coldness of the air. Suddenly the wolves disappeared. He was left alone in the Arctic wilderness. Though cold it felt pleasantly warm; the moonlight shone brightly through the ice crystals hanging on the trees; the snow was soft, and he could almost hear the great stillness in the air. As he skied across the snow, the meadow seemed like a crystal fairyland. He felt completely calm, at rest, finally at peace.

This was years ago. He hasn't had the dream again and he knows he never will. He won't, because his last dream solved the puzzle.

Do you have a recurring puzzle in your life that you have been trying to solve? If you have a pleonastic dream, it may help you find an answer. You can do it wide awake. Do the following exercise to get you started.

Homework

EXERCISE 15.1 A Recurring Dream

Step 1. If you have had a pleonastic dream—a recurring dream throughout your life—remind yourself of what it is about.

Step 2. Don't primarily pay attention to the contents of the dream, the place, and the people in it, or the emotions you have when you dream it. Instead, look for the overall theme, the puzzle your brain is trying to solve. The theme doesn't have to be anything hidden from you when you are awake. You may be quite aware of the puzzle. For example, in Mark's dream the important feature was not that there were wolves, or that he was alone in the wilderness of Alaska, or even that he was afraid. His dream provided him with his life-puzzle. His particular puzzle was that he had to face his frailty as a human being. He knew he was plopped onto this earth temporarily and surrounded by very powerful forces that he could not control. He also knew he wouldn't live forever, that someday he would die and cease to be. His puzzle was how do I go through life knowing all this. Do I hide? Do I run? Do I fight it? Do I barricade myself against these overpowering forces trying to keep them from getting me?

Step 3. If you found your puzzle and your theme, does a solution come to mind? If it does, would the solution help you? Would it help those you love or who love you? Would it be useful for all of us (the rest of humanity) to solve the puzzle in the same way? For example, Mark discovered that face to face with his core frailty, he could not barricade himself against it—for it was always there behind the wall; he could not run away from it—because it was part of him and runs along with him; he could not attack it—because he had no weapons strong enough to overcome it. All he could do was to accept it; accept that he is a frail human being like the rest of us. But (and this is a most important "but") he decided that he must continue his life in the direction he wished to go and not let the fear of his own insignificance swerve him from his course. He could continue his walk in the moonlight, fully knowing that this bungled and botched part of him could trivialize him at any time by destroying him. For him the art of living was to continue his journey through life without letting the knowledge of the frailty of his nature turn his step or alter his path.

It may be a good lesson for all of us.

chapter 16

Cultural Point of View
The World According to Australian Aborigines

Man's nature, his passions and anxieties, are a cultural product; as a matter of fact, man himself is the most important creation and achievement of the continuous human effort, the record of what we call history.

ERICH FROMM

IN THIS CHAPTER

• Understanding that our culture teaches us how to look at the world

• Seeing that some of our problems are caused by the categories we have learned

 Many of our major beliefs originate in our culture. Not only does our culture provide us with our values and our customs, but also it gives us the very point of view through which we interpret everything around us. We are so immersed in our culture that we learn to see the world only through its eyes, and we are not even aware that there may be another way of looking at life. When we encounter another cultural viewpoint, we immediately reject it as being a cockeyed, primitive superstition. We are certain that our way of looking at the world is the only correct, the only natural way.

A good example of a different viewpoint is a story in a book by George Lakoff, the noted linguistic professor (1987). The title of his book is *Women Fire, and Dangerous Things*, and one of the main stories in it talks about the Australian tribes who speak the Dyirbal language. It shows how differently they look at the world.

In the Dyirbal language, every noun is preceded by one of four categories. In essence, everything in the universe can be divided into these categories: Bayi, Balan, Balam, or Bala. Whenever the Dyirbal name anything, they introduce it by identifying the category that the object falls under. These categories are more than linguistical; they also show how the speaker relates to the object, so that different emotions, behaviors, and values are associated with each group. But the four categories are not what those from Westernized, industrialized cultures would expect.

To see how different their categories are, do the following exercise. It can be done quickly and should be fun. It is the best way I know to show how different cultures teach such different views of our world.

Homework

EXERCISE

16.1 Dyirbal Categories

Step 1. Look at the following objects (Figure 16.1). They are some of the most common objects in the Australian aboriginal environment.

Step 2. Make up four categories in which each of the objects may be placed. Please limit your categories to only four. They can be any kind of categories you wish, but pick those that feel most natural for you.

Step 3. Look at each item shown below and put them in one of your four categories.

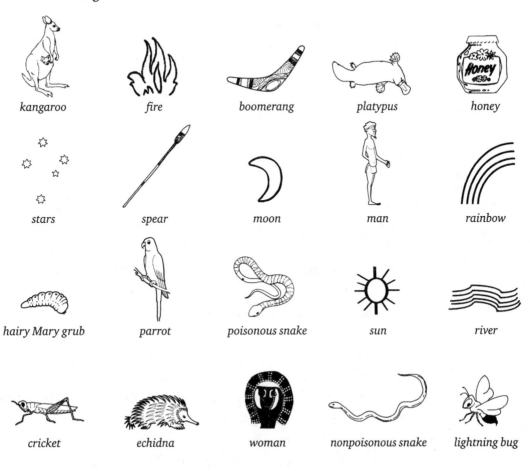

Figure 16.1 Dyirbal categories

Step 4. Now compare your categories to the Dyirbal ones.

WESTERN VERSUS DYIRBAL CATEGORIES

EXAMPLE Many Westerners choose the following categories which seem most obvious to them.

- *Natural phenomena*: rainbows, rivers, the sun, stars, the moon, and fire
- *Animals*: snakes, parrots, lightning bugs, hairy Mary grubs, crickets, echidnas, kangaroos, honey (product of bees), platypus
- *Manmade goods*: spears, boomerangs
- *Humans*: men, women

The above groupings reflect Western logic rather than Dyirbal culture. The correct Dyirbal categories are:

- *Bayi*: men, the moon, boomerangs, kangaroos, nonpoisonous snakes, rainbows. This category often produces an animated, excited feeling in the listener.
- *Balan*: women, the sun, fire, poisonous snakes, hairy Mary grubs, spears, rivers, stars, lightning bugs, parrots, platypus, echidnas, and crickets. Items in this category are often feared.
- *Balam*: consumable items like honey, fruit, and edible leaves. These items are often desired.
- *Bala*: anything not in the above three groupings. These items the Dyirbal will often feel neutral about.

See, it's simple. If it is not obvious why these things are grouped in these ways, a brief explanation may help the non-Dyirbal reader.

Dyirbal categories come from their culture. Men and the moon are in the first category because in Dyirbal mythology, the moon and the sun are husband and wife and men are descended from the moon. Men use boomerangs to hunt kangaroos and nonpoisonous snakes, so they are placed here. Rainbows are included because the souls of men who die as heroes turn into rainbows.

Women and the sun are both in the second category because all women descend from the sun, which is considered female. Fire, poisonous snakes, and the hairy Mary grub sting like the sun so they are all included. Spears also fall into this category because this entire category includes the concept of dangerous things (hence the title of Lakoff's book). Rivers are included because water from rivers puts out fires. Stars and lightning bugs shine like the sun, so they are included. Parrots and many other birds are believed to be the spirits of human females. And in Dyirbal myth, crickets are old ladies.

Understanding the Dyirbal categories requires that we set aside the logic system that we were culturally born into. Even in attempting to do so, some Westerners would wrongly see the categories as cockeyed, the product of primitive, uneducated brains. Many of us would wrongly believe that if these aboriginals were smart like us, they would see that their categories are just primitive superstitions while ours are the only correct ones.

But there are no natural or correct categories, theirs are as good as ours. Our categories seem correct simply because we grew up in our own culture and we think our view of the world is the only natural one. But to the Dyirbal, our categories would be cockeyed.

 There is no absolute correct way of looking at the world. We have all learned to perceive things in certain ways because our culture has taught us to do so. Because different societies teach different points of view, there are no apriori or necessary groupings—there is no natural way of looking at things. All cultural categories are arbitrary. Our cultures, our societies, and our language teach us how to view things. The groupings may have nothing to do with the way the world is, whatever that may be, it's just the way we have been taught.

The languages that we all use are metaphorical in nature. In other words, we understand one experience by comparing it to another. These metaphors are cultural and reveal some of the most fundamental values of the society we live in. Our metaphors tell us what to see, how to cope with the world, and how to interact with other people.

Some readers might be wondering, So what? Who cares? Possibly, we *should* care.

Take about five minutes to do the next exercise. It may enlighten you about why the Dyirbal categories may be relevant to you. It may even help you discover the origins of one of your personality traits.

 ## 16.2 Your Personal Categories

Read the steps and all the examples below before you begin the exercise.

Step 1. Pick one of your personal traits that bothers you. Try to find one word that describes it (e.g., impatient).

Step 2. Look in a good thesaurus and collect all of the metaphors you associate with the trait. Pay particular attention to slang expressions (e.g., ants in one's pants, itchy, short fuse, jumpy, agitated, jittery).

Step 3. Where did you learn to use these metaphors to describe your trait? (e.g., When I was young I had difficulty sitting still. My parents said I was too antsy.)

The following examples of Jim and Martha reveal what they discovered by doing the exercise.

WHAT A MAN!

EXAMPLE

Jim was a good-looking, single 25-year-old man of average height. He worked as a rancher, was kind and considerate toward women, and had a homespun kind of country charm. But he felt depressed because he didn't think he was aggressive enough and was shy with women.

He picked the word *inferior* as his central trait (Step 1). He looked up the word in a thesaurus and picked the following phrases as the most accurate description of his feelings about himself (Step 2).

Came up short	Bargain basement	Less than
Lower than	Small time	Puny
Under	Lightweight	Two-bit
Small potatoes	Lowly	Mickey mouse

Jim associated "inferior" with the metaphor of shortness and smallness because he perceived that the size of a man is associated with his ability to defend and protect women. He grew up on a ranch in West Texas and his culture had taught him that a man of average height or who was short was less capable of doing this (Step 3).

He countered his metaphor when he recognized that the invention of the bow and arrow, the slingshot, guns, automatic weapons, and nuclear bombs have blurred the importance of male size to a great extent. His favorite counterphrase was, "I will protect you from those nasty nuclear weapons, my dear." When he changed his metaphor, his feelings of inferiority lifted.

BLOW UP

EXAMPLE

Martha was a well-bred, 46-year-old married woman who was afraid of her emotions. She had grown up in an upper-class British family. She went to private prep schools based on the continental model. In her culture, it was low class to feel or show any strong emotion. Emotions were considered petty bourgeois and a sign of lack of breeding.

When she did the exercise, she picked two traits. She thought she was generally anxious and angry (Step 1). When she looked up other words for anxiety and anger from a thesaurus, she identified the following metaphors (Step 2):

Anxiety: losing control, on tenterhooks, out of one's head, hysterical, berserk, shaking like a leaf, overwhelmed, about to explode, falling to pieces

Anger: blowing your top, losing it, exploding, flipping your wig, freaking out, having a fit, hitting the ceiling, having a hemorrhage, blowing a gasket

She felt the emotions of anger and stress were dangerous, and so to protect herself from these feelings, she had created a narrow emotional safety zone. If her emotions ever rose above the zone, she would get scared and retreat from wherever she was.

Why did she view feeling anger and stress as so dangerous? No traumatic event had occurred in her history that could have caused such a concern. It appears she simply categorized these emotions as dangerous because of her cultural background. Her culture had labeled these feelings in such a way that she associated danger with them.

The words she picked were more than just phrases; they were the ways she viewed emotions, and they prescribe how she would experience having these feelings. Like the example of the Dyirbal, the core categories prescribe the glasses through which she saw the affective world. They were basic reflexive reactions that Martha had learned from the time she was young, and she did not believe that emotions could be perceived in any other way.

Her definitions show how she categorized emotions. She perceived them as energies inside a container. Anxiety and anger were the energy, while her body was the container. If emotional pressure became too strong, the container could explode. Descriptions like, "falling to pieces, exploding, blowing a gasket, hitting the ceiling," demonstrated her perception. She was afraid of emotionally exploding, so whenever she felt the slightest fear or anger she became terrified that the feeling would build to an uncontrollable level and she would go insane or have a nervous breakdown. In her mind, she would only be protected if she kept these emotions inside a narrow safety zone; she had to control her environment completely to keep her emotions from growing.

Martha's view of emotions was damaging. To remove her fear of emotions she had to change her metaphor. She had to realize her view of emotions was culturally based and not grounded on scientific evidence. She found that the following description of emotions was far more helpful.

Human beings don't have gaskets that can be blown. Nobody hits ceilings, and the tops of our heads don't explode when we get upset. These descriptions come from a 19th-century metaphor that explained human physiology in terms of hydraulic systems. A more useful way to look at emotions is to think of an electrical circuit. Either the switch is on or it is off, but the energy doesn't build up inside of us any more than the energy builds inside a television set when we shut it off. We don't have to fear our emotions; we just have to feel them.

It wasn't easy for Martha to change her metaphor. It was part of her basic model of the world, so she held on to it tightly. But gradually, over time, she was able to change it. When she did, her fear of emotions disappeared. She accepted fear and anger as a normal human process—distressing at times but not dangerous. She started to extend her emotional safety zone so that she could experience the full range of her emotional life.

 Ultimately, our metaphors should best come from our personal experience in the world, not just from others. If we become more open and aware of the reality that exists outside of our cultural group (our family, our race, our religion, our nation), we will be able to see that many of our cultural metaphors are not useful. We will learn that all trees aren't green, all men aren't aggressive, all women aren't bad at math, all Muslims aren't terrorists, and all New Yorkers aren't rude. Mostly, however, we will learn that the people in our cultural group aren't always right.

chapter 17

Who's to Blame?
When Bad Things Happen to Us

Life is a long lesson in humility.   JAMES M. BARRIE

IN THIS CHAPTER
- Grasping why we blame others
- Assessing how much control we have

When something goes wrong in our lives, some of us have one readily available, all-encompassing, perfect solution that makes us feel better: someone must be to blame. It feels reassuring to find some person who is culpable because it makes us human beings feel we aren't helpless corks in a fickle, cosmic ocean.

We can blame anybody. Sometimes we blame ourselves, but most of the time, we try to find someone else to tie to our problem. It may be a spouse, a boss, a business, or a government agency—anyone.

Once we pick those who are "it," we make them pay for our problem. And there is a wonderful way for us to do this. It's a great way; it's the American way, sue them!

To see how popular this ritual is, look at some recent lawsuits.

BLAMING OTHERS

EXAMPLE

- There was a flood in Oahu, Hawaii due to some heavy torrential rains. Some houses were destroyed and an elderly man died. His wife sued the local council for damages.

- A basketball fan sued the coach of his local professional team because the team was having a losing season.
- A woman in Florida sued the community because she hurt her retina looking at a partial eclipse of the sun. She said the local papers hadn't sufficiently warned her.
- Several parents have sued record companies because they thought their children were psychologically damaged after listening to rock music.
- Doctors take their careers in their hands every time they practice their profession. Anytime an operation doesn't work or a treatment fails, physicians are vulnerable to a suit.
- A man drinks too much and gets into an auto accident, but sues the bartender for serving him the drinks.
- People in California sued the local council because they were attacked by a mountain lion.
- In Colorado some skiers skied out of bounds but sued the ski resort because of an avalanche.

What underlies some of these suits?

 A major reason for these suits is emotional not just economic. There seems to be a core belief particular to the American culture, that if something bad happens than someone is to blame—not *something*, but *someone*. Many of us do not accept accidents, bad luck, acts of God, or the individuals' bad judgments as acceptable causes. The belief is that natural accidents don't happen. If something bad occurs than there must be some human being or collection of human beings who caused it or who should have prevented it from happening.

It is a curious 21st-century belief. Can you imagine a 19th-century pioneer Kansas farmer suing someone because his crops failed, or his barn caught fire, or a hailstorm hit his field, or a bear attacked him, or his son became a bum, or his daughter got smallpox and the country doctor couldn't help? No, it wouldn't have happened. Even if the mechanisms for suing were as comprehensive then as they are now, the farmer would have felt it immoral to steal money from others because of his own misfortunes.

Before the present day, most of humanity accepted that bad things could happen by accident. They looked at nature as big and powerful while they considered human beings as small and fragile. They believed these powerful forces could overwhelm humanity at any time. They also viewed the human race as a fallible species incapable of doing everything right. They accepted that humanity has a bungled and botched side. They would have considered thinking that humans were perfect was sacrilegious because it implies perfection only reachable by God.

But the world has changed. Many people no longer believe that a fickle and powerful nature constantly surrounds us. We experience a world built mostly by human hands. We are surrounded by superhighways, transcontinental jets, sprawling cities, space shuttles, canals, irrigation projects, concrete dams; and nature (when noticed at all) is more of an afterthought—a park in the middle of a city, a dammed up river, a tree seen between the skyscrapers. Nature beheld on such a small scale appears weak and impotent in comparison to the might of human creation.

We therefore, switched our belief about nature and humanity. We now assume that any catastrophe or misfortune occurring in our lives is man-made not naturemade. There are no acts of God anymore. If something bad happens, some person is to blame. So, instead of cursing the gods, we curse humanity, and now we have a way of fighting back—we sue.

But it's an illusion, 21st-century humanity is mistaken. Because man-made objects surround us most of the time, we have become excessively impressed by our own power and might.

Our great grandparents were aware that lurking outside our cities, towns and villages, lived an overpowering force that pulls its strength from the same power that revolves our planet around our sun, our sun around our galaxy, our galaxy around a million galaxies in a vast almost incomprehensible universe. In comparison, humanity is microscopic and absurdly puny.

To demonstrate this point, you may find it useful to rate how much control you have over the most important things in your life, like family, health, career, friends, and love. You may be surprised by the lack of control you have over many of these. Do the exercise and find out.

Homework

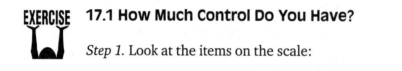

17.1 How Much Control Do You Have?

Step 1. Look at the items on the scale:

no control   25%   50%   75%   total control

Step 2. Go through the following list and give a percentage describing how much control you feel you have over each item. The scale ranges from 100% control (e.g., being able to move your finger) to 0% control (e.g., being able to keep the Milky Way galaxy from sliding into a black hole). Place the letter for each item on the above scale.

(a) my gender   (b) my weight

(c) my race   (d) my early environment

(e) my parents   (f) my education

(g) my health   (h) meeting a potential mate

(i) being rich   (j) picking my career

(k) my appearance   (l) where I live

(m) catching a cold   (n) my death

(o) who my friends are   (p) my religion

(q) _____   (r) _____

Most people said they had no control over their gender, who their parents were, or their race. They judged they had only a little control over their early environments, catching a cold, and their health. They also thought that they had only 50% control over who they married (there is a lot of luck in meeting one's mate), becoming rich (if one's parents are rich it really helps) choosing their friends (whoever one happens to bump into), picking their careers (whether there's money for college) or where they lived (where one can get a job). Yet, these factors are among the most important influences in our lives and will greatly affect our happiness on earth.

We need to remind ourselves that we are just creatures on this planet, not the creators of it. We also need to recognize how fragile we are. As far as we know, this is the only planet in our solar systems that can sustain us, and the planet does so only reluctantly. Even on earth, our existence is tenuous. We can live only in a three mile vertical zone of the planet. Only 4% of this whole surface can support us. We can't breathe water; we can't handle the pressure of our ocean trenches, or above our mountaintops. We need a very narrow temperature zone not too hot, too cold, or too dry. We need exactly the right amount of atmosphere to breathe and to keep the cosmic forces outside our planet from destroying us. And we need exactly the right chemicals in our bodies and around us (not too much of one thing, or too little of another) to continue to live. If Earth were just 1% farther from the Sun or 5% closer, we would not exist at all. Considering the immenseness of the cosmos, it is a miracle that we are here.

 From time to time nature reminds us about how arrogant some of us have become and teaches us a lesson. When this occurs, there is nobody we can sue, except God.

18

Superstitious Thinking
The Law of Association

It is bad luck to be superstitious. ANDREW W. MATHIS

IN THIS CHAPTER
- Looking at the cause of some superstitions
- Finding the origins of our own

Most of us would like to believe we are not superstitious because we feel it would be a sign of intellectual weakness if we were. But it is the rare person who doesn't have some superstitions.

 Superstitions are often formed because of the way our brain works. They develop based on a basic psychological principle—the law of association. Our brain is so built that it connects any two things that occur together. When one of the paired items takes place, it pulls in the other one. It doesn't mean the items are related in any other way or that one item caused the other; it just means if they both occur at the same time, the brain will associate the two items.

Remember the last time you heard a song you hadn't heard for many years? Did it bring back memories from the past?—for most people it does. Waves of pictures of earlier time come flooding into our consciousness. We remember where we were, who we were with, what we were doing. Perhaps even more interesting, the music often recreates an emotion we had from the earlier time, whether sadness, or joy, or excitement.

This is a powerful fact; the research behind it is overwhelming; and it is important, yet many of us make mistakes because we don't recognize this fact. At times, almost all of us ignore it. Because of this, we develop superstitions.

EXAMPLE

Ken's family took a vacation at Atlantic City when he was 7. While looking in some stores on the boardwalk, he became separated from his parents. He couldn't find them for hours and panicked. Finally, a police officer saw him and took him to the police station where a couple of hours later his parents showed up. He calmed down and after a few days of tension, everybody forgot about the incident.

But Ken didn't, at least a part of him didn't. One day, many years later, he was walking down the street to go to work as a stockbroker. He walked by a travel agency and saw a poster of a small Caribbean resort sitting in the middle of a turquoise ocean. For most people the scene would have engendered a calm, peaceful feeling; but for Ken, he immediately experienced tension. It puzzled him that it lasted for several days.

Ken looked for an explanation for his tension. He did a quick perusal of popular literature and found explanations such as—he must be bored with his marriage, so he wants to escape to a tropical island, but this feeling produces guilt, so he gets anxious. Or the ocean is an archetypical image representing that safe, secure, and nurturing time when he was inside his mother's womb, and he secretly wants to return. Or his job as a stockbroker overstresses him and his inner child wants to play hooky again. Or he has a fear of success and the tropical island reminds him of his fear.

Because we know Ken's history, we can guess that his reaction was based on superstitious conditioning—the law of association. The poster of the ocean produced fear because of what had happened when he was 7. But Ken didn't remember the earlier incident. After getting some help, he learned the tension was caused by the old event.

There are many explanations for why we feel as we do—they are almost endless, but the point here is that most of us don't look for the law of association first. Maybe we should consider that we could have learned some bad associations. Some bad feelings could have become paired to some odd stimuli.

The following exercise is somewhat involved but it is a good way to find some of the associations that may be causing one of your superstitions. When you have some time and it is important enough to you to find the cause of a superstition, try the exercise.

Homework

EXERCISE

18.1 Finding the Cause

Step 1. First read the worksheet example on page 120, "Traveling George."

Step 2. Pick a superstition whose cause you don't know. (For example, lets say George has a superstition that something bad will happen to him when he travels. As a result George often feels tense when traveling by air or when taking a long car trip.)

Step 3. Look at Worksheet 18.1, "Searching for the Cause of Your Superstition." In the first column (the left-hand column), list all the possible causes of your superstition that you can think of. In our worksheet example, George lists that he could be afraid of travel because:

- I thought I could get into an accident.
- I got very tired.
- I drank too much caffeine.
- I kept worrying about something at work.
- I felt I was not in control of the plane, train, or bus.
- I had too much time on my hands.
- I didn't get enough sleep.
- I didn't eat right.
- I felt rushed.
- I felt lonely.

Step 4. In the next columns (columns 1–5) think of five situations where you had the superstition that caused you to feel upset. Think of the specific events in as much detail as possible so that you can recall exactly what happened. (In our example, George remembered two plane vacations, one auto holiday, an interstate bus trip, and the time he took a short boat excursion).

Step 5. In the final columns (columns 6–10), find five more instances as similar as possible to the first five, except that your superstition did *not* occur (e.g., George recalled two other plane trips, two other interstate auto holidays, and one other long bus journey where he did *not* feel upset).

Step 6. Now go through all the possible causes you have listed and mark columns 1 to 5 (when you felt upset) with a "+" whenever that cause was present in the situation. Do the same for columns 6–10 (times when you didn't feel upset). In our example, George marked all 1–5 columns next to the "I felt lonely," item, but he didn't mark any of the 6–10 columns. Feeling lonely is a possible cause, because every situation when George had the superstition he was feeling lonely, but he never had the superstition when he wasn't feeling lonely.

Step 7. Calculate your results. The likely cause of a superstition should be present in most of the situations where you had the emotion but rarely in the situations where you didn't. The greater the difference between the two types of situations (5–0) the more likely you have found the cause (i.e., the likely cause of George's superstition when traveling was feeling lonely). He was not afraid of the plane crashing, getting into an accident, or being trapped. He was only tense when he felt lonely while traveling.

People who did this exercise looked for things that happened when they experienced a superstition, but didn't happen when they weren't superstitious. They looked for thoughts, feelings, or experiences that occurred right before the superstition appeared.

EXAMPLE OF WORKSHEET 18.1
TRAVELING GEORGE

What is your superstition?

I am afraid that something bad will happen to me when I travel.

POSSIBLE CAUSES	Situations in which you had the superstition					Situations in which you did NOT have the superstition					DIFFERENCE (1–5) – 6–10)
	AIR TRIP 1	AIR TRIP 2	CAR TRIP 3	BUS TRIP 4	BOAT TRIP 5	AIR TRIP 6	AIR TRIP 7	CAR TRIP 8	CAR TRIP 9	LONG BUS 10	
1. I thought I could get into an accident.	0	0	+	0	+	0	0	+	0	0	+1
2. I got very tired.	+	0	0	+	0	0	+	0	0	+	0
3. I drank too much caffeine.	0	0	+	0	0	0	+	0	0	0	0
4. I kept worrying about something at work.	+	+	0	+	0	+	0	+	+	0	0
5. I felt I was not in control of the plane, train, or bus.	+	0	0	0	+	+	+	0	0	+	−1
6. I had too much time on my hands.	+	+	+	+	+	+	+	+	+	−	+1
7. I didn't get enough sleep.	+	0	+	+	0	0	+	0	+	+	0
8. I didn't eat right.	0	+	0	+	0	0	0	+	0	+	0
9. I felt rushed.	+	+	0	0	0	+	+	0	0	0	0
10. I felt lonely.	+	+	+	+	+	0	0	0	0	0	+5

18.1 Searching for the Cause of Your Superstition

What is your superstition? _____

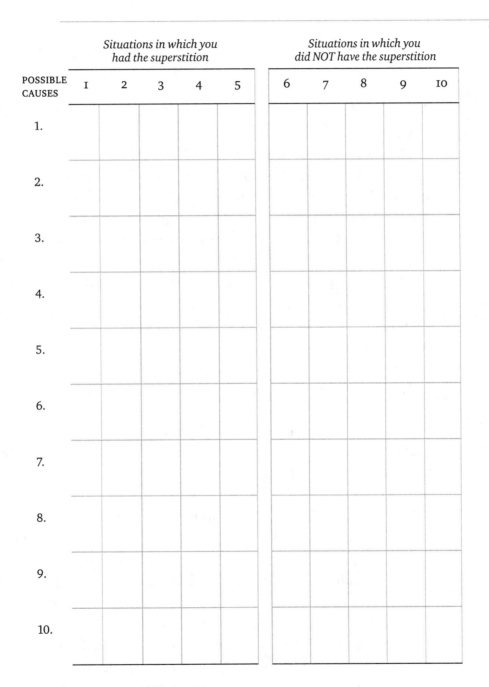

POSSIBLE CAUSES	Situations in which you had the superstition					Situations in which you did NOT have the superstition				
	I	2	3	4	5	6	7	8	9	IO
1.										
2.										
3.										
4.										
5.										
6.										
7.										
8.										
9.										
10.										

The following story shows how complex and obscure some superstitions may be.

FAIR WEATHER

EXAMPLE Ronald was a middle-aged man who lived in Denver, Colorado and who occasionally had a sudden superstitious feeling that caused anxiety. He had a feeling that something was terribly wrong and this feeling would occur once every four or five months or so. But he had no idea as to the cause. He was curious as to why he had this superstition and decided to do the "Finding the Cause," exercise.

He made a careful list of every time he had the superstition, and made an extensive list of the possible causes—the things that happened right before he felt superstitious. The items on the checklist were things like: Was I angry? Sexually frustrated? Was I having problems in my marriage? Had I changed my eating habits? Was there trouble at work? Had I been extremely tired or depressed? Did I drink a lot of coffee?

There were more than 80 items on his list, but he didn't find anything significant. Most often, a person doing this exercise would find one or more items that would always occur right before each superstition, but would never occur without it. But Ronald could find no associations—no pattern appeared; there were no common triggers for his superstition.

Ronald continued looking for the cause because he was curious as to whether he would ever be able to figure it all out. But it was difficult. He had his superstition so infrequently that it was hard to find any associations. Finally, one night several months later, his superstition appeared again. Ronald reviewed everything that had happened during the day, everything from the time he woke up to the time he felt the first pangs of fear. He explored his actions, his thoughts, his feelings, his remembrances, what he had eaten that day and so on. But he still didn't find anything, there was nothing significant, no unusual traumas, frustrations, or conflicts—just an average day until the superstition appeared. He kept searching. He had been watching TV, so he found a *TV Guide* and reviewed all the shows he had watched that day to see if one of them may have been the trigger. He found nothing. He had read the morning paper, so he reviewed the news stories of the day, national and international. Still nothing. He skimmed the sports section, the cartoons, the editorials, and the advertisements, still zero.

Finally, right before he was about to throw the paper away, he noticed the daily weather forecast. It said an unusually high-pressure front would be coming through Denver at about 10 o'clock in the evening. It struck him that this was the same time he had gotten anxious. He searched through his memory to recall if he felt a change in the weather right before he felt anxious.

He remembered that he did. He felt this eerie feeling right before his superstition. He couldn't describe it, but it was like the pressure on his skin felt different—stronger or something."

He couldn't recall exactly when, but he did remember feeling this sensation before.

On a hunch, he went to the library and pulled out the weather reports for each of the previous times he had felt his superstition. He found a common element in all the situations. He discovered that before each superstition, the barometric pressure was unusually high and it was exactly the same on each of these days. Exactly! How strange. How could barometric pressure cause a superstition? After getting some help and more detective work, he uncovered the explanation.

About 15 years before, Ronald's father had died suddenly. One day while at work, Ronald received a call from a local hospital. His dad was in an automobile accident and was in critical condition. He was told that he must come to the hospital quickly, for his father might not last long. He jumped into his car and rushed to the hospital trying to arrive before his dad died. He was anxious thinking he would not make it in time. We can guess what the weather was like—an unusual high-pressure system was moving through Denver. When he finally arrived at the hospital, it was too late. His father had died.

Strange as it may seem, we can see what happened. The grief, anxiety, and guilt Ronald had about his father dying were associated to the barometric pressure. He didn't recognize it, of course. But his brain connected the two events. Later on in life, long after the incident, his brain still held the pairing. Every time the barometric pressure reached exactly the same level, it triggered the superstitious feeling.

One may reasonably ask why the superstition became connected to the barometric pressure rather than to some other stimulus, like the temperature, the time of day, driving, cars, accidents, hospitals, or anything else, but we don't know. All we do know is that something about the original incident made the barometric pressure most salient and most receptive to being paired.

Once Ronald found the cause it was easy to counter the effects by creating new associations to barometric pressure. Today, he no longer has superstitious anxiety when a certain pressure system moves through Denver.

This case is a good example of how any superstition can become associated with any stimulus. Everything the brain is aware of can be paired with any emotion. Social scientists have observed many stimuli that caused superstitions: cats, the color red, cloud formations, acid rock music, full moons, the movie *Citizen Kane*, South American animals, a deep breath, books on astronomy, green bathrooms, having a full stomach, making love, and thousands of other things.

 One reason we don't understand our superstitions is that we keep looking for weird explanations for our feelings, like repressed sexual desires, hidden aggressive impulses, lack of Vitamin E, our birth star is in the seventh house of the moon, our psychic energy is out of balance, and other similar explanations. At such times, we had best look first for the immediate associations surrounding our superstitions. With some good detective work, we may solve some of our emotional mysteries.

Part III

Analyzing Your Beliefs

chapter 19

Analyzing Beliefs
Sniffing Out the Trash

All truths are easy to understand once they are discovered; the point is to discover them.   GALILEO GALILEI

IN THIS CHAPTER
- Exploring the various ways to determine the validity of our beliefs
- A usefulness checklist

Many of us probably believe that we can easily tell whether our thoughts, beliefs, or attitudes are trash or not. We don't think we need any special instruction on the matter. We feel we can immediately determine false, pungent beliefs from true, clean-smelling ones. Do we need training to detect that an apple is rotten or that a pencil is broken? Do we have to buy a book to teach us how to figure out whether our thoughts are real or make-believe? Surely not—we just know!

The question is, how do we know? How do we recognize that anything is true or false, useful or damaging, clear or fuzzy? The answer is that we are left with what the rest of humanity has had available throughout its history. We have to use these methods to ascertain whether something is so or not. Fortunately, or unfortunately (depending on your point of view), we have only a limited number of methods available to determine the reality or unreality of anything. The major ones are:

- Our physical senses
- Consensus
- Divine inspiration
- Tradition
- Reasoning
- The scientific method

Having filled out your Master List of Core Beliefs (see page 47), you are now ready to use one of the above methods to decide whether the beliefs on your list should be kept or thrown into the trash. You don't want to throw away those that are real and useful. Although it is possible to change any belief, it is not advisable to do so and can be downright damaging. Cultists, propagandists, slogan masters, and unethical sales entrepreneurs can deceive people using cognitive change techniques. The result is that procedures designed to help people, get twisted to achieve power or monetary gain. The purpose of CRT is not to make us feel good; it is not a form of cognitive tranquilization where all pain is gone and where we are left with a Disneyland world of pleasant pastels. The real world sometimes hurts, and real life can produce real grief and real sadness. The purpose of CRT is to help us see the world with a clearer eye, more usefully, and without minimization or exaggeration. Useful beliefs help us survive, develop, grow, and enhance our lives; nonuseful ones do not.

IS THERE A FIRE IN MY BEDROOM?

EXAMPLE

Here are four long-established methods to determine the validity of our beliefs.

Our Physical Senses

Our senses can be a powerful way of determining some facts. For instance, if someone asked us whether there was a fire in our bedroom we wouldn't turn to external sources to find the answer. We wouldn't use an *authority*; we wouldn't call the fire chief and ask, "Excuse me chief, but since you are an expert on fires, is there a fire in my bedroom?" Nor would we use *consensus* and take a vote of the people sitting in our living room, "Because 70% of us think there *isn't* a fire in the bedroom, we can keep watching the game."

We wouldn't use *tradition*, "I have never had a fire in my bedroom before, so I can't have one now." Finally, we wouldn't even use the *scientific method*. We wouldn't develop a scientific study, with hypothesis, and statistical probabilities to find out. We wouldn't conclude that there is no fire because the probability that any random room, in anyone's home, at any given time, is less than 1 in 10 million.

What we would do is obvious. We would get up and go into the bedroom, look for flames, try to smell smoke, touch the floors and walls to feel if they were hot. We would use our senses.

Taking Out Your Mental Trash

But can we use our senses for all of our beliefs? Do we think we can sniff out false beliefs in the same way we sniff out bad apples? Do we somehow, magically believe that we can sense that something is false, or pick up its pungent odor, or taste it sourness, or hear its discordant cords? We know we can't. Thoughts, beliefs, values, attitudes, opinions, and all the other cognitive processes we have, are abstractions. It doesn't mean they are not real and don't exist; they do and we are aware of them because they are in our own brains. But they are nonsensual elements, that aren't observed by any one of our senses. We can't see them, hear them, taste them, smell them, or lick them. Therefore, trying to use our senses to discover whether our thoughts are rotten is like trying to touch, taste, or smell abstract concepts like justice, virtue, or freedom. We can't do it.

Consensus and Tradition

The same can be said for consensus and tradition. In certain areas of knowledge the only way to tell what is correct or incorrect, is by finding out what most people think. To know what picture is beautiful, or what music is good, or what gem is valuable, we must get a consensus and we must look to tradition. A Ceylon sapphire is not valuable because of any intrinsic quality of the rock, other rocks are harder, or clearer, or stronger. It is valuable because such sapphires are scarce and people are willing to pay a lot of money for them. Consensus and tradition make them valuable.

But we can't use these methods to determine the truth or falseness of our beliefs. We can't because these are our own beliefs, not those of others. We are not trying to judge what *everybody* should believe. We are only trying to determine what our *own* beliefs should be. So the job is ours to figure out, not someone else's.

The Scientific Method

Some of us finally turn to science because it has the advantage of being less arrogant than the other methods. It has become the truth-finder for many people and many have flocked to it for answers to important questions. Science takes nothing on authority or as a result of an intuition. A scientist is not supposed to accept anything on faith or reject anything without evidence. Science is based on reasoning and experimentation with the facts and only the facts used to guide us in accepting or rejecting any concept.

It has taken 500 years for humanity to come up with this method. From the Renaissance through today, it has been the most effective method of advancing our knowledge about the world. Because of it, we have cars, planes, electric lights, telephones, television, penicillin, a smallpox vaccine, and countless other changes in our world. It is flexible and fair and has probably advanced human knowledge more than any other method. That is why many of us use it all the time and believe in it.

But science has a major problem—time. It takes a surprisingly long time to identify even a minuscule part of a useful principle, and it can take many years, if not decades, to establish a useful law. Scientists can spend their entire life just finding the truth or falseness of a small hypothesis of one little, subpart of an esoteric theory. For example, in the middle of the 20th century, many scholars hoped that the social sciences would help humanity by finding out the causes of such social ills as prejudice, hatred, violence, and war. After 50 or more years of research, these sciences have yet to deliver an answer. Apparently studying human beings is a lot more difficult than studying the physical world. It will take a lot more time.

But when we try to turn the scientific method to address the truth or falseness of our own beliefs, we get frustrated. We become confused about how to assess such thoughts as, "All we need is love," "In my heart I know I'm right," or "I am inferior to others." Even if we could break down our thoughts into concrete hypotheses whose truth or falseness could be ascertained, it would take a great deal of effort and a long time to come up with an answer. While we may admire the methods of science and we may wish to continue to use them, we know we don't have the time. We could spend months studying the validity of just one of our beliefs, but we have too many diapers to change, pet fish to feed, toenails to clip, life to live, to waste our time on examining all the hundreds of beliefs we have floating around in our heads.

So what do we do, give up? No! We don't have to be sure of things in order to make a decision. We don't need certainty. We just need to know that we are moving in the right direction. And there is an easier way for us to figure all this out.

What is Useful?

We might wish to give up our search for the exact truth of our beliefs. Instead, we may wish to redirect our search to what is useful. Whether or not our thoughts are ultimately true or false may be less important than if they are useful. And we can ascertain whether they are useful, without polling our community, following traditions, or doing complicated scientific experiments. We just need to make a decision.

The following exercise is designed to help you decide if your beliefs, values, and attitudes are useful (based on Maultsby, 1984). To do the exercise, pick a belief from your Master List of Core Beliefs—any one of those thoughts that you are interested in and are not sure about— and fill out the checklist by answering each question with a "yes" or a "no."

Homework

EXERCISE 19.1 Usefulness Checklist

1. Does the thought make me feel better?	YES	NO
2. Does the belief improve my relationship with others?	YES	NO
3. Does the attitude help me solve problems?	YES	NO
4. Does the value help me accomplish my goals?	YES	NO

Rule. Your thought is useful if you answer, "yes" to every question. After all, what's the point of believing in a thought that doesn't make you feel good, solve some problem, improve your relationships, or help you reach your goals. If you answer "no" to the questions, your belief is a stinker and you should get on the phone and call the trash truck for a special pickup.

EXAMPLE OF CHECKLIST

Belief. "I need everybody to respect me."
Usefulness Checklist. This thought makes me feel terrible. I am always worried about somebody out there who may disapprove of me. It destroys my relationships with others because I am constantly bending over backwards to please everybody, and they end up being disgusted with my sycophantic behavior. It creates worlds of problems with others because they never know what I think and really feel. If my goal in life is personal happiness, this attitude will totally prevent me from ever achieving it.
Conclusion. Not useful (0 out of 4).

Belief. "It's terrible when things go wrong."
Usefulness Checklist. Since things are always going wrong, I always feel terri-

ble. I try to be a perfectionist, which only annoys everyone around me and creates more problems than I had in the beginning. If my goal in life is success, my belief is taking me farther and farther away from reaching it.
Conclusion. Not useful (0 out of 4).

Belief. "People should be different from the way they are."
Usefulness Checklist. This thought keeps me constantly angry with everybody, all the time, about everything. And so far as hurting my relationships, I don't have to worry about this, I have no relationships left because of this belief. For some reason people don't appreciate the all-wise and all-knowing plan I have prepared for them.
Conclusion. Not useful (0 out of 4).

Belief. "I ought to be happy all the time."
Usefulness Checklist. Well, of course, this kind of thinking has a magical effect on me. It multiplies my unhappiness by a factor of four. Not only do I get unhappy at times, like everyone else on the planet, but also because of my belief, I get angry with myself for getting unhappy because I have convinced myself that I must always be happy. Each new disappointment brings forth more unhappiness, which causes more disappointment, which brings forth more unhappiness ad infinitum. Finally, the only thing left of me is one gigantic ball of unhappy-disappointment rolling across the land.
Conclusion. Not useful (0 out of 4).

Belief. "I can't do something unless I'm in the mood."
Usefulness Checklist. It does make me feel good at times to think this way because then I don't have to do anything. So the answer to the first question in the Usefulness Checklist ("Does the thought make me feel better?") is, "Yes." Unfortunately, the answers to the other questions are a resounding, "No!" My relationships stink because other people get upset when I don't show up for lunch or don't turn in my report on time; and for some reason they don't accept my excuse that I just didn't feel like it. And as for, "Does the attitude help me solve problems?" my problems seem to be multiplying because I didn't feel like doing my bills, or opening a savings account, or fixing the toilet. It seems I am getting farther away from my life goal of having pleasure and avoiding pain. I seem to have a lot more pain lately.
Conclusion. Not useful (1 out of 4).

I hope the reader has seen that whether our beliefs are true or not may be considerably less important than whether they are helpful to us. If they aren't useful, this alone is more than sufficient reason to get rid of them. The only remaining thing to do, then, is to ask our self one final question:

5. Do I want to get rid of my thought?   YES   NO

If you answer "No," this is your choice. As a free human being, you have a right to decide for yourself no matter what any checklist says. But if you answer "yes," you can kiss your thought goodbye, for its days are surely numbered.

chapter 20

Gut Feelings
Can We Count on Our Intuition?

*The whole problem with the world is that fools and fanatics are always so
certain of themselves, but wiser people so full of doubts.*
BERTRAND RUSSELL

IN THIS CHAPTER
• Examining the accuracy of intuition
• Finding the source of our intuition
• Assessing the correctness of our
  gut feelings

Some people believe that in their hearts they know they're right. They observe their intuitive feelings and believe they have this deep felt sense about what is true and false that flows in a cavern somewhere inside their minds. They honor this sense as the key to all knowledge, as an almost spiritual vision of the truth. But is there such a thing?

The "in-my-heart-I-know-I'm-right" people claim there is and that their gut feelings are never wrong. Is there a part of us that just knows without having to do research or use logic? Do we possess this sixth sense deep inside us that tells us the truth?

It would be a marvelous thing if it existed. Having a part inside us that knows true knowledge instantaneously and is never wrong would be the solution for our busy lives. Information from books, TV, the Internet, movies, and magazines bombards us constantly. There are so many different opinions, explanations, judgments, and speculations about everything that many of us feel lost in a maze of contradictory viewpoints. We don't know which are the correct ones. It's too confusing. It takes too much work to figure it all out, and we don't have time to do the research. But if we could forget this traffic jam of contradictory viewpoints and simply trust our guts, we would have a clear road to understanding. The trip is quick, easy, and doesn't cost anything.

People wax lyrical about this inner sense. When working on some theory that is all tangled, they get tired of looking for evidence, or testing hypotheses, or gathering data. It takes so much time to unravel everything, and it's boring. At times like this, they remember how many people work on problems. They hear people suggest, "You don't have to do all this work; all you have to do is trust your heart."

This wellspring of truth we are all supposed to possess is difficult to locate. If it does exist, where does it reside? When we say, "I have a gut feeling about what is true," or "In my heart I know I'm right," we can't really mean it. These are just expressions people use to describe the sense. Obviously, no organ in our stomach or chest can give us knowledge of what is true and false. How could it? Our organs consist of cells, tissues, and blood. How could true knowledge reside in one group of tissues rather than another? How could correct knowledge inhabit any tissues at all?

Many of us have searched inside looking for the source of our intuition. We have practiced focusing on our deep felt sense. And surprise, surprise, you know what, some of us actually do find this feeling, this sense of what is true, and what is false. It feels certain, and complete, and solid, and all the rest. Just as people say it does.

Eureka! All these years of wasted effort doing research to find the truth, and all they had to do was to listen to their guts or hearts. Well maybe, maybe not.

Some of us have the sneaking suspicion that our collective guts or hearts may be fooling us. Even though this inner sense is confident, almost arrogant in its certainty, over time we notice that it has made some mistakes, and some of these have been real whoppers. After all, people have believed in Santa Claus, the Easter Bunny, the Tooth Fairy, and a flat earth. This knowledge was once unshakable, but where are these beliefs now? Most of us have assigned them to our mental attics where we keep our other childhood toys.

If you really want to know whether your intuition is correct, do the following homework exercise on your gut feelings about people.

Homework

20.1 Test Your Intuition

Record your results on Worksheet 20.1, "Test Your Intuition"

Step 1. Pick 10 people who were once strangers, but you later learned to know very well. Focus on the first time you met them.

Step 2. Try to remember what kind of people you first sensed they were. Did you feel they were honest? Were they smart? Had they suffered a lot in life or have they traveled through life unscathed? What did you feel the strangers' childhoods' were like—had they grown up in loving families? Were their parents divorced? Things like this. Remember your first gut feelings and write them down.

Step 3. If you feel confident that you now know the person quite well and have learned a more complete history of his or her past, make a judgment as to whether your gut impressions were right or wrong.

Step 4. If you find that your gut feelings were wrong, try to determine exactly how and why you made the mistake. List the type of mistakes you made (e.g., didn't know them well enough; judged too much on their appearance; I had a prejudice against this type of person; I listened too much to what other people had said about the person).

Step 5. What guidelines can you give yourself in the future so that you don't make the same type of mistake again (e.g., get to know a person first; pay less attention to surface appearance; recognize your prejudices; ignore gossip about the person).

WORKSHEET

20.1 Test Your Intuition

Name	*Initial gut feelings about the person*

Decide if your gut impressions were right or wrong about each person. If wrong, list why.

Type of mistake I made:

_____

_____

_____

Things I can do in the future to avoid this type of mistake:

_____

_____

_____

_____

People who have done the exercise report that their intuitions were right about 30% of the time. Not bad, considering they knew almost nothing about the strangers when they first met them. But this percentage was based on averages. There were some people whose gut guessed right almost every time, while some others were usually wrong.

Why are some people's intuitions so wrong most of the time, particularly when their impressions were so strong? Some of these people felt sure that one stranger had come from a broken family, or had a lot of money, or was dishonest. They later found out they were wrong. When they went back and looked at each of their mistakes, they tried to discover why their intuitions had misled them so.

There were many reasons, but one seems to underlie them all. Personal stereotypes poisoned their judgments. Most of the time, they weren't even aware of the stereotypes that lurked in their shadowy preconscious, and only certain types of people activated them. Apparently, some strangers trigger some underlying stereotypes.

For example, consider Karen.

KAREN'S GUT

EXAMPLE Karen's gut feeling told her that a mechanical engineer she had just met was probably a cold, left-brain, nonemotional person. She was certain he came from a high pressure, high achieving family, and probably had many problems with intimate relationships. Her gut said he was an unfeeling, boring, conservative person. This kind of thing. But the truth about this engineer turned out to be the opposite. He wrote poetry, painted landscapes, loved to listen to opera, had a wonderful sense of humor, read Eastern philosophy, and loved to immerse himself wild hot springs in the nude.

Why did she misread him so? Answer, because of her cultural stereotypes about mechanical engineers and certain other types of people as well. Her cultural biases were that engineers are cold and aloof; psychologists are all weird; blondes are bimbos; musicians are junkies; fat men are jolly; models are vain.

The exercise may have shown us the secret about some of our gut feelings.

This marvelous thing we call our intuition, this beautiful sense inside some of us that sees things so clearly, this brilliant source of truth and wisdom, may consist of just one thing—stereotypes. A gut that we honor so may be

Taking Out Your Mental Trash

full of overgeneralizations, narrow mindedness, myopia, and twisted observations. Some of us have been fed these warped overgeneralizations since we were infants. Our intuition feels so spontaneous and certain because it lies deep inside the lower levels of consciousness that our reasoning has little access to. It just pops up whenever we meet someone of a certain type.

Some of us have an intuition that is wrong seven out of ten times because our gut only drags up our learned stereotypes about peoples' looks, or how they sound, or what type of work they do, or where they come from, or what their nationality is.

 This is it. For many of us, our intuition isn't a sacred grotto of knowledge; it's a subterranean cavern of irrational generalizations accumulated over a lifetime. It doesn't teach us the truth; it exposes our malignant fears, our cultural biases, and our own insecurities.

This insight puts the glory of our intuition in a completely different light. Our gut doesn't teach some of us who people are; it prevents us from seeing who they are. Stereotyping people keeps us from even bothering to learn about them. We already know that engineers are nonemotional, bikers are criminals, or football players are dumb. The door is closed, the information is in. No need to look further because in our hearts we know we are right.

chapter 21

Who Says So?
Are Authorities Always Right?

Every great advance in natural knowledge has involved the absolute rejection of authority.
THOMAS H. HUXLEY

IN THIS CHAPTER
- Examining our need for authority
- Over-obedience to some authorities
- Surveying the authorities we have used in our life

Believing that authorities are correct, usually doesn't come from our own experience with authorities, but from what society has told us. We have been taught that we need various experts to tell us what is true and false or right and wrong. We use authorities all the time. To determine whether the pain in our chest is a sign that we have a heart problem, we don't see, hear, or smell a heart problem; we don't have our friends vote on it, and we don't conduct an experimental study. We go to a doctor. Diagnosis is a complicated business, so we leave it to the experts who have spent years of training and clinical practice to help us decide.

Throughout our lives, we have relied on different authorities. Because we were little and weak as children, we figured grown-ups knew what was true and eventually would reveal it to us—when we grew up. Our first authorities were our parents. They are so powerful to a small child that we figured their mighty power was immediately translatable into mighty truth. Alas, as we got older their power faded and along with it our certainty that what they were telling us was true.

As preteens we often picked another authority—our older peers. Those of us in grade school often thought high school students were smart and streetwise and had things all figured out, so we imitated them. But when we went to high school we found out we still didn't know much, so we looked elsewhere. Some picked college students or professors, others chose successful business or professional people who had earned a good living. But if we became a college student or ran a successful business, or earned a professional degree, we realized we still didn't know that much, so we had to hunt down other authorities who might clue us in.

Some of us made a sojourn into esoteric faiths because we figured maybe the truth has been revealed to a few shamans or gurus who would share it. But we were confounded by such a huge number of sages and wise mystics, preaching different viewpoints that we became confused about who was genuine and who was a false prophet.

Others of us turned to the authority of popular opinion—the will of the majority. Possibly the *individual* cannot find what is truth and what is right. Maybe truth is only shown to *groups* of people. After all, it is the principle of democracy, isn't it? The individual can be mistaken because of personal biases and prejudices, but in a mass of individuals, these biases are often canceled out. Indeed the majority may have the best chance of seeing the good and the truth.

But in certain ways, this method turned out to be just as bad as the others. If we look at human history, we find that the majority of humanity used to believe in all kinds of silly things, like the earth is flat or there are witches; you can cure disease by bleeding with leaches; the earth is the center of the universe; women are inferior to men; kings have the divine right to rule. So much for the majority. At times in our history, popular opinion has been just another word for popular ignorance.

Overreliance on authorities can cause great problems, as the following example reveals.

OBEDIENCE TO AUTHORITY

EXAMPLE

Yale psychologist Stanley Milgram, conducted some famous studies in social psychology that revealed that people will obey authority to torture innocent persons (Milgram, 1983, 1992). During his experiments, people denied their own consciences to inflict pain on others.

The setups for the experiments were similar. Subjects came to the Yale University psychology laboratory in response to a newspaper ad. They agreed to participate in studies they thought would examine the effects of punishment on learning. A hardheaded experimenter required the subjects to become "teachers." Their job was to teach students a list of word parings by delivering shocks of increasing intensity for every error the student's made. In some cases, the shock got quite high with the students screaming in agony. The "students" were actually stooges who received no real shock, but the "teachers" didn't know this during the experiment.

The purpose of the study was to see how much the "teachers" would increase the shock. In front of them they had switches labeled as, "Slight Shock," "Very Strong Shock," "Danger: Severe Shock," and the last switch said "XXX." Most people thought the "teachers" would stop at a mild level when the "students" shouted, "Hey, this really hurts." But to the surprise of everybody, 63% of the "teachers" went to the highest level (the "XXX" switch) even when they heard the students scream and beg them to stop.

The obedience of the subjects to authority greatly disturbed Milgram, other social psychologists, and the public when they heard about it. They were distraught that the "teachers," would be so obedient to authority. The study was repeated many times, but it produced the same results.

Why were the "teachers" so obedient to authority that they were willing to inflict pain on their fellow human beings? The answer may lie in the "teachers" beliefs. Milgram found that most of the "teachers" believed that they were inferior to authority. They thought:

"Authority is right because it is so powerful."

"Authority must know what it is doing."

"They know more than I."

"Authority will punish me if I don't do what they say."

Those of us who, like the "teachers," believe these types of thoughts will be more likely to do harm to others in the name of authority. We must never deny our own compassionate values and own good sense no matter who tells us to do so.

Homework

21.1 Who Have Been Your Authorities?

The following is a list of "authorities" people have relied on. Look at them and see which ones have been most important to you. Consider different time periods: your childhood, adolescence, and adulthood.

Step 1. Look at the people in the list below and decide if you ever used them as an authority.

Step 2. Identify the specific authority (e.g., if you picked a parent, which parent?).

Step 3. Pick the subject matter for which you considered them an authority (e.g., "I went to my mom about relationships and my dad about business").

Step 4. If you stopped using them as an authority, when and why did you stop? (e.g., "When I left home to go to college, I picked other people as the experts").

Step 5. Compare what authorities told you, with what your own experience in life taught you. Which judgments were more accurate?

AUTHORITIES

Parents	Older peers	Professionals
Grandparents	Neighbors	Spouse
Brothers, sisters	People of my social class	In-laws
Aunts, uncles	People of my race	Boy or girlfriend
Teachers	People of my gender	Media personality
Coaches	People of my national group	
Professors	National leaders	*Others*
Family tradition	Philosophers	
Bosses	Popular figures	_____
Political figures	Authors	_____
Ethnic group	Historical people	_____

No matter what authority you picked, it is important to realize that you were doing the picking; therefore, in a sense you were using yourself as the authority, at least the authority for choosing. Maybe this is the way it should be.

The obvious question about using authority is, what experts do we ask to find out whether our life is worth living, or whether we should get married, or are we truly happy? There isn't anyone else to turn to, but ourselves.

 Consider all the authorities we have used in our lives: from sports heroes to movie stars, TV personalities to college professors, successful business people to well-known professionals, gurus to majority rule. If we can't count on these authorities, who will we rely on? It may be we have outgrown the need for authorities, and we will have to figure things out on our own. It may be that our own experience is our highest authority, the touchstone for all validity. No other person's ideas, points of view, or values are as expert as our own experience with the world.

chapter 22

Finding the Good Reason
How We Fool Ourselves

A person usually has two reasons for doing something: a good reason and the real reason.
THOMAS CARLYLE

IN THIS CHAPTER
• Identifying a damaging fallacy
• Finding the real reason

Most of us probably believe that our attitudes are based on carefully thought out principles. But this kind of thinking has a flaw that pollutes the clarity of our logic. It is called "Finding the Good Reason" and is defined as defending a position by picking the most favorable sounding argument, rather than choosing the real reason.

 Our brains have this nasty little habit of making things up just to make us feel good. It doesn't matter that a thought is false or that we lack good evidence for believing it, we accept it just the same for the very basic, simple reason that we feel better about ourselves when we think this way.

It means that we have an opinion first, and then think of a good reason to have it. We search around for the best-sounding argument or the most rational explanation for what we already believe. We then offer our chosen rationalization as the sole reason for our belief. The explanations we give often have nothing to do with why we believe as we do. We simply make up logic or evidence to support our opinion. Our attitude does the driving; our evidence hitchhikes along for the ride.

Finding the good reason is a very damaging fallacy. It destroys our perception of the truth. But the most damaging thing about this fallacy is that we stop looking for accuracy at all. Instead, we spend our time searching for the most convincing way to prove that we are right. This leaves little time and less energy to find out whether we were right in the first place. The result is that we have masses of people roaming around spewing their dogmas, denigrating their opponents, and hawking their views of the world. If they used even a small part of their time and energy searching for the facts, we would all be better served. Finding the best reason locks our problems in place and keeps us from solving them.

Many of us recognize the tendency in ourselves to make things up, but we don't see the process as clearly in other people. We know what we are feeling, but we don't know what others feel. For example, have you ever watched a TV show where some well-known experts were talking and felt envy at how clearly they could explain difficult subjects? Were you overwhelmed by their ability to persuade others and reason so cleanly about ideas you were unsure about? Their reasoning seemed so lucid and certain. They could explain their thoughts so clearly. In contrast, you knew your thoughts about the subject were murky and shallow. You wish you had at least one moment in your life when you could experience the peace of such clear thinking.

We are sure that such clarity must come from years of research and specialized knowledge about a subject. Surely, someone could not become so confident without a deep logical mind, a brilliant memory, a total dedication to the truth, and the skill of a detective in discovering the facts. Many of us are awestruck and feel inferior in comparison.

But should we feel inferior?

In most cases, probably not! Most likely, these people simply have done a better job in finding a good reason for their positions than we have. Or they could have learned to explain their reasons more convincingly. Some people are better actors than we are.

It is important for all of us to recognize our human tendency to make up the best reason for whatever we think. The following exercise can help us offset this tendency.

Homework

EXERCISE

22.1 Finding the Worst Reason

Step 1. Select some of your opinions about various controversial matters such as a life hereafter, politics, males and females, the military, law enforcement, the environment, gays, abortion, America, the economy.

Step 2. Write down the best reasons you can think of for believing as you do. Pick the reasons that put you in the most favorable light. Totally ignore whether or not they are true.

Step 3. Actively search for the worst reasons for your opinions. Pick the least flattering reasons for believing as you do. Put these next to the best reasons.

Step 4. Having both the best and worst reasons sitting together, go out and try to find the real reasons.

EXAMPLE

BEST AND WORST

Some of my clients who did this exercise found the following best and worst reasons for their beliefs:

Person: A man in denial about his drinking problem.
Best Reason: "I had a poor unfortunate childhood."
Worst Reason: "I am a drunk who won't admit it."

Person: A woman who had stopped taking risks and had withdrawn from life.
Best Reason: "I am an emotionally sensitive person who can perceive dangers that others miss. 'Fools walk in where angels fear to tread.'"
Worst Reason: "I'm a coward who doesn't have enough guts to face life."

Person: A highly successful businessman with martial problems.
Best Reason: "My spouse is insensitive to my needs."
Worst Reason: "I am a spoiled brat who is not willing to pull my own weight in the relationship."

Person: A local magistrate who was ticketed for speeding.
Best Reason: "These cops have nothing to do but harass poor honest citizens."
Worst Reason: "I am an arrogant son-of-a-bitch who thinks the law shouldn't apply to me."

Person: A wealthy woman who was a strong political conservative.

Best Reason: "I am a patriot who wishes to maintain the best policies that my country has taken decades to develop."

Worst Reason: "I want to hold on to all the money I made under the old system, and I don't want to share it with anybody."

Person: A man who was politically liberal.

Best Reason: "I want to improve society in every way possible so that it becomes more equitable and beneficial to all people."

Worst Reason: "I don't have the skill, industry, or guts to make it in a competitive world, so we should change everything to give me a better chance in a new system."

Person: A college professor who had difficulty controlling his anger and annoyances.

Best Reason: "I have a higher sense of justice and fairness than the rest of humanity and have the duty to be upset when I see injustice."

Worst Reason: "I think I'm greater than God and that the whole universe should work exactly the way I want it to."

Person: A politically active man who worked for a third party that had never won any elections and never pulled in more than 10% of the vote.

Best Reason: "The party is in a readjustment period so we can prepare to run the country in the 21st century. We are the party of the future."

Worst Reason: "I like backing losers and hopeless causes because we can spend our time carping from the background. Since we'll never get elected, we will never have to stand and deliver."

Person: A middle-level manager of a logging company.

Best Reason: "There needs to be some logging in the northwest because people require wood for their houses and loggers need to support their families."

Worst Reason: "We want the money now. To hell with the future."

Person: A paid employee of an environmental group.

Best Reason: "People need natural beauty and places for recreation."

Worst Reason: "I already have a job and a wood house, so I don't care if others don't and are put out of work, just so I have some trees to hug."

Person: A Marine Corps colonel.

Best Reason: "We always will need our armed forces because the good will of the rest of humanity can never be counted on."

Worst Reason: "I love fighting."

Person: A young man who burned his draft card.

Best Reason: "War should always be the last measure any society takes. We should first exhaust all other alternatives, and I mean all."

Worst Reason: "I'm too chicken to fight."

 This exercise is more difficult than it appears. Most people who did the exercise found it hard to find a good reason for the opposing point of view or a bad reason for their own. It is hard for us to go against our strong opinions. Some people might find they can't do the exercise at all.

With practice and scrupulous self-honesty, someday, we may be able to remove our best and worst reasons and substitute our real reasons.

chapter 23

The Law of Parsimony
How to Have Clear Thoughts

Everything should be made as simple as possible, but not one bit simpler.
ALBERT EINSTEIN

IN THIS CHAPTER
- Understanding the law of parsimony
- Components of the law

We may have hundreds of thoughts, beliefs, and attitudes to consider. Which ones do we keep and which do we remove? There is a useful method to help us clear out our mental trash. It's called the law of parsimony. It is one of the most helpful ideas in understanding ourselves and the world around us.

At its most basic, the law means that, all things being equal, the simplest explanation is the best. A small book by Quine and Ullian (1978), two famous Harvard philosophy professors, explains the principle well. They describe the law of parsimony in detail and give many common everyday examples that demonstrate the law's power. Here is one of their examples.

WHERE'S MY CAR?

EXAMPLE Picture that one afternoon you get in your black '05 Ford Explorer SUV and drive to the supermarket. You park next to the shopping cart stall and go into the store. An hour later, you come out pushing a cart full of groceries. You look at where you parked your car and you see a black '05 Ford Explorer there. What do you conclude?

The answer is so obvious that most people don't see the point of the question. Obviously, you conclude that it is your car—the same car that you left in the parking spot when you drove in. You may ask, "Of course. What else could it be?" Well, it really could be a great number of other things. For instance, someone might have stolen your car and driven another black '05 Ford Explorer SUV in its place. Or you could be hallucinating—you just think you see your car there, or it could be a holograph of your car, or it could be a VW bug disguised to look like your car. Well, you can see what is happening. Only your imagination limits what it could be.

But the difficulty with the whole story is, by what logic do we reflexively answer that it is our car? How do we know it is not one of the alternatives? Do we use authority? No. No authority tells us it is our car. Consensus? No, we didn't take a vote of people in the parking lot to determine if it is our car. Has God revealed it to us? It is unlikely that God would do our homework for us. How about science? Does the scientific method prove that it is our car? No, we didn't conduct a controlled experiment that proved that our car was sitting there; we just automatically assumed it was. So on what basis do we assume it's our car, and how are we so certain that we feel we don't even need to consider the other possibilities?

The usual answer is that we use our logic, our reasoning. We assume it is our car because this is the most probable explanation. Since we have gone to the store 99 times before and have always found our car where we left it, we assume that this hundredth time will be the same as the previous 99 times. We think it has the highest probability. We admit that other explanations are possible, but we believe they are so unlikely that we don't think we should waste our time considering them.

Most people would think this is a good explanation—very satisfactory. Our logic tells us to pick the most likely possibility. End of discussion, right?

Wrong! Our logic is mistaken. Many philosophers starting with Hume and ending in the modern day with Popper, assert otherwise. They suggest that just because something has happened a million times before, there is no guarantee, or even a probability that the next time it will happen again. Just because the sun has risen on all previous days, we have no right to expect that it must rise tomorrow.

Why not? Why can't we believe there is a high probability that the sun will rise tomorrow simply because it has done so for the last 5 billion years?

The reason we can't is that there is no logical connection between tomorrow's sunrise and all the previous sunrises. They are independent events. As Hume explains, imagine that there are two perfectly accurate clocks which are set one second apart. On the hour, one strikes and a second later the other invariably strikes. Does the first clock cause the second to strike? Are the two clocks connected? Clearly they are not. And it doesn't matter if we have heard the two clocks strike a thousand times, the first clock still doesn't cause the second to strike.

Thinking that independent events are connected in some mystical way is called the gambler's fallacy. This is the thought that one chance event influences another chance event. For instance, what is the probability of getting a head when you flip a coin? Fifty percent. Now, suppose you got 10 heads in a row. What is the probability you will get a head the next time? The answer is the same, 50%. It doesn't matter how many heads you got in a row, a hundred or a thousand, the probability is only 50% that you will get a head the next time. Many people think that probabilities build up, that the coin "knows" after a hundred heads that it is supposed to land as a tail pretty soon, so the impetus for a tail gets stronger and stronger. Obviously, however, this is absurd. Coins aren't great thinkers and are worse rememberers. In fact, you can't count on a coin's memory; a coin has no sense.

Your car is no smarter than the coin. It doesn't remember it was in the parking lot 99 times before. It doesn't know whether it is a holograph or a negative hallucination, or if Mr. Spock has transported it to the planet Vulcan.

Much of modern philosophy is convinced that we cannot prove concepts like cause and effect, probability, and chance. If they are right, we may never be able to find out whether our thoughts are valid or not.

So, we are back where we started. Philosophy is at the same place that we have been, which simply stated is, "Who knows?" We can't be sure of anything: authority, intuition, consensus, revelations, logic, or science, they all fail. We still have no good reason for assuming it's our car, even though we make this assumption all the time, and we make it without question.

Undoubtedly, this whole discussion will strike many people as absurd. Nobody in their right mind would think of these other options. Everybody would conclude that they saw their car. It is obvious.

Yes, it is obvious. But the reason it's obvious to every normal human being is the law of parsimony (or Occam's razor). The law means only this: the simplest explanation is the best. It is such an unpretentious concept, but it answers the car riddle, while science, authority, and consensus do not.

This law is so ingrained in us that in situations like the one with the car in the parking lot we pick the simplest, clearest, least complex explanation and don't even consider the others. We immediately assume it's our car and forget the alternatives. We use the law a thousand times every day, and we do it so automatically that we aren't even aware of using it.

In any situation, our brain picks the simplest, least complex interpretation of an event, and we are satisfied with this interpretation unless later information contradicts it. It is automatic and ingrained in our species.

The law is useful for more than finding cars in parking lots. The following homework exercise will let you see how this law may operate in many other areas in your life.

Homework

 EXERCISE

23.1 Who Done It?

Imagine you are in the following situation.

THE SCENE

You work in an office and one of the expensive laptop computers has been stolen. The boss asks you to find out who took it. You discover it had to have been stolen from the supply room between 3:00 p.m. and 3:15 p.m. on Friday. The supply room was locked and during this time and only three people had keys—Al, Bob, and Carl. Al has an alibi, because he was at a marketing meeting from 2:30 to 3:30 on Friday. Bob also has an alibi because one of his coworkers said he was in the cafeteria with him during this time. Carl claims that he was sitting in his office filling out papers, but we only have his word for it. There are many other possibilities here. Maybe Al gave the key to a colleague in order for him to steal the computer while Al was at the meeting. Maybe Bob's friend is lying and they both met before hand to come up with the alibi. Maybe someone else got a key before the office began keeping an accurate count of the keys and they had planned to steal the laptop weeks ahead of time.

Therefore, the possibilities are that Al, Bob, Carl, or someone else stole it. But who? You can use the law of parsimony to find out.

Look at the three sublaws. They may help you pick the best suspect. When you finish, see if you can apply these laws to decide who is the likely thief.

The Three Sublaws of Parsimony

Step 1. The most conservative explanation. When we are looking for the cause of something, we should pick the most conservative explanation first. "Conservative" means to pick the explanation that conflicts the least with what we already know. For instance, if we squeeze our toothpaste and nothing comes out, we could conclude that the laws of physics have been mysteriously suspended for our tube of Crest, that for this moment in space and time, the second law of thermodynamics does not apply (for every action there is a reaction). As we have seen before, just because the toothpaste has always come out before is no guarantee it will come out this time. But the law of parsimony causes us to reject this notion out of hand, we don't even consider it. Instead, we conclude that the most conservative explanation is that something is stopping up the end of the tube or that we are out of toothpaste. Mystery solved.

Step 2. Look for the easiest explanation. The law of parsimony also tells us to search for the answer that requires the least energy, the most modest hypothesis. Consider this example from Quine and Ullian's book, *The Web of Belief* (1978, p. 68).

> Suppose a man rings our telephone and ends by apologizing for dialing the wrong number. We will guess that he slipped, rather than that he was a burglar checking to see if anyone was home. It is the more modest of the two hypotheses, butterfingers being rife.

The car analogy is also a good example. The interpretation of what we see in the parking lot that requires the least amount of energy is that it is our car. It would take a great deal of energy to remove our car and substitute a holograph, or transport it to another planet, or steal it and replace it with another one of exactly the same year, model, and color. Our brain picks the explanation that is most modest and requires the least amount of effort.

Step 3. Pick the least complex answer. Third, the law impels us to pick the simplest answer. The least complicated interpretation is preferable to entangled explanations. For example, a Freudian theorist might suggest that women are afraid of snakes because snakes represent the male organ, and those women who have repressed their sexual feelings will develop a phobia about anything that symbolically can be associated with the penis. But this is a very complex explanation. The least complex is that women and people in general are afraid of snakes because poisonous snakes can kill us if they bite us. If the rejoinder is, "Why then are people afraid of nonpoisonous snakes," the answer is that it is often difficult to tell the difference between one and the other.

Results of Exercise

Most people who did the exercise said that their first suspect was Carl. It was their most parsimonious explanation. Al, Bob, or some other person were also possible, of course, but for one of them to do it, would require more complex, less conservative, and more energy (e.g., Al had to give the key to someone else, Bob needed to get a colleague to lie for him, and someone else would have had to have gotten a fourth key months before).

It is important to note, here, that the rule of parsimony does not mean that all unfamiliar, high-energy, complex explanations are wrong; the rule only means that you should pick the simplest explanation first, and choose complex, unusual answers only if the simplest one doesn't fit all the facts.

But what if . . . ?

Let us add to the exercise, slightly. Imagine that we checked Carl's office computer and found out that he had faxed 20 minutes of complicated accounting information during the time when the laptop was stolen. For Carl to take the computer, he would have had to prepare the fax the night before and then arranged to send it automatically at the right time. He could have done this, but since it would have taken a lot more time and energy, most people would doubt that he did it.

We would then move to the next most likely suspect, Bob. We would make him our first choice if we thought his colleague in the cafeteria could be lying for him. Of course, we would have to get some evidence that the colleague would be willing to lie. But if we discovered that they were not friends but competitors, it would seem unlikely that a competitor would be willing to lie for Bob.

We next would consider Al. Maybe Al didn't stay throughout the whole meeting. We would check with other people at the meeting to find out. If Al's alibi held up, we would conclude that none of the three original suspects were likely, and we would be finally left with the possibility that someone else had made an extra key to the supply room.

explanation first. We eliminate it only if the facts do not support it. Then we pick the next simplest explanation, and then the next. We gradually work our way up the ladder of complexity until we find the most parsimonious explanation remaining that still fits with the facts.

 In the future, if you find yourself faced with a puzzle such as why someone treated you badly, or where did you park your car, or what is the cause of your emotion, or where did you leave your purse, or why did you fail in this or that project, or who stole the laptop, look for the most parsimonious answer, first. The simplest explanation is the best.

Taking Out Your Mental Trash

chapter 24

Our Cosmic Dance
What Should We Believe?

> *Human beings, vegetables, or cosmic dust—we all dance to a mysterious tune, intoned in the distance by an invisible piper.*   ALBERT EINSTEIN

IN THIS CHAPTER
- An extended metaphor
- Exploring the birth of our beliefs

Are all our beliefs relative and of equal value? It would bother most of us if this were so. It would seem to be part of the wishy-washy values of our modern, sophisticated 21st-century view of the world. It would suggest that there are no absolutes, that deciding whether our beliefs are valid or not is simply a matter of wispy, constantly changing opinion, that we can hold any belief or value and indiscriminately substitute one for another. But is this view correct?

This book instructs us to throw out our unsound beliefs, so how are we going to do this if we can't tell the difference between the real ones and the unfounded ones? If all beliefs and values are relative, does this mean there is no reality outside of human judgment and no standards to lean on?

To answer this important question and to understand if your beliefs and values have no more substance than a fleeting cloud, I ask the reader to go on a bizarre fantasy trip. The metaphor I use may seem far-fetched, but if you complete the journey, you may see that its underlying message is at the very heart of this book.

Take an imaginary journey to Earth's distant past.

LIFE IN A PRIMORDIAL POND

EXAMPLE Imagine that you are a molecule floating around in a primeval pond 3 billion years ago on planet Earth. It is steamy hot, the horizon is full of erupting volcanoes, scarlet clouds are illuminated by a red oversized sun, and hundreds of lightning bolts thunder and crackle around you. The pond you are in is a chemical stew, a mixture of water, oxygen, nitrogen, carbon, methane, ammonias, hydrogen sulfide gases, all being churned up by the lightening bolts.

The pond is an amorphous mass of blinking, clicking, odorous, tactile, pulsating, moving chemicals. But you don't see, hear, smell, or feel anything because you have no eyes, ears, nose, or feelings. For now, you are just part of this mass, floating around randomly and bobbing up and down.

Suddenly, you notice a boundary starting to form around you. A membrane has appeared which separates you from the chemical soup of the pond. It encloses you so that now you have your own discrete chemical stew, your own miniature pond inside the larger one. Because you are enclosed and distinct, you gradually begin to develop a separate internal chemistry, detached from what is going on around you. You are now a "you" rather than an "it." You have become alive. At the same time, you notice other molecules forming membranes, which encase and disconnect them. You look at the pond, and now there are millions of little self-contained chemical boats like you inside the larger sea of whirling chemicals.

You split into two, then four, then 16, then more. Around you others are dividing, combining, and getting larger. Soon you become a complex organism.

You do not understand why you became alive. Something truly mysterious and magical has happened. You don't know why you are here, but you revel in what you have become. All you know is that some mighty power, a force way beyond your poor ability to comprehend, has given you life. An invisible, cosmic piper has planted a mysterious tune in you—a tune that drives you to survive, to reproduce, to develop, to grow, to expand.

Initially, you have no sensitivity to various aspects of the pond around you; you respond to the gross movement of the water, the gravity, the currents, and the tide. Later, a part of your membrane is thinner and you become sensitive to the different light quantas in the pond. You learn from trial and error that light increases your chances of getting food, so every time you sense light, you move toward it. Eventually, after eons of time, this part of your membrane will become eyes. Next another section of your mem-

Taking Out Your Mental Trash

brane develops a sensitivity to the noise vibrations in the pond. You learn to move away from the clicking sounds because you have discovered that when you get close to the clicking, something there hurts you. Ultimately, this sensitivity will develop into ears. You also notice other organisms developing other senses to respond to different aspects of the pond.

When your internal chemistry becomes complex enough, you start developing primitive circuits and schemas (later in the far distant future, to become beliefs, thoughts, and attitudes) about those aspects of the pond that are useful to you. Initially you only know that light is good and clicking is bad. But gradually you learn to differentiate one kind of light from another and to notice that there are different types of clicking.

As you move around the pond, you explore it, test it, and learn more about it. You pay particular attention to the other chemical boats around you. It is like a microscopic dance between you and the pond. Sometimes the pond leads by sending you different signals that you have to recognize and adapt to; sometimes you lead, by moving into a new area of the pond where you send out probes and wait for a response. Over time, you learn to differentiate certain aspects of the pond, learn to distinguish one chemical boat from another, and develop some primitive rules about how the pond operates.

You continue to dance. As you learn more and more about the pond, you develop increasingly complex internal thoughts, beliefs, schemas, and interpretations. You even form a memory to recall what you have learned. Those thoughts that are mistaken and not useful are eliminated; those that are useful and that help you survive, reproduce, and enhance, are retained.

Our dance continues to the present day. Over the years, centuries, millenniums, and eons, the beliefs created by the little self-contained chemical boats and the pond have become highly integrated. Our thoughts are now very complex. They are so developed that we humans (the most intricate organism in the pond) no longer passively observe the pond, we push, and probe, and change it, making it fit to our needs. And our thoughts, beliefs, attitudes, and values now encompass a far greater pond. Our pond is no longer a small pool of tepid, bubbling chemicals in a primeval volcanic landscape; it is a pond that includes the whole earth, the solar system, and the universe beyond—a cosmic pond.

And what lessons do we learn from our imaginary journey? If we look closely, we can see that our best beliefs and our most useful attitudes have emerged directly from our dance with the pond. The key word here is direct. If we are in constant interaction with our environment and we continuously probe and prod for answers, the feedback we get from the world is very useful. But if our beliefs and attitudes come from outside our dance, they often lead us astray.

The treatment for mistaken beliefs is to get back into direct contact with our pond and to learn to dance again. This exercise may help you do this. It will be a good review of the major principles taught in this book.

Homework

EXERCISE 24.1 The Cosmic Dance

Step 1. Go to your Master List of Core Beliefs (p. 47)

Step 2. How many of these beliefs came from your own direct experience with the world? That is, did you learn them from repeated interactions with people and your physical environment (i.e., they came from your own personal dance with your pond)?

Step 3. How many came from other sources? That is, you learned them as a result of traumatic emotional experiences, or from tradition, your parents, your other authorities, your culture, your early childhood experiences, your superstitions, and your own wish fulfillment? *Read the examples below.*

Step 4. Decide to throw into the trash all those attitudes that you got from somewhere else and retain only those that came from your own experience with the pond.

WHY ALL THE MENTAL TRASH?

There are five major reasons why most of us have developed defective beliefs.

Traumatic Experiences

Some thoughts we believe out of fear. We may have been so scarred by life that we exaggerate life's dangers and decide to hide away from the world (e.g., "Run, away from all danger"; "Traumatic life experiences must always dominate me"). We may have had experiences that were so emotionally traumatizing that they distorted all our later attitudes. We mistook a few bad steps for the whole dance.

Early Experiences

Sometimes we haven't updated our beliefs since we were young (e.g., "I need everybody in my group to like me"; "Appearance is everything"; "There is one true love"). We were too young to correctly interpret the meaning of life. We practiced an old dance and didn't notice the tune had changed.

It Makes Us Feel Good to Think This Way

Some beliefs we held because they flattered us by making us feel strong and powerful so that we could forget our fragility (e.g., "Our inner guide is always right"; "We intuitively know our true selves"; "Our minds are all powerful"). We must always remember that we are creatures on this planet, not the creator of it.

Overreliance on Others' Opinions

Some opinions we affirmed because we relied too much on what other people told us. We honored other people's experiences and demeaned our own (e.g., "Experts are always right"; "Someone is to blame"; "One group of people is inherently better than another"; "There is only one natural, correct way of looking at the world"). It must be our own dance, not someone else's. We cannot dance by the numbers.

Tired of Fighting

And some opinions we believed because at times we got weary of life, and wanted a quick and easy answer that didn't take too much effort (e.g., "One should take the path of least resistance"; "I am inferior"; "I can't help what I think"). We can't sit out our dance with our environment.

 But underneath all these reasons, there is one central, one key reason why we learned these trashy beliefs. They were never *ours* in the first place. Others taught us them; powerful emotions inflamed them; distorted childhoods twisted them; flattery enticed us toward them; weariness of spirit resigned us to them. None of these distorted beliefs originated from our own direct intercourse with the world, our dance with our cosmic pond.

 As long as our beliefs come from our own dance with life, they are useful and will help us survive, develop, grow, and enhance. If we stop dancing with the world, we cease to be. Life is to be experienced; life is to live.

Part IV

Changing Beliefs

chapter 25

Countering
Fighting Back

Change is the constant, the signal for rebirth, the egg of the phoenix.
CHRISTINA BALDWIN

IN THIS CHAPTER
- Mastering countering techniques
- Being assertive with yourself
- Key principles of countering

Change is difficult; it takes effort. Most people find it easier to continue in the same old way rather than to put forth the effort to try something new. But people can change. We see them change all the time, learning new skills, trying new experiences, shifting their attitudes. How many people believe the same things they did at 5, 15, or 25? If people don't change, they die.

Yes, we can change our attitudes, and we do so all the time. This chapter discusses how we can reverse our thought processes even after years of thinking in the same manner.

One of the most obvious ways to change our beliefs is as old as the human race, argue against them. If someone expresses an idea we don't agree with, we counter it. Disputing, challenging, and arguing are all ancient methods older than Plato's dialogues. Today these techniques are used by virtually everyone, in all kinds of situations, from barrooms to college classrooms to presidential debates.

 We can use this same method to change our own beliefs. We can counter our erroneous thoughts, dispute our damaging attitudes, and challenge our useless beliefs. These counters are thoughts that we throw against our beliefs. A counter can be one word, "Nonsense!" It can be a sentence, "I can't be better than everyone, in everything, all the time." It can be a question, "Why is it terrible, horrible, or catastrophic if this person doesn't like me?" Or it can be an epigram, "We are all ignorant, just about different things." It can be a counterimage, picturing our feared colleague as a big duck wearing glasses and a jacket and tie, or it can be a philosophy, "The purpose of life is not for me to protect, hide away, and shield myself from all possible misfortunes; the purpose of life is to take some risks."

Many of us have been able to argue effectively against others' beliefs, yet we may have been unable to argue against our own beliefs, and worse we may never have even tried. The following exercise gives us some practice.

Homework

EXERCISE

25.1 Self-assertion

Use Worksheet 25.1, "Countering Practice"

Step 1. Pick one of your beliefs from your Master List of Core Beliefs (page 47), and focus on it.

Step 2. Put your belief into one concise sentence using the first person singular ("I must, I should, I need to, I can't, I shouldn't, I am," etc.) For example, "I must have everybody like me; I shouldn't have made the mistake; I can't stand being upset; I am a failure."

Step 3. If necessary, recast your sentences to show the underlying assertion (i.e. the statement you are making to yourself claiming there is a connection between two things). For example:

Statement: "I am scared."
What you are really asserting: "Something is dangerous."

Statement: "I need to be competent to feel worthwhile."
What you are really asserting: "Competence equals self-worth."

Statement: "I can't survive without a man."
What you are really asserting: "Men are physical necessities."

Statement: "I shouldn't make mistakes."
What you are really asserting: "Perfection is possible for human beings."

Taking Out Your Mental Trash

Statement: "All you need is love."

What you are really asserting: "All human problems can be solved by feeling the emotion called love."

Statement: "It's terrible that I didn't get the promotion."

What you are really asserting: "One of the very worst things that can happen to any human being in life is not getting what he or she wants."

Statement: "It shouldn't have happened."

What you are really asserting: "The universe should follow my rules."

Step 4. Develop a list of counterarguments against your assertions. Use the principles below to help you develop your counters.

KEY PRINCIPLES OF COUNTERING

EXAMPLE

1. *Counters should be directly opposite to your destructive beliefs.* Oppose the belief forcefully. For example, a counter that states, "It is impossible to succeed in everything I do" is better than, "It is often quite difficult to succeed in everything I do."

2. *Develop as many counters as possible.* Ten counters are twice as good as five; 20 are better than 10.

3. *Counters should be believable.* Make sure your counters are realistic and logical. Don't subscribe to the power of positive thinking, in which people often tell themselves positive lies. Instead, stress the power of truthful, realistic thinking and say true things to yourself, not just platitudes. For example, although it may feel good to think, "Life gets better with each passing day," it's not true, some days things get worse.

4. *Practice, practice, practice.* Repeatedly counter your damaging beliefs. Many months will be needed for some tough thoughts. Most people balk at this investment of time and energy saying they've already tried countering to no avail. After discussions with these people, we usually discover that they have argued with themselves for only an hour or two some Sunday afternoon. It is important to understand that you must argue against a belief as many times as you have previously argued in its favor. It may take an hour a day for a year to overcome a lifelong core sentence.

5. *Make your counters concise.* Many people turn their counters into "dissertations." Counters should be written in the vernacular so that they can be easily remembered and immediately thrown against the old thought whenever it pops up. For example a counter such as, "Tough shit that he doesn't love me!" is better than, "In the myriad course of human interchange, it is unfortunate that one sometimes encounters a person who does not exhibit reciprocal amorosity."

Step 5. This is the most important step. Countering in an automatic, mechanical, and unconvincing way makes countering useless. The ideal counter is a belief that pulls in a hierarchy of values, perceptions, experiences, and emotions drowning the damaging thought in powerful currents flowing in the opposite direction. Short phrases or slogans are useful when they are tied to strong counteremotions.

Since countering is more than an intellectual process, pulling in strong emotions will help you change your damaging beliefs. To understand how, consider the following analogy.

THE "MELTED WAX" THEORY

EXAMPLE Thoughts are like wax impressions in our brain. They are often formed when we have a strong emotion like fear or anger. These emotions act on our thoughts like heat, causing them to liquefy and reform into new beliefs.

When the heat of high emotional arousal has dissipated, the thought is solidified. To change the belief we have to either chip away at the wax impression, which takes a long time, or reheat the wax so the thought can be remolded. If we get angry and assertive enough with our useless thoughts, it is like heating them up so that we can pour them into a new mold.

The intensity of emotion that you invest in a counter is the key to your success. Disputing is most effective when you argue against a thought with strong emotion in a high state of arousal. An intense emotion virtually eliminates the repetitious, mechanical parroting that so often renders counters ineffective. It is often helpful to be angry against your belief before you counter. After all, your damaging beliefs have caused you emotional pain, why should you treat them tenderly? Frequently only an aggressive dispute can elicit a strong, enough emotional level to overturn a strong damaging thought.

Step 6. Practice using your counters whenever you think of your core belief. One way to do this is by "image practice." Picture thinking the core belief until you have it clearly in mind. Once the belief is clear, shout "Stop!" to yourself, and immediately dispute and argue against it using all the counters you have developed. Fight the old belief as hard as you can with powerful emotions. Continue until you feel the belief become distinctively weaker.

25.1 Countering Practice

1. My Master List Belief:

_____

_____

2. Write a concise sentence of belief using the first person singular:

_____

_____

3. Recast sentence showing what I am really asserting:

_____

_____

4. Counterarguments to my belief:

   (a) _____

   (b) _____

   (c) _____

   (d) _____

   (e) _____

   (f) _____

   (g) _____

   (h) _____

   (i) _____

   (j) _____

5. Counters Checklist

   Is the counter opposite?

   Is the counter realistic and logical?

   Is the counter short and written in the vernacular?

   Does it pull in your counter emotion, values, and experiences?

   Does it have emotional strength?

THE STORY OF PHILIP

EXAMPLE

Philip was a single, very attractive young man in his 20s, studying to be a lawyer. Despite being an accomplished tennis player, sturdy, and 6'5", he was extremely shy with women. He couldn't ask a woman out for a date. He had no difficulty being assertive with men and handled male confrontation appropriately. He began the exercise by isolating his core sentence; he thought women were weak, fragile creatures who must be protected by men. He viewed himself as a complete lummox, a Baby Huey who shouldn't step on the sensitive toes of these delicate creatures.

Philip's personal history indicated that his father had taught him this idea. Apparently, the father feared that his son's large size would make him too aggressive with women, a problem the father had experienced himself when growing up. As a result, he taught his son to be extremely careful not to hurt women. The lesson had been so effective that Philip hadn't dated for two years and was so nervous around women that he said practically nothing in their presence for fear of bruising their delicate feelings. As a result, women rejected him out of hand as an extremely dumb, though attractive, jock.

During the fourth step of the exercise, he developed a long and accurate list of counterarguments against his core sentence. However, when he tried to use them, he would counter so passively that his arguments were ineffective. It was at this point he was taught to imagine the following scene.

THE BOXER ANALOGY

EXAMPLE

I am a fighter, but my opponent isn't in a ring, he is in my head. My opponent is the core belief that women are extremely fragile. This belief has been beating me up for years, making me inordinately shy around women, and preventing me from developing normal relationships. Even though I logically know this belief is false, I haven't convinced myself. I have hardly been fighting it at all, and on those rare occasions when I do fight, I do it so weakly that the belief easily overpowers me. It keeps giving me a black eye. I must start defending myself and fight back whenever this belief enters my head. I can't appease it. It's like dealing with any other bully; the more I give in, the more ferociously it will come back next time to beat on me. I must start attacking this belief as hard as I can.

Initially the thought will be stronger than I, and will win the fight. But if I persist, I will gradually become stronger and it will become weaker. After a

Taking Out Your Mental Trash

while, I will begin to win some of the time, then most of the time, until finally it won't come back anymore. Let's start fighting back.

It took some time, and it wasn't easy, but Philip was able to counter his core sentence effectively. As the old belief got weaker, he got stronger and started to ask women out. Soon he was dating regularly and became increasingly interested in one particular woman.

 To do this exercise effectively, it is crucial that you understand a key point. *Attack your beliefs, but not yourself.* It is helpful to call your beliefs silly, stupid, or ridiculous, but it's important never to call yourself these names. You believe the sentence because you have been taught it, and anyone with the same background and experiences would have believed it. There is nothing wrong with you; there is only something wrong with your thinking. It is a subtle but critical distinction.

Although it usually takes a long time to weaken many damaging beliefs, countering occasionally produces dramatic reversals. Many people have been able to quickly remove sentences they had held for years because they became intensely angry at continuing to think the same old way (see Chapter 30, "Quantum Leaps," for more details).

 While this exercise may be quite useful, like all techniques it doesn't help everybody. Sometimes it can even make people feel worse. We must use it carefully and only when it feels right. Since the exercise accelerates our emotional level, we shouldn't use it if we are already superagitated. At these times being a good, soft, kind, teacher to yourself is more appropriate and more helpful (see Chapter 9, "Our Secret Teachers," for more help).

chapter 26

Alternative Beliefs
The Rule of Primacy

Hesitancy in judgment is the only true mark of the thinker. DAGOBERT D. RUNES

IN THIS CHAPTER
- Understanding the rule
- Finding alternative beliefs

Many people believe in the Rule of Primacy. The rule means that we pay more attention to our first beliefs than to our later ones. These primal thoughts can be about anything: our first opinion of a new idea when we first heard it; our first assessment of whether someone was guilty or innocent of a crime; our first beliefs about the world when we first left home; our first job; or our first romance.

The trouble with our first beliefs is that they are usually wrong. Many of us impulsively intuit the meaning of a given event and then stick to this initial thought, assuming that it must be correct. Later beliefs, though often more accurate, only rarely seem to implant themselves as solidly as the first. For example, some of us continue to believe that crossing our eyes too much can make us permanently cross-eyed, or shaving makes our hair grow back thicker, or that we should feed a cold but starve a fever, because we heard these beliefs when we were young. Once implanted, primary beliefs can be very difficult to change.

When our first beliefs are negative, they may cause lifelong distortions and misjudgments. Early twisted thoughts may harden our perceptions into concrete that a lifetime of later beliefs doesn't crack.

We can't stop ourselves from having first thoughts, nor should we. What we need to do is to realize that these beliefs have a high chance of being incorrect. It is useful for us to replace some of our first thoughts with alternative beliefs. The following exercise may help you do this.

Homework

EXERCISE 26.1 Alternative Beliefs

Use Worksheet 26.1, "Alternative Beliefs"

Step 1. Pick four thoughts from your Master List of Core Beliefs that you once assumed were true, but now know are false. The attitudes could be about anything: your first opinions about a new idea you just heard; your first beliefs about a potential danger; your first thoughts about why something bad happened; your first impression of yourself.

Step 2. Write your original thoughts on Worksheet 26.1 under "First Belief." Try to remember the wording you used when you first had the thoughts.

Step 3. Think of at least four alternative beliefs. Pick substitute thoughts that would have been more correct and more helpful at the time. Write them on Worksheet 26.1. See the examples below to help you find the type of alternatives being suggested.

Step 4. In the future, if your first mistaken thought returns, immediately think of each of your four alternatives.

Here are examples of how several people did the exercise.

BREAKUP

EXAMPLE A single, 25-year-old woman had just broken up with her boyfriend.

First Belief

There is something wrong with me. I am inadequate, and I'll probably never develop a lasting relationship with a man.

Alternative Beliefs

1. I haven't met the right man.
2. I don't want to give up my freedom right now.
3. My boyfriend and I didn't have good chemistry together.
4. My boyfriend was afraid to commit to any relationship.

BAD LUCK

EXAMPLE

After years of driving his car with a rabbit's foot hanging from the mirror, a man decided to throw it away. The next day he felt a little anxious when driving to work.

First Belief

See, I knew it. I needed the rabbit's foot to keep me from getting into an accident; without it, I'm sure to have one.

Alternative Beliefs

1. I'm anxious because I don't have my crutch anymore.
2. My rabbit's foot certainly wasn't lucky for the rabbit.
3. My tension is the price I pay for the years of silly thinking I kept feeding myself.
4. Tough! I am driving to work without it just the same.

SAGEBRUSH

EXAMPLE

A man was driving down an Arizona highway late at night and saw a shadow in the road ahead.

First Belief

It's tumbleweed, and I'll drive right through it.

Alternative Beliefs

1. Maybe I should slow down and find out.
2. It's a rock and will crush me like a peanut.
3. It's a smudge on my glasses.
4. It's a UFO from the planet Zattor which came to earth to do rectal probing (see Tip on next page).

Taking Out Your Mental Trash

Legs

My husband says I have fat legs.

First Belief

My legs are grotesque. I'm deformed. I feel like I shouldn't wear shorts because everyone will see my legs. Nature gave me a raw deal.

Alternative Beliefs

1. He was angry with me for not having dinner ready. He knows I'm sensitive about my weight and was trying to hurt me.
2. He is going through his midlife crisis and wants me to look like an 18-year-old so that he'll feel younger.
3. He has fat legs and is projecting.
4. He's an idiot!

For this exercise to be effective, the accuracy of your alternative beliefs is not essential. What is essential is for you to realize that alternative thoughts are possible and that your first belief is not magically true simply because you thought of it first. Alternative ways of thinking help you weaken the certainty of the first belief and helps you learn to suspend your initial judgment until you can obtain more information.

26.1 Alternative Beliefs

First Belief:

_____

Alternative Beliefs:

1. _____
2. _____
3. _____
4. _____

First Belief:

_____

Alternative Beliefs:

1. _____
2. _____
3. _____
4. _____

First Belief:

_____

Alternative Beliefs:

1. _____
2. _____
3. _____
4. _____

First Belief:

_____

Alternative Beliefs:

1. _____
2. _____
3. _____
4. _____

chapter **27**

Changing the Past
Historical Resynthesis

You can't depend on your eyes when your imagination is out of focus. MARK TWAIN

IN THIS CHAPTER
• Finding the roots of your beliefs
• Correcting old mistakes

Sometimes it is not enough simply to know the origins of a belief and develop alternative thoughts (last chapter), we also need to learn how the old belief changed over time. Many of the attitudes we have today are only the most recent reincarnation of the beliefs we had during our childhood and adolescence. To change a present day thought, we may have to go back through each period in its past to pull it out by all its roots. It may appear to be impossible, but it isn't—consider the metaphor below (Figure 27.1).

EXAMPLE

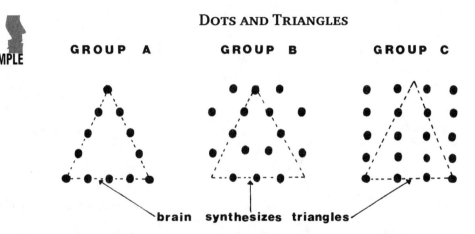

DOTS AND TRIANGLES

Figure 27.1 Dots and triangles

The dots stand for our little bits of experience. These may be the place we were living, the relationships we had, our predominant emotions, what we were doing, or other raw bits of information we had about our self and our environment. The dots alone don't mean much to us. They are raw bits of disorganized information and have no meaning on their own. They become alive only when we put meaning into them.

If our brains were machines, we would have grouped the dots into the best patterns they revealed—triangle for the first; oval for the second; and square for the third. But our human brains don't simply scan data, we transform it. We create patterns based on habit and emotions and what other brains have taught us. As children, we may have correctly perceived triangles; as we grew, we may have continued to see triangles because of habit or strong emotions, even though circles or squares provided a better fit. We can spend our entire lives seeing triangles simply because we saw them when we were young.

As children, we may have looked at our lives and the world around us as big and incomprehensible. The pattern we formed may have been that we were weak and small (the triangle). At this stage in our life, the pattern may have been accurate.

But as we grew older the world changed. We were less weak and powerless (the circle and square), but many of us continued to think the same, simply because we were used to this old view, or because others insisted that we were still weak, or simply because we never got around to updating our information.

It is often difficult for us to change our present view because it has such strong roots in our past. But, if we are to accurately see the world and ourselves, change must take place.

The following homework exercise is one small step in updating our beliefs.

Homework

EXERCISE

27.1 Resynthesizing Earlier Critical Events

Use Worksheet 27.1, "Changing the Past"

Step 1. Refer to your Childhood or Adolescence Lists of Critical Events (Worksheet 5.1, page 32 or Worksheet 5.2, page 33). Pick out one of those critical events. Don't pick the most upsetting, pick one you feel comfortable considering.

Step 2. As you have done before, recall the event and remember what happened and how you felt.

Step 3. Remember precisely what you said to yourself about the event at the time. What did you tell yourself that got you so upset? What did you conclude about yourself because of the event?

Step 4. Look at what you now believe through your present adult eyes. Use all your present knowledge and mature understanding and correct what you said to yourself then. What do you know now that you couldn't possibly have known as a child or adolescent? What do you see now with your present understanding and knowledge of the world? Try to find the mistake in thinking you made years ago.

Step 5. Correct the mistake. Say the truth to yourself now, the truth that you didn't see, or couldn't see before. Remember your correction.

27.1 Changing the Past

Critical Childhood or Adolescent Event

Situation: _____

_____

Emotion: _____

Early Belief

What did you say to yourself then that got you upset?

_____

_____

What did you conclude about yourself because of the event?

_____

_____

_____

Corrected Belief

Looking back, what was the mistake in your thinking?

_____

_____

_____

Now, as a mature adult, what is the correct belief?

_____

_____

_____

THE STORY OF MARK

EXAMPLE

Mark suffered from travel anxiety. He learned to travel to most places and performed most activities without undue fear, but he hadn't mastered one fear, he still couldn't fly.

Like many people with this problem, Mark didn't fear the plane crashing; he was afraid of getting panicky while airborne. He feared being trapped on a plane while having an anxiety attack and being out of control.

After counseling with a cognitive therapist, he found several early critical events in his life that led to his fear of traveling.

Ages 2–6

Critical event: Overprotected by mother.

Early belief: Life is dangerous and I need someone to protect me. I can't handle this world by myself.

Corrected belief: My mom overprotected me because of her own fears, not because of my supposed weaknesses. Life was no more dangerous for me than for anyone else. I can handle the world as effectively as others.

Ages 6–12

Critical event: Spoiled.

Early belief 1: Life should be as easy as it once was.

Early belief 2: I shouldn't have to feel pain.

Corrected belief: Because of my early distorted learning, I developed a false expectation that I should have my wishes fulfilled without much effort. This belief is not only false but is damaging to me. People have to work to get what they want. The sooner I learn this, the happier I will be.

Ages 12–16

Critical event 1: Rejected by peers because he acted spoiled.

Early belief 1: It's horrible if everybody doesn't like me.

Early belief 2: If I am perfect I will be liked.

Early belief 3: I need to control everything to be perfect.

Corrective beliefs: The other kids didn't like me because I was a spoiled brat and I demanded that they treat me the way my overprotective mom did. Of course, my peers would have none of this. My perfectionism and attempt to control everyone were the causes of their rejection.

Critical event 2: Saw a fellow student vomit in class and observed that his classmates rejected the student.

Early belief: People will reject me unless I control everything physical going on inside my body.

Corrective belief: No human being can control all of his or her physiological symptoms, many of which are instinctual. Attempting to do so causes huge problems; I am spending all my time and energy trying to control something that can't be controlled. People are far more likely to reject me if I become a control freak.

Critical event 3: Anxious about getting sick in a car during a cross-country trip. Started to fear anxiety itself.

Early belief: Now I must control everything psychological going on in my body so that people don't reject me.

Corrective belief: Anxiety is distressing but not dangerous. I am spending my life watching my mind work instead of living.

Critical event 4: Whenever he considered taking a plane trip he would get panicky.

Early belief: I won't be able to control my fear in a plane, and I won't be able to escape, therefore I will be trapped in an intolerable situation.

Corrective belief: So what if I get scared and embarrass myself? I have tolerated it for years now so how is that intolerable? It would be better if I just let myself get scared than spend my whole life trying to control all these feelings and make myself miserable by hiding in my house, while experiencing little of the pleasures of life at all.

The emotions connected to early critical events can be very powerful. Therefore, this exercise is best done under the guidance of a counselor. If you are trying it on your own, go carefully and only pick an event that you feel you can comfortably handle. If despite your caution, a problem occurs, contact a counselor.

chapter 28

Making Choices
Getting Out of Our Ruts

The strongest principle of growth lies in human choice.　　GEORGE ELIOT

IN THIS CHAPTER
- Examining the ruts we get in
- Breaking the routine

We recognize that many things we do in life are a result of habit. If we look at our average day, we may see many routines: the time we get up, which shoe we put on first, where we place our car keys, the route we drive to work without thinking about how we got there, checking our Internet mail first when we get to the office, the place we have lunch, our routine before going to bed, and so on. Often, we only notice our habits when something gets out of place—when we lose our keys or when our alarm clock doesn't ring. When the routine is broken, we get confused and have to start making choices and decisions about things that we have previously done by rote.

It is fortunate that we do things by habit. Otherwise, we would find ourselves exhausted. Those of us who have lived in another country, discovered that our routines got so broken and everyday tasks were so different that we needed far more energy just trying to make it through a day. Much of our mental energy was spent on making choices about the everyday common things, such as how to figure out the strange looking telephone numbers, or remembering to drive on the correct side of the road, or having to learn to travel around city streets with strange sounding names. We had to spend our energy on learning things that we used to do by rote, so we had little energy left to do important business or personal decisions. It may have taken us months before we learned the new routines.

When we are young, our lives are full of small, daily individual choices. Maybe only a third of what we do is by habit. As we get older, we turn more and more of our earlier choices into routines. Thirty something people may have half of their activities based on habit, for middle aged people it may be three quarters; and for the elderly, almost all activities may be based on habit.

But there is an unfortunate aspect to doing things by habit alone. We stop making decisions. We take choice out of our lives. So long as our routines are useful, they don't cause problems, but as soon as our environment changes, we can find ourselves unable to make new decisions. We are so stuck in our old habits that we can't choose a new path.

Consider an important case.

RELATIONSHIP RUT

EXAMPLE

Cynthia was an attractive, successful professional woman of 36 who had dated the same man for five years. He was a bachelor who never wanted to be tied down by marriage. So she knew he would never commit, but he was comfortable. She always had someone to take her to shows or go on vacations with. He was reasonably attractive, rarely made excessive demands, and treated her reasonably well. He wasn't exciting and their relationship was routine, but it felt comfortable like a pair of old shoes. She was constantly advised by her girlfriends to leave him, but she could never get the energy to do it. She had gotten too accustomed to his phone calls on Wednesday night, to their Saturday dates, to his occasional flowers, and to his greeting cards on holidays.

If she wanted a full long term commitment, it was obvious what she needed to do. He was a cul-de-sac boyfriend. She couldn't change him, so either had to accept the dead-end relationship or leave. Everybody she knew, male and female, young and old, told her to leave. But she kept trying to escape the obvious by reading every pop book on, "How to Make Your Boyfriend Commit," "How to Straighten Out Your Man," "How to be a Total Woman," "How to Turn Him On So that He Screams for More." But nothing changed. The relationship just chugged along inside the deep five-year-old rut.

Taking Out Your Mental Trash

Then one Wednesday night Cynthia was home waiting for her boyfriend to call. She was just sitting there alone in the living room feeling bored. There seemed to be no escape from the rut she was in. When the phone finally rang, she did something unique, something she hadn't planned to do—she just sat there and let it ring. The phone rang and rang until she finally answered it. To the shock and amazement of her boyfriend, for the first time, she declined their Saturday date. She said she just wanted a break. Nothing special, but just a little time off. Well, of course, her boyfriend panicked and was sure something major had happened. He called again that night and again on Thursday and Friday; and he had never done that before. She went out with him again the following week, but she insisted they go bowling, something they had never done together before. In later weeks, she demanded they go out on a Friday or a Sunday rather than Saturday. She skipped other dates sometimes for two or three weeks in a row.

After more time she realized that she had changed. She was now making all kinds of choices and decisions about the relationship—when to go out, where to go, when to skip a date. She was no longer going out just because of habit. She was out of her rut. And then a strange thing happened. When she was free from the routine, she realized she didn't want the relationship any more. She discovered there was nothing holding it up but habit. Later, one Wednesday evening, she ended the whole thing. She never went back on her decision or doubted it for a moment. A few months later she found a more appropriate successful professional man who was not afraid to commit. Ultimately they got married.

If you discover that you are in a rut, and you would like to do something about it, the following exercise may help.

Homework

EXERCISE

28.1 Breaking the Routine and Making Choices

Step 1. Pick one of the routines that you have been following for years that bores you. You can pick an aspect of your daily schedule, your work routine, your relationships, or your leisure activities. The following list may get you started.

what you have for lunch	times of days you shower
types of books you read	when you exercise
vacations	Sunday morning routine
when you call your relatives	sports you play
when you read your e-mail	TV shows you watch
how you greet a friend	where you shop

Step 2. Pick one routine, just one, and very gradually change some component of it. Make the small changes one at a time. For example, if you think your vacations are in a rut, you can change the time (go in May rather than July); change the place (take a vacation to the mountains rather than the seashore; go by train rather than fly); or change what you do (try horseback riding rather than swimming).

Step 3. Each time you do the activity, change one more component of the routine.

Step 4. Keep making changes until you feel the routine fading and the old habit melting away.

 As you break up the routine, you will begin to see you are automatically making more and more choices. Each choice is taking one step out of the rut. The more choices you make, the more you take back control of your life.

chapter 29

Breaking Through the Dam
Why Change is Difficult

If we don't change direction soon, we'll end up where we're going.   PROFESSOR IRWIN COREY

IN THIS CHAPTER
- Forcing changes
- Confronting our selves

Climbing out of our ruts can be difficult because it requires more than simply making a choice. It is a necessary first step, but if all we needed to do were to make up our minds, it would be easy for all of us. We would never have to pick up a book like this, or go to a friend for advice, or see a counselor. We would only have to decide, and, presto, change would occur. In the abstract, change requires making a choice, but in real life we don't change simply because we want to; we often change only when we have to.

 Most people will continue to suffer through any problem until some crisis forces them to change. Even then, during the crisis, people will avoid changing as long as possible. They will postpone the inevitable until they absolutely, positively cannot avoid it anymore. It is sad, because people have to unnecessarily endure all the additional emotional pain and waste so much time.

Maybe the best way to understand the process is to consider the following metaphor.

EXAMPLE Picture life experiences as a river flowing toward the ocean. So long as our experiences are flowing freely, with all the currents, whirlpools, and eddies allowed to move at their own pace, we are healthy. But as soon as the river is stopped up, as soon as our experiences become rigid and customary, our life stream becomes stagnant. We stop growing and changing. Our fear of change can dam up our river. The dam can be so strong that only extreme pressure will break it. We attempt to do everything we can to avoid breaking through the dam. Like a river, we may have tried to flow around it or over-flow our banks. But when all these escapes are blocked, when the river has no place to go accept against the dam, and when the pressure gets strong enough, the dam is broken, and our life flows freely again.

When we are sufficiently fed up with a problem, when we are sufficiently tired because of years of avoidance and delay, we may be ready to burst through the dam and do something about the problem.

But don't take my word for it; see for yourself by doing the brief exercise.

Homework

EXERCISE ### 29.1 Dam Busting

Step 1. Pick some problem that you had in the past but don't have anymore. Try to find something that continued for several years. It could be any kind of problem: a concern about your health that you never took care of, a drinking or drug problem that you always put off facing, a long-standing difficulty in a relationship that you hadn't solved, a work problem that you kept on letting go instead of handling. Pick any problem that you want, but be sure to pick something that you *have resolved*.

Step 2. Think back carefully to the time when you began to solve the problem. Were you in a situation when you were forced to make a decision? Was there pressure on you that required you to take action: something you couldn't avoid, something you couldn't ignore, something you couldn't minimize? In terms of the metaphor, was there something that stopped up the water in your dam, something that prevented you from going around the dam so that your only choice was to continue to have the problem or bust through the dam?

Many people who did the exercise report that they changed because, at the time, the alternative of doing nothing became unacceptable. They felt they had to change.

Managing Ourselves

In trying to make changes in our lives, we can be either too hard or too soft on our selves. We are too hard when we put too much pressure on ourselves and expect to change too quickly or too much. Change is a form of growing and we must be like a gardener. We can become impatient or frustrated and start to pull on ourselves to grow faster. Change, growth, and healing take their own good time; they do not operate according to the dictates of our hopes or demands. We had best weed our gardens, provide a fertile ground, and then wait for the blossoms of change to appear.

But sometimes we are too easy on ourselves. It is an understandable mistake. We want to be nice. Wrestling with a problem causes pain and we want to reduce the pain as quickly as we can. We don't look behind the pain, so we rush in and try to rescue ourselves from the hurt. This makes us feel better temporarily but often with the consequence that the problem remains intact.

Often, however, our rescuing can be a big mistake and ultimately may hurt us a great deal more. The emotional pain we human beings feel may be a signal or sign that something is wrong. In a sense, it is like a physical pain that tells us that some body part is injured and needs our attention. The pain of a splinter in our foot tells us to look for the splinter. If we quickly numb the pain, we will leave too many splinters. Likewise, emotional pain motivates us to find the cause. When we remove the pain too quickly, we make it more difficult, sometimes impossible, to find the root of our hurt.

AVOIDING REALITY

The best example of this type of mistake is found with alcoholics and addicts. Initially they deny and ignore their alcohol or drug-induced problems, hoping that the problems will go away. But they keep on using just the same. Next, they look for some deep-seated unconscious, hidden reason for their use. They often find something, but the knowledge doesn't change anything because they keep on using, just the same. Next, they try to change their use. They start telling themselves, "I'll use cocaine just on the weekends"; I'll only have two beers a night"; " I'll snort only at parties"; "I'll switch from liquor to wine." These strategies may appear to work for a while but in the end, it's always the identical result, they keep using just the same.

Many recovering alcoholics and addicts report that all their attempts to rescue themselves from the problem made them feel better temporarily, but at the cost of keeping their addiction going. These attempts reduced their pain a little and buffered them from feeling the full natural consequences of their addiction.

Addicts and alcoholics began their recovery only when they told themselves the truth. What truth? The truth that they were hooked, that drink or drugs were destroying their families, their health, and their ability to be happy, and that the best way to turn their lives around was to admit to their addiction and stop all use. Often the only way some alcoholics or addicts could see this truth was to be trapped into a situation caused by their addiction that they couldn't get out of. They reported that they had to stew long enough in their own messes until they perceive what a personal holocaust their drug use had produced. Only then could they break through their dams (McMullin & Gehlhaar, 2004).

Sometimes in life, we have to forsake all our denials, our evasions, our excuses, and our rationalizations, and go ahead and break through our dams.

chapter 30

Quantum Leaps
Changing Ourselves Dramatically

Even a thought, even a possibility, can shatter us and transform us. FRIEDRICH NIETZSCHE

IN THIS CHAPTER
• Understanding rapid change
• Rules for quantum leaps

It appears that change is mostly gradual. People usually change at a very slow pace. Whether it's learning to ride a bicycle, play a guitar, master a foreign language, build a successful marriage, or change a belief or attitude, it takes work and years of practice. It's like climbing a mountain. Most of us slowly climb from one rocky crag to another, gradually making our way up the precipice. If we reach the top, we have a clearer view and feel stronger because we made it. Unfortunately, some people give up half way; they lack the patience or endurance to keep climbing until they reach the top.

 The overwhelming majority of people change only gradually, but occasionally some of us make dramatic shifts. All of a sudden in a few days, we may change a way of thinking that we have believed for most of our lives. It's as if we are climbing the mountain when unexpectedly, all at once, we jump to the summit, a quantum leap.

These leaps are fascinating. How could people who believed the same nonsense for 30 years suddenly stop believing in it at all? How could they change in a few days or a few hours what has taken a lifetime to build? What are the principles behind these leaps?

The following example shows how one person was able to make a quantum leap.

OLD TIME RELIGION

EXAMPLE One Saturday afternoon a tent revival meeting was held in the countryside, not too far from a southern college campus. At the meeting was a young man named Roy. He was a local boy attending college on a football scholarship and majoring in PE, but he had a problem. He drank heavily. Because he was drinking too much, he was suspended from the team. If he didn't stop, he was in danger of being expelled from school.

Roy had wandered into the meeting in an open field where there was a large canvas tent sheltering 400 folding chairs. People meandered into the seats from all sides. In the front was a preacher pleading with the audience to change their ways.

Roy and the others listened to the preacher describe the horrors of hell, and some people were getting more and more upset. Then the preacher instructed the audience to renounce the devil and come to God now. "Walk right up to the front of the tent and stand with Jesus." In the beginning only a few came forward. After awhile the aisles were filled with people walking to the front. Roy went up with the rest.

The preacher thanked Jesus for saving these sinners, and then he described in detail what heaven was like. He said that in heaven, we would gather with all our friends and relatives, that all our physical infirmities would be washed away. We would be forever young, we would talk with the prophets, and we would be soothed and comforted. Then the people sang some hymns (almost everybody sang) and the revival ended.

Roy returned to campus right after the meeting. In a few days, he had stopped all his drinking. After a few months, he had returned to the football team and was doing well in school. He never went back to drinking.

Roy made a quantum leap. He made a 180-degree shift away from what he was to what he would become. He had transformed his life. He never looked back. And it all seemed to have happened because of one Saturday afternoon at a tent revival meeting.

DISCOVERING QUANTUM LEAPS

EXAMPLE

Over the years, I have observed many people make quantum leaps. While most people had to struggle and plod along making changes in slow, minute steps, I also saw people like Roy who made dramatic shifts. I hadn't understood why some people could make these shifts until one day I visited a university library. I was researching some articles for a book and thumbing through an old psychology journal. In it, I noticed an article about hidden images. These are drawings, which look meaningless on first appearance, but after looking at them for a while a picture suddenly appears. One particular drawing caught my attention. It was a sketch of a cow (Dallenbach, 1951, pp. 431–433). At least that's what the text said it was. But I couldn't see anything. It looked like just a mass of meaningless blotches, so I pushed it away. A few weeks later, I went back to the same library and was looking in the same journal. I saw the cow picture again but still didn't see the cow. I thought, "Stupid picture. There is no cow!" So, I pushed the article to the side and worked on something else. But right before I left the library, I accidentally glanced over at the picture sitting on the side of the desk and suddenly the image emerged—the head and forequarters of a cow. The shift was not gradual; it occurred all of a sudden, a visual metamorphosis, a perceptual quantum leap.

Immediately I thought of people like Roy. They had seen something all of a sudden. Perhaps the two processes were the same. Maybe seeing an image pop out of a drawing is the same as having a new attitude pop up in our brain. True, one is a perception while the other is a conception, but the process could still be the same. If we could figure out how an image suddenly leaps out from these drawings, then maybe we could discover how some people make quantum leaps.

Over the years, I have collected many of these pictures for study. Some colleagues must think twice about having me appear on a panel or workshop—"If we invite Dr. McMullin, he may show his damn pictures again." But these pictures are the best analogy I have found to explain a complex principle of how people change their attitudes. They are the Rosetta Stone to understanding dramatic shifts and growth. They explain how people make quantum leaps.

The best way to understand these quantum leaps is to do the exercise below.

Homework Exercise

EXERCISE

30.1 Find the Cow

Step 1. This is the picture of the cow I mention above (Figure 30.1). Look carefully at the drawing and try to see the cow. There is one in the drawing. The drawing shows the head and forequarters of the cow. She is turning toward the front looking at you. Hold the picture up and see if the cow emerges.

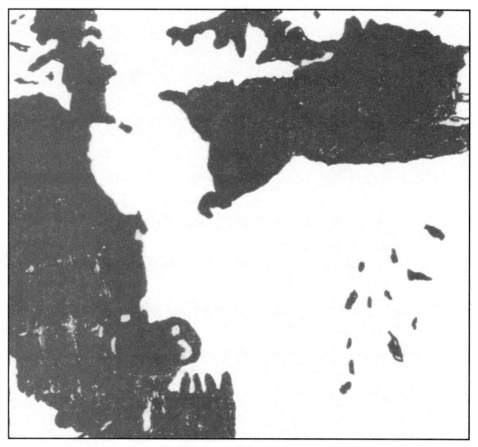

Figure 30.1 Hidden cow (Dallenbach, 1951). From *American Journal of Psychology*. Copyright 1951 by the Board of Trustees of the University of Illinois. Used with permission of the University of Illinois Press.

Step 2. What did you see? Most people don't see the cow immediately. In fact very few do. If you didn't, don't be concerned. Continue to look for it whenever you get a chance. Eventually the cow will emerge. Realize that this is the most difficult picture in my portfolio, and it takes time (often weeks) before you see it. You will see the cow when your brain is ready. Don't give up.

The interesting thing about the picture is the process we go through to see the cow. How are we suddenly able to see something that we haven't been able to see at all? It's not the drawing, which remains the same whether we see the cow or not; it is not our eyes. Whether we recognize the cow or simply notice meaningless blotches, the image on our retina is the same. It's not our optic nerve, the information shooting up the nerve and reaching the occipital area of our brain is the same. The only difference in what we see is how our brain organizes the raw data available to it. Our brain interprets the drawing into meaningless blotches or into a cow. When we change from one image to another, our brain makes the transformation. Only our brain causes the quantum leap.

What counts about the exercise is not whether we see the cow or not. The important things are the rules we use to discern and comprehend things. How are our brains able to create the cow? What principles lie behind being able to see nothing to being able to see the cow?

What method did *you* use?

Some people answer quickly. They say it's easy, all you do is look at this or that part of the picture, and the cow emerges. If you inspect the left, you notice part of the cow's right ear; near the bottom is the nose; about in the middle is the cow's left eye. Despite the apparent logic of this view, it is incorrect. It's not where we look; it's what our brain does with what we see. We can stare at only one spot in the drawing and recognize the cow without altering our focal point.

The way our brain generates a cow in the drawing is the same way our brain makes quantum leaps. The picture is the key. What is true for the picture is true for our thoughts, attitudes, and values.

Quantum Leap Rules

Through research, scientists have discovered five elements that seem essential for both seeing hidden images in drawings and changing long held beliefs. These principles are at the heart of all quantum leaps.

Willingness

We have to be plucky enough to look at things in a new way. If we dogmatically and rigidly hold to our old viewpoint, then there isn't any room in our brain for a new attitude. If we didn't see anything in the picture and then rigidly insisted that there was nothing to see, no other way of looking at it, then we would never see the cow.

The same principle is true for our beliefs. If we are sure we are right and we permit no possibility that we are wrong, then we will never change what we think. One man was like this. He was sure he was a weak, passive, wimpy person. As a result, he always tried to compensate by acting tough and mean—the short man syndrome. Well, the truth was of course that he wasn't what he thought. He wasn't weak or passive at all, just the opposite. He was far too aggressive. But because of his perception, he kept on trying to make himself tougher and meaner. He forced himself to the point where he became so obnoxious that no one wanted to be around him; he was fired from jobs and lost his friends.

When he was shown his mistaken self-perception, he refused to listen. He dogmatically rejected that he could be wrong and refused to accept that there may be another way of looking at himself. He was sure he was weak and passive and that was that. He refused to look at himself differently. So he never did change. He still can't hold a job and has no friends or intimate relationships because of his hyperaggressiveness.

Guidance

The second principle behind quantum leaps is guidance. To see something new, it helps to have someone to guide us who already sees the new viewpoint. If we want to make a quantum leap, the best coaches are those who have already leapt. They know exactly what to look for and can guide us as to where to look. It is easier to find the cow when we are told we are looking for a cow. If we thought we were looking for a meridian of longitude, we would all still be looking. It's helpful to have someone who sees the cow teach us how to find it.

It's the same for changing our attitudes. Someone who believes in the usefulness of a new attitude can teach us to see it. Self help groups such as Alcoholic Anonymous or Recovery, Inc. can be very helpful. Cocaine addicts benefit from listening to recovering addicts, anxious people learn from people who have overcome their fears, while people suffering from grief, find survivor groups helpful. All these recovered people have made a quantum leap and can show the beginner how to do it.

Flexibility

The third principle is flexibility. We need to try different strategies to make a perceptual leap. In order to see the cow we had best try different methods.

Maybe we need to look at different parts of the drawing, or bring it close to our eyes, then look at it from farther away. Maybe we need to put the picture away for a while and then look at it later. But we need to vary our strategy.

It's the same thing for our beliefs. To change an attitude we need to look at our beliefs in different ways until the shift takes place. People who keep doing the same thing repeatedly, never change. We can use different strategies. The basic idea is to make the old attitude weaker and inject strength into the new one. We can tie the new belief into some powerful, personal memory that has a strong emotional hook. We can reinforce ourselves whenever we see the new belief and punish ourselves when we see the old. We can divide the beliefs into parts and try to shift these parts before we shift the whole. But the main thing we need to do is to experiment and try some new methods until the shift takes place.

Time

Changing our viewpoints takes time. The brain needs time to process the information until the new perception comes together. If we stopped looking for the cow after a few seconds, we would never see it. We have to keep looking until the image emerges.

It's the same principle for changing a belief, or a value, or an attitude. It takes time. It may require only a few minutes to shift the image in a picture, but it may take months or years to change a philosophy. No matter how long it takes, it's important to continue to work at the change. Otherwise, we will never make the quantum leap. Our brain will make the shift when it is ready. If we keep trying to change, some morning in the future we will wake up and have what is called an "Ah ha" experience. The perception we have been searching for will suddenly appear. Our brain will click everything all together in a clear, powerful, certain perception. We will have made our quantum leap.

Repetition

One of the unfortunate aspects about quantum leaps is that even after we have transformed the way we think, we may still leap back. The cow picture shows the process. If we put the picture away and look at it at some future time, we may only see the meaningless blotches again and not see the cow. It's unfortunate. We can feel all excited and happy about changing our attitudes, and then a few weeks later we wake up thinking the same old nonsense again. It can be depressing. All the work and then we crash back to the beginning again. But nothing terrible has happened. After thinking in a certain way for 20 years, it is not surprising that our brain shifts back to the old way whenever it gets half a chance.

The solution for these backward leaps is the same as for the drawings. Practice seeing the new way—practice, practice, practice. If we want to see the cow every time we look at the drawing, we should keep on practicing. After a time (it can be weeks) we will find it harder and harder not to see it. Likewise, if we keep retreating to our old belief, we should keep practicing seeing the new one. We may have to make the same leap repeatedly until it becomes permanent.

 It is possible to change any attitude, belief, value, opinion, or even any prejudice using the above principles. Like Roy, we are not stuck with any of our old attitudes, no matter how ingrained in us they may be; no matter how deep the roots lie inside; no matter how ancient their origins. We can correct our mangled thoughts and our fouled up attitudes. Knowing this, if we don't change, it is our own responsibility.

chapter 31

Living by Our Core Values
Making Our Lives More Meaningful

Happiness is that state of consciousness which proceeds from the achievement of one's values.

AYN RAND

IN THIS CHAPTER
- Appreciating the importance of our values
- Making value bridges

After we have removed some of our damaging beliefs the obvious question that pops up is, "What do we replace them with?

Some people go through life by living day to day. They try to solve problems, avoid anguish, experience some amusement, and get through the day without bumping into some great catastrophe. Living day by day is fine. It is a choice we all make and it is even recommended by some sages who encourage us to live in the here and now and not ruminate about the past or worry about the future. For some people, in poorer parts of our world, just surviving another day and helping their loved ones survive represents a great triumph.

But most people seem to want more out of life. They wish life to have more meaning than just making it through another day. They want to feel that life has a purpose. They want goals that last more than a day, a month, or a year. They want to be moving on a track with an end destination always in mind throughout their lives. If they get off the track, they feel life has lost it purpose. They feel they need to keep their goal clearly in mind to make life fulfilling.

The key to a purposeful life is following one's basic values. These can be religious, social, or individual. We choose them, and we make the choice early in life. Our basic values are deeply rooted within our concepts of reality and the meaning we give to why we are here on the planet. They define for us what counts as important and what doesn't. So long as we follow our basic values, we feel we are staying on track and living with a purpose. To be satisfied with our lives, we need to engage in activities that are congruent with our values. But when we notice an important discrepancy between our values and our behavior, we get troubled. We feel our lives have become incongruent and aimless.

To feel fulfilled we need to get in touch with our personal hierarchy of values, and then observe if we are doing in life what we said we should be doing.

There are many ways to determine our values, but the following exercises are a good start. They suggest we ask ourselves a series of basic questions. The answers we give can provide us with a good picture of ourselves.

Homework

EXERCISE 31.1 Your Basic Values Hierarchy

Read the list below before you begin the exercise.

Step 1. Find your values. Make a short list of the values you think are most important to you. You can use the table below as a guide, but be sure to add your own items if one of your values is not included.

Step 2. Be careful. It is difficult to find our true values. You must take particular care to look for values that others reject or that are socially unpopular (e.g., hedonism, power, etc.). It is crucial that you pick what you personally believe, not what may be the most socially correct values or the values that would be best for humanity. For this exercise, it doesn't matter what society thinks, it is what you think that counts.

fame	adventure/excitement	exceptional skills
friendships	artistic/creative	salvation/goodness
knowledge/understanding	helping others	freedom
wealth	justice	security/safety
kindness/charity	beauty/style/grace	mastery
pleasure	health	other
spouse/family	democratic	
power/control	tolerance	

Taking Out Your Mental Trash

Step 3. Rank your values. You could order your values from the most important to the least important; it would be quick and easy. Unfortunately, it probably would also be wrong. Our ability to fool ourselves about such matters is quite high. Because we like to think approvingly of ourselves, we have a strong tendency to select the best sounding values.

A better way to rank yourself is to imagine that you are in different situations that throw one value against another, so that you have to pick one over the other. For example, if the values of, "spouse/family" and "freedom" are on your list you would imagine being in a family or living alone and then asking yourself, "Which would I rather have—the security that comes from living with others who care for me or the freedom of being single but perhaps feeling somewhat lonely?"

These types of imagined situations and questions, repeated over the range of the values you selected, should eventually lead you to the construction of your own personal hierarchy.

THOMAS'S LIST

EXAMPLE

Thomas was a 35-year-old professional man who liked politics. He had run for student council in college, read numerous books on politics, and was familiar with most political issues. He was active in all kinds of local and state politics in different states and worked on several candidates' campaigns. When he did the exercise, he picked four values: wealth, friendship, health, and freedom.

When he imagined conflicting scenes that pitted each one of his values against the others, he discovered the following answers.

Question 1. Wealth or friendship?
  Answer: Wealth

Tom imagined that he was living 10 years in the future. He owned a beautiful mansion by the ocean. He had several antique cars, an expensive stereo and DVD system, a kidney-shaped pool, a gym, and a tennis court. He had all the material goods that he had ever wanted. But, he was living by himself, had almost no friends, and few people ever visited him. He compared this picture with a contrasting scene. He was living in a modest three-bedroom home in the suburbs; he had an 8-year-old Ford, a borrowed stereo system, and had to use the local park for exercise. He paid all his bills but had to watch what he spent. However, he was the most popular person in his community. He was immensely liked by his neighbors and had a great number of friends. He was constantly invited to parties and people would visit him all the time. When comparing the two scenes, Tom chose the one where he was wealthy.

Question 2. Wealth or freedom?

    Answer: Freedom

Tom pictured again that he was living 10 years in the future. He imagined that one day he decided that he was tired of where he was living and what he was doing. He pictured himself being able to take off to live and work in Fiji or New Zealand. He imagined he could sell his house and store his goods, and do this all in a couple weeks. In contrast, he pictured that he couldn't settle his affairs while living in the mansion with the swimming pools and the tennis court for at least a year. When comparing the two future images, he chose freedom.

His other choice was:

Question 3. Health or friendships?

    Answer: Friendships

By imagining a number of scenes, asking and answering a series of questions, it became clear to Thomas. His hierarchy of values were:

    Highest value: Freedom
    Second: Wealth
    Third: Friendship
    Lowest value: Health

Once you have discovered your basic values, you may find them helpful in straightening out your life. If you have a feeling of incongruence between what you value and what you have been doing, you can get yourself back on track. Look at some of your old thoughts and beliefs and see if they fit with your basic values. If not, you can change them to new beliefs by using your basic values as a bridge. Homework 31.2 will show you how.

Homework

EXERCISE **31.2 Value Bridges**

Use Worksheet 31.1, "My Value Bridges"

Read the examples on page 205 before you begin the exercise

Step 1. Pick one of your beliefs from your Master List of Core Beliefs that still bothers you, and note what value it represents. To understand what I mean, I will go back to our example of Thomas, the 35-year-old businessman who loved freedom. Imagine that Tom had this thought on his Master List: "I should be very concerned about getting cancer." This thought would represent a health value, important to Tom, but not as important as his higher values of freedom, wealth or friendship.

Step 2. Now pick one of your higher values and use it to counter the lower valued belief. For example, Tom could counter his overconcern about his health by thinking, "If I keep obsessing over getting cancer, I'll become so boring I will lose all my friends. Who wants to be around a hypochondriac all the time" (friendship value). Or, "I'll spend all my money on unnecessary tests, and phony cancer prevention scams" (wealth value). Or, "I'll lose my freedom to travel and go where I want to because I'll be afraid of getting cancer in a faraway land without adequate medical help" (freedom value).

31.1 My Value Bridges

1. *Old Belief:*

_____

_____

Higher Value: _____

New Bridge Belief:

_____

_____

2. *Old Belief:*

_____

_____

Higher Value: _____

New Bridge Belief:

_____

_____

3. *Old Belief:*

_____

_____

Higher Value: _____

New Bridge Belief:

_____

_____

Taking Out Your Mental Trash

Examples of Value Bridges

EXAMPLE

Old Belief: It would be very bad if my husband's colleagues did not approve of me.

Higher Value: Christian religious beliefs.

New Bridge Belief: To truly follow Christ's teachings, don't strive to be popular and appeal to what people think. More importantly, Christians should use their God-given inner conscience and aim for what is right rather than what is fashionable.

Old Belief: Everything I try to do ends up in failure.

Higher Value: Endurance, "When the going gets tough, the tough get going!"

New Bridge Belief: I am not in control of whether I succeed or not. I am only in control of my effort. I will always strive and try to learn from my failures so that I can be more successful in future attempts.

Old Belief: She left me for a younger, more successful man.

Higher Value: What is realistically true.

New Bridge Belief: I'm good, but I am not better than all the other men in the world.

Old Belief: I must have a man in order to be happy.

Higher Value: Self-respect.

New Bridge Belief: I would rather like myself even though alone, than hate myself living as a slave to a man I disliked.

Old Belief: If I take this job abroad, I'll leave all my friends.

Higher Value: Stimulation and adventure.

New Bridge Belief: I would die of boredom here sooner than I'd die of loneliness there.

TIP

Without values, life is a mistake. Values are the mental homes we have chosen to live in. They give our lives purpose and meaning. To be truly happy, we need to return home frequently.

chapter32

Beyond Payoffs
What Inspires Us to Do Things?

Satan: There is no difference between my followers and the followers of God—both serve for pay. BASED ON ROBERT FROST

IN THIS CHAPTER
- Examining human motivation
- Finding your payoffs

Are we all totally motivated by external rewards and punishments? Is our only motivation the same driving force as that of other animals, to seek pleasure and avoid pain? Is this the only purpose of our existence on this planet? Are we no different from laboratory rats that press levers to get food pellets, and avoid shock grids? Are we the same as dolphins who jump through hoops to be paid with fish? In the excerpt above, is Satan right that all human beings do everything for the only purpose of receiving some kind of payoff? This chapter offers some possible answers to these questions.

In the social sciences, some theorists, who are called radical behaviorists, believe that payoffs are exactly the reason people behave in the way they do. They call it the *principle of reinforcement*—any behavior that is reinforced, increases, while any behavior that is not, extinguishes. Case closed?

Well, not quite. Many people recognize that we do things for rewards. After all that's why most of us work, or study, or save money. But we have a lot more difficulty understanding why some people engage in certain, non-payoff-like activities.

Several types of acts puzzle us, like sacrificing ourselves for another;

charging a machine gun nest in times of war; running into a burning building to save a child; or doing or not doing something where there is little or no possibility of receiving an external reward or avoiding punishment.

Where is the external payoff for all these activities? According to some radical behaviorists, we shouldn't do these things. But of course, we do, so maybe there is something wrong with their theory.

There is. The theory is much too simple when applied to human beings. We are not the same as rats, pigeons, guinea pigs, dogs, or other mammals, we have some more complex characteristics that affect our behavior. We have language and the ability to look at the world in a symbolic, metaphorical way. We have a far larger brain relatively speaking than pigeons or rats. Our thoughts, beliefs, imagination, and fantasies create a huge, symbolic, inside mental world that in many cases overwhelms the simple rewards and punishments of the outside physical world.

 Human beings can be rewarded or punished by all kinds of symbolic, non-physical events such as frowns, smiles, and verbal compliments and criticisms. More importantly, we are crucially influenced by our own opinion of ourselves in terms of self-praise and self-punishment (praising ourselves for good behavior and blaming ourselves when we did something wrong). Internal opinions may be overwhelming, even when they are largely disconnected from external consequences. In other words, lower animals may do something because they receive a food pellet or avoid something because they received a physical shock. But we human beings often do something because we tell ourselves it is the right thing to do, or avoid something because we think others would disapprove. We don't need external payoffs to control our behavior. We can be rewarded or punished by our own thinking even when the thinking is devoid of external reinforcement or punishment.

Let's look at some examples.

DRUG USE

 Doing things that hurt us (like taking crack cocaine) does create ultimate pain, but the pain comes much later after the pleasure. People who use a damaging drug may do so to get a "rush." Some people are stimulus junkies and they love the feeling of endorphins pumping in their brains. Like Don Juan, who sought out dangerous affairs with married women, they seek the "rush." That's why some people enjoy roller coasters, driving fast, bungee jumping, skydiving—the rush.

Now the difficulty, of course, is that the rush is temporary. It lasts only a few minutes or a few hours. Afterwards the cocaine addict will start crashing and the alcoholic will start going through withdrawal. Yet, despite all this, many people choose the few minutes of pleasure over the days of pain. They may think that this time the pain won't happen; or they may simply ignore the pain because they want the pleasure so much.

CRIMINAL BEHAVIOR

EXAMPLE

If the payoff for chemical abuse is the rush, what is the payoff for criminal activity? Another rush? The rewards of intimidation? The financial gain? All of the above and still more. One of the most surprising things about criminals is what they tell themselves about the crime they committed. The majority of felons don't think they did anything wrong. By this, I don't mean they insist they are innocent. We all know about this aspect. Almost everybody in jail claims that they are innocent of the crime. What I mean is that even those who privately admit that they committed the crime still deny that what they did was wrong. It may have been against the law, but in their eyes, it wasn't wrong. It is curious. Most convicted felons offered a guiltless, blameless reason for breaking the law. They have said:

"Everybody steals, but I had the bad luck to get caught."
"She deserved to be bashed because she was such a bitch."
"Those rich people in those big houses have all the money; I have none.
I had the right to break in a take all I could."
"I did the world a favor by attacking the bastard."
"I fenced the goods for my friend because I was just trying to help him."
"I held up the store because I needed the money."
"I hit the cop because he was hassling me. I had the right."

Very few criminals think they are bad or wrong for what they did.

It's a human trait. Many people find it extremely difficult to think badly of themselves. Apparently, people's self-concepts require them to see themselves in the best possible light. They may have committed some horrible acts, but they will somehow justify them in the end. For example, some multiple rapist/murderers think they are agents of God, punishing women for their licentious ways. In their eyes, their acts were not evil, they were legitimate because they were only carrying out the will of God by removing evil

Taking Out Your Mental Trash

women from the world. It appears some people can rationalize any act if they try hard enough.

So, the payoff for many lawbreakers is not only the money they make, the rush they feel, or the frustration they express. It is also the positive feeling they get from their own convoluted rationalizations.

Of course, the ultimate consequence of their criminal act is punishment, imprisonment; and this they don't like. But punishment doesn't change their behavior because they amazingly don't connect the punishment with the crime. Psychologists have asked prisoners in jail, "How come you ended up in here?" Few ever said, "Because I violated the law." Instead most answered, "Because Joe turned me in, that son of a bitch." Or, "The cops found the crack in my car when they pulled me over for speeding." Or, "The bitch screamed so loud after I hit her that the neighbors called the cops." When they are asked, "What could you do in the future to avoid ending up in prison again?" Instead, of saying things like, "I shouldn't rob stores, deal cocaine, or assault my wife," they say, " I have to get rid of Joe!" "Don't speed when you have crack in the car!" Or, "Get myself an old lady who doesn't scream so much."

It proves a point about punishment. For punishment to work, it's not enough for it to be strong. What is more important is that the person being punished must see the connection between his act and his punishment. Most lawbreakers don't see this connection because of their mangled, fouled-up way of thinking. They feel they didn't do anything wrong, so there is no reason for them to stop their criminal behavior.

HEROIC BEHAVIOR

EXAMPLE

What possibly could be the payoff for those heroes and heroines who give up their lives, those people who sacrifice themselves for others?

In some cases it may be simple, the admiration for their acts. "Isn't Mr. Smith a wonderful human being," is a very powerful symbolic payoff if you are Mr. Smith. Even if only a few people watch our sacrifice, we can imagine all of humanity applauding. How many young men have pictured their girlfriend's adoring gaze as they mentally imagined charging that machine gun nest. The fact that his girlfriend is unlikely to think, "You are such a big, strong, wonderful hero," but more likely to believe, "I don't want to marry an idiot who charges machine gun nests," is irrelevant to the fantasy.

In our daydreams, we may imagine the whole universe admiring us. A good example of this principle is Mark Twain's inventive story about being praised in heaven. In the story, a very rich man, Mr. Langdon, received a letter from the Recording Angel in heaven because he gave $15 to a starving widow. Of course, if we imagine it happening to us, we would imagine it without Mark Twain's wonderful irony.

Part of the letter is as follows:

> (The excitement in heaven about your contribution reached its peak a few days ago) . . . when the widow wrote and said she could get a school in a far village to teach if she had $50 to get herself and her two surviving children over the long journey, and you counted up last month's clear profit from your three coal mines—$22,230—and added to it the certain profit for the current month—$45,000 and a possible fifty—and then got down your pen and your check-book and mailed her *fifteen whole dollars*! Ah, Heaven bless and keep you forever and ever, generous heart! There was not a dry eye in the realms of bliss; and amidst the hand-shakings, and embracings, and praisings, the decree was thundered forth from the shining mount, that this deed should out-honor all the historic self-sacrifices of men and angels, and be recorded by itself upon a page of its own, for that the strain of it upon you had been heavier and more bitter than the strain it costs ten thousand martyrs to yield up their lives at the fiery stake; and all said, "What is the giving up of life, to a noble soul, or to ten thousand noble souls, compared with the giving up of fifteen dollars out of the greedy grip of the meanest . . . man that ever lived on the face of the earth?" (Twain, 1962/1887, p. 107)

 If we look at the rewards and punishments for human beings, they seem qualitatively different from getting a food pellet, or avoiding an electric shock. They are symbolic, metaphoric, and caused in large degree by our internal opinion of our self. These internal rewards may be so important that they overwhelm even very powerful external negative consequences. They may even be more important than life itself. Consider the man who saved the lives of several passengers in a plane crash in the Potomac River.

A RIGHTEOUS MAN

 Many readers may remember this incident. It was several years ago. A plane tried to take off from Washington, DC but crashed in the ice-filled Potomac River in midwinter. Several passengers were able to escape as the plane was sinking. But the water was so cold that the survivors rapidly became numb and were unable to swim. A rescue helicopter arrived and lowered a sling. TV cam-

     Taking Out Your Mental Trash

eras showed a man, who had escaped earlier, help other passengers onto the sling. He could have gotten on himself, but he helped others first. But the water was so cold he became numb and never made it to the helicopter. By helping others first, he died. And he died anonymously; no one recognized his picture. That's the whole point. He was too far away and too indistinct to be identified at the time. His name was not recorded. Where was this man's reward?

Some commentators have suggested he did it for religious reasons, "He has no greater love then to lay down his life for his friends." But we don't know if he was thinking religious thoughts. Maybe he was an atheist. Of course, we will never know his motivation, but why would anyone give up his or her life for a stranger? Would we? We will never know unless we are tested. It's this haunting doubt about ourselves; whether, when it comes down to it, we would find the strength. Almost everyone who saw the scene on television admired his act above other acts of heroism because it seemed so very unselfish.

Or consider another example of a heroic act in a very different context.

NEVER GIVE UP

EXAMPLE

It was a few years back in the New York marathon. The race had finished hours before. It was late in the evening. The TV was showing interviews of the day's winners. Almost as an aside, the camera panned to a live shot of a man still way back on the course. He was without legs, pushing himself on a type of skateboard. His hands were bandaged and bloody, but he still continued to push with all his effort. He was on some back streets where almost all the spectators had long since gone. There were only a few people watching—an old couple, a man coming home from work, a wino sitting on a curb, and about six or seven adolescent kids.

As he was coming up the street the few people there acted embarrassed for him, they looked away pretending they didn't see him. But not the adolescents; they appeared to be mocking and taunting him. We can imagine them saying, "Don't you know the race has been over for hours, old man?" "You need a motor for that thing. Trying for the slowest time? What an asshole!"

But he seemed to ignore them and kept looking straight ahead, pushing with all his might. Just then, he passed the people watching, and they saw his face. Then a remarkable thing happened. All these people who had been ignoring or mocking him, started to cheer him—not just polite cheering, but shouting and screaming at full volume encouraging him to continue. They were jumping up and down, running next to him, pleading with him to keep trying, patting him on the back. The street kids were cheering louder than anyone else. And it wasn't phony, mocking cheering; it was the gut busting, soul driving, powerful kind of cheering.

Why the change? Why all of a sudden did they stop mocking and start cheering him? We don't know, but we can make a strong guess. It could be that the spectators suddenly recognized what was really going on inside of this man. Maybe they saw that it didn't matter that he was hours behind the winning time. It didn't matter that there were only a few people there to watch him. The people may have recognized that this man was doing everything he could to finish the race. He was putting in every effort, all the energy he could muster to keep on going. And it was this energy and spirit they understood and admired.

Do you believe as this man did? To find out, do the following easy exercise.

Homework

EXERCISE

32.1 Payoffs

Use Worksheet 32.1, "Payoffs"

Step 1. Think of four major endeavors you did in your life for no obvious external rewards or punishments (e.g., giving money to a charity; doing volunteer work; helping someone without his or her knowledge; or trying as hard as you could to accomplish something even though you knew you wouldn't get a prize or receive recognition).

Step 2. Think about each of these endeavors. Why did you do them? Can you identify your underlying motivation? (e.g., "Help someone else; it was the right thing to do; I felt an obligation," etc.)

Step 3. Looking back, now, do you think your reason was a good one? (e.g., "No, I was really wanting to be rewarded for what I did, but I kept this reason hidden from myself." "Yes, that was my only reason"; or, "I did it for several reasons, some good, some not so good."

Most people have found that they did numerous things in their lives for reasons other than gaining some external reward or avoiding some external punishment.

Ultimately the greatest payoff for human behavior may not be external rewards or punishment, not money, or pleasure, or avoidance of pain, or even the promised reward of a better life hereafter. The real payoff may be pouring all our being into reaching a goal whether it be winning a race or saving another's life. The immature human only sees the immediate gain or loss in each situation, but the person who knows the pain of life seeks the long-term goal. The reward for the marathon man and the man who rescued the passengers is far grander than the immediate reinforcement of the moment. It is the ultimate payoff of using all our energy, all our ability, and all our strength for one grand final push, striving for a goal until we reach it or die trying. The goal is irrelevant; it's the striving that counts. This is what makes our species so exceptional. This is why we dominate this planet. This may be the payoff of life itself.

32.1 Payoffs

1. *Past Activity*

What was your underlying motivation to engage in the activity?

Looking back, now, do you think your reason was a good one?

2. *Past Activity*

What was your underlying motivation to engage in the activity?

Looking back, now, do you think your reason was a good one?

3. *Past Activity*

What was your underlying motivation to engage in the activity?

Looking back, now, do you think your reason was a good one?

4. *Past Activity*

What was your underlying motivation to engage in the activity?

Looking back, now, do you think your reason was a good one?

Part V

Seven Beliefs to be Trashed

chapter**33**

The Atari Syndrome
Belief 1: I Am Inferior to Others

Have no fear of perfection—you'll never reach it.   SALVADOR DALI

IN THIS CHAPTER
- Grasping the importance of practice
- Assessing the amount we have practiced

Feeling inferior is a universal belief that we all have on occasion. Most of us feel that we are inferior to someone, in something, at some time, and it bothers us.

One reason we all have this thought is that it is true, yes, true. If we play the comparison game, we can almost always find someone better at X then we are. Even those few individuals who are truly better at X than everyone else will be constantly looking over their shoulders to see who may be catching up to them. And even these people notice that although they may be better than others in X, they are mediocre in Y and absolutely terrible at Z. Nobody can be better than everyone in everything. Thank God, what a boring life that would be: nothing to strive for, no competition, no chance of improving. There really wouldn't be much purpose in being alive.

Since we are all inferior in someway, then it's silly for us to be upset by something that is universally true. We know this is correct, but many of us stay upset just the same. There are two major reasons for our silliness. We may think that people's worth as human beings is dependent on their achievements, which if true means we should kill all the poor, weak, old, ugly, sick, or uneducated to make room for us more worthwhile folks. Or we may think that if we are very successful, than other people will like and respect us, which is contradicted when we notice how we actually feel about those people who are richer, smarter, prettier, or more powerful than ourselves.

But there is a third reason for our silliness that we may have missed. I call it the Atari syndrome, and I coined it after watching my children play when they were growing up.

VIDEO GAMES

EXAMPLE

My two daughters Linda and Michele use to play Atari video games when they were children. They loved the games and played every chance they could. It was very instructive to watch them. Each preferred one type of Atari game to all the others. I don't know why. Maybe one preferred the characters of one while the other liked the strategy of the other. One daughter liked a game called *Adventure*, which had dragons, swords, and chalices, while the other preferred *Superman*, which had the Man of Steel chasing Lex Luthor all over Metropolis.

Because they liked different games, they played the one they liked far more than the other. They played their preferred game at least 10 times more often. You can guess what happened. They grew very skilled at one while less skilled at the other.

So far no problem; they kept playing the game they liked. But occasionally they would play together and compete with each other on these two games. Then the sparks would fly.

If they played *Superman* or *Adventure*, the one who had practiced the most would always win. She would then like it more and play more, while the loser would hate the game and play even less. Naturally, their abilities in these two games grew farther and farther apart. Future contests became increasingly one-sided.

It got so bad after a while that they couldn't play these two games without ending up in a brawl. The one who lost in *Superman* would start yelling, "She cheated; She is a rotten person who always cheats. I hate her and I won't play with her ever again." The one who lost in *Adventure* would say, "I stink. I'm no good. She is better than me in everything. I can't do anything right. I'm not going to play this stupid game again."

Their anger was surprising at least for the outside observer. They couldn't see what was going on. They didn't know why they were losing. One daughter thought her sister won because she had more talent, or more endurance, more concentration, or more guts. The other thought her sister was sneakier, or luckier, or cheated more.

But they were both wrong. Looking in from the outside, you could easily see.

The reason one was better than the other was simple. It is the reason that many people refuse to accept, the Atari syndrome. Simply stated, it is, " We are good at what we practice." That's it. That's why my daughters were good at different Atari games. No mystery at all.

The principle applies to many areas besides video games. In fact, there are very few areas where it doesn't apply. Unfortunately, most people ignore the lesson. Like my daughters, people attribute achievement, skill, and talent to everything but practice.

Here are some examples of our failure to consider the Atari syndrome. One of our culture's favorite explanations for excellence is that some people are born with talent. This concept feeds our romantic, dramatic impulses. Practice is boring and sounds very mundane. But talent, particularly great talent, appears to our sense of mystery and wonder. We can't understand it; we can't predict it. It seems to come out of nowhere imposing its will randomly on undeserving children. So when we wish to explain why some people do things exceptionally well, we shake our heads, sigh, and say it's just some natural, God-given gift, the result of the fickle finger of fate.

The truth is broader. The concept of natural talent doesn't take into account the Atari syndrome. Lurking behind the skills of many geniuses lie years of practice. Most of this practice is hidden, buried in childhood. Many of our most talented prodigies practiced extensively when they were quite young. For example:

WOLFGANG AMADEUS MOZART

Mozart wrote his first symphony at the age of 8. He became one of the world's most prolific composers. When he died, at the young age of 34, he had composed 41 symphonies and many operas—769 compositions in all. Not only was he prolific, but his music radiates with a captivating humanness that many people judge as rarely equaled and never surpassed in musical history.

His ability was so manifest that we can attribute much of his genius to inherited talent. His father Leopold was a court violinist and his mother's father was a court musician. Together, they undoubtedly provided an excellent genetic foundation for music, but heredity alone doesn't account for all his skill. The additional factor was practice—the Atari syndrome. Starting at the age of 3, Mozart spent countless hours at the keyboard, perhaps to emulate his older sister Nannerl and to please his father. During his childhood, he spent three hours in the morning and three hours in the evening devoted to musical practice and composition (Solomon, 1995, p. 39).

Talent be what it may, there would be no preeminence, no world-level skill without the Atari syndrome.

Do a few calculations in the next exercise and determine if the Atari syndrome applies to you.

Homework

EXERCISE

33.1 Counting the Hours

Use Worksheet 33.1, "Hours of Practice"

Step 1. Pick three things that you are good at. They can be big things (e.g., I can speak three foreign languages) or little things (e.g., I can kill flies with a rubber band). If you can't find anything at all, immediately skip to the section on depression in this book.

Step 2. Next, pick three things that you are not good at (e.g., speaking in public or playing Scrabble). If you can't find anything, immediately skip to the section in this book on too-high self-esteem.

Step 3. Now do a rough calculation. Compared to most other people your age, how much more or less time did you spend engaging in the activity? Did you practice about the same? Two times more? Three times more? If you did less practice than the average person, how much less? Was it two times less? Three times less?

Step 4. Remember early practice (as a child) is worth far more than later practice (as an adult).

Step 5. In what activities did you put in the most practice?

33.1 Hours of Practice

1. Something I am good at: _____

2. Something I am good at: _____

3. Something I am good at: _____

1. Something I am bad at: _____

2. Something I am bad at: _____

3. Something I am bad at: _____

Amount of practice compared to other people my own age. Put an "X" on scales below.

Good at:

1. −3x   −2x   −1x   0   +1x   +2x   +3x

2. −3x   −2x   −1x   0   +1x   +2x   +3x

3. −3x   −2x   −1x   0   +1x   +2x   +3x

Bad at:

1. −3x   −2x   −1x   0   +1x   +2x   +3x

2. −3x   −2x   −1x   0   +1x   +2x   +3x

3. −3x   −2x   −1x   0   +1x   +2x   +3x

The result of the exercise is dependent on what activities you picked for your scales, but most people found that the more they practiced, the better they were. But it is also true that the better they were the more they wanted to practice. And of course, this makes perfect sense.

Some people who feel inferior to others expect to be good at something even if they haven't practiced; they seem to believe that their skill should jump out fully formed. They may accept that the Atari syndrome is important in playing musical instruments, learning a foreign language, or competing in athletics, but they fail to see that it applies to many other endeavors. We should not be surprised that people who practice making money usually are richer; those who practice gaining power usually have more power; and those who practice getting other people to like them usually are more popular. There are few areas in life where the Atari syndrome doesn't apply.

 Of course, practice isn't everything. Inborn ability is still important. Look at some accomplished athletes. It is doubtful you could play center for the Los Angeles Lakers if you were 5' 9" (the average height of the American male), or be a successful professional tennis player if you had slow reflexes, or an Olympic skater if you were born with an inclination to be 70 pounds overweight. But also remember how many years of practice these athletes spent—the years of shooting baskets; the thousands of dollars spent on tennis lessons before they were 10; the waking up at 4 a.m. every morning in order to get to practice on the ice rink.

Genius is one percent inspiration, 99% perspiration. (Thomas A. Edison)

chapter 34

True Love
Belief 2: There is One True Love

Love is the triumph of imagination over intelligence.   H.L. MENCKEN

IN THIS CHAPTER
• Critiquing a fable
• List of relationship fallacies

One of humanity's oldest fables is about love. Although many of us consider this myth to be very romantic, its effects on our relationships can be devastating.

OUR MISSING HALF

EXAMPLE
The ancient tale describes how, in primeval times, men and women were not separate creatures. God had originally blended male and female into a single human soul. But one day an evil demon, jealous and resentful of God's creation, magically split the human soul into two parts—male and female. He hurled the divided parts into the North Wind, scattering them across the earth. From that time on, all men and women had to spend the rest of their lives trying to find their missing half. There was only one ideal, perfect match for each person. If they found their missing half, their one true love, they would become whole again and eternally blissful. If not, they would forever wander the world searching—forlorn and inconsolable.

BIG IDEA
This fable teaches a damaging moral and creates unrealistic expectations. Many individuals reject good potential mates because they find a faint blemish in them. In their minds, their one true love can have no flaws. They may

go through scores of relationships looking for the perfect mate, and reject good, promising partners simply because they find a flaw. When they discover the futility of their search, it may be too late to find anyone at all.

The moral underlying the fable may be the source of many relationship problems. In some cultures over half of the marriages ultimately end up in divorce. Typically, these relationships start out well. A young man and young woman date and fall in love. Initially, it is romantic and exciting, but then after a few years, the relationship loses its excitement; the couple gets bored and they become disillusioned.

While there may be many reasons marriages break down, loss of novelty, sexual boredom, in-law problems, financial insecurity, loss of an extended family system, easy divorce, infidelity, and so on, the idea of the perfect other half lurks behind many of these failures.

The myth's danger lies in its lesson; it teaches the young to expect a lot from marriage—the perfect union, one true love, becoming whole and complete.

The fable is not limited to any one culture. People from different parts of the world differ only in their definition of true love or the perfect marriage, but they don't differ in their expectation for it. Americans may define a successful marriage by the accumulation of wealth and high status. To an Australian, it may mean companionship. A Pacific Islander often measures success in terms of serenity and having lots of babies.

Expectations climb mountains while reality sits there trying to put on its socks. The reality of married life crashes down on the "one true love" fable. The American couple may hit an economic recession; the Australian wife encounters male "mateism"; and the Pacific Islander discovers that it is impossible to mention serenity and babies in the same sentence.

The fable may have spawned other fallacies about relationships. Among them are these:

- In order to be happy, we need our spouse to love us all the time.
- When our spouses make mistakes we should criticize and blame them.
- In a good marriage we will only have sexual desires for our spouse.
- We should be concerned and upset when our marriage is not ideal.
- Our spouse causes all of our marital problems.
- Successful marriages should solve or at least greatly reduce the emotional problems we had before we married.
- Loving each other is all it takes to have a good marriage.
- We should love steadily all the time.

- A good spouse puts up with any problem the partner has—such as alcoholism, bad temper, abuse, or infidelity.
- It is good for partners to be emotionally dependent on each other.
- Simultaneous orgasms are necessary for a good sex life.
- When our spouse treats us badly, it's our fault for not being a good enough partner.
- Good marriages don't have major problems.
- Our partner should know our needs and desires without having to ask.
- If we love each other enough, we don't have to work on our relationship.
- To have a happy marriage, we need our spouses to act the way we want them to.
- Love is a mysterious thing and no one knows what it is.
- Children always make a marriage happier.
- Loving couples never argue.
- Love and marriage go together.
- Marriage should cure loneliness.
- When the romantic feelings fade it means there is something wrong with the marriage.
- In good marriages couples do everything together.

In all human endeavors, preventing problems from occurring is preferable to correcting them, and there is no more important endeavor where this is true than affairs of the heart. It may take months or years to change a distorted perception, while preventing the distortion in the first place is a lot quicker and a lot less painful. Love is such an overwhelming emotion that clarity of thought needs to come before love arrives, because it is almost impossible to have it afterwards. The following exercise may help you prepare and improve the clarity of your thinking about relationships.

Homework

 EXERCISE

34.1 Relationship Trash

Step 1. Review each of the fallacies about relationships mentioned above.

Step 2. While reading, imagine the worst possible consequence of believing each thought (e.g., "If I keep believing there is only one true love, I will reject everybody as soon as I find the first flaw"). Let your imagination run wild. Let yourself go. Picture the worst in as vivid detail as you can (e.g., imagine saying good-bye to a kind, good, interesting person because you found some flaw). When you have imagined the worst possible consequence, you can stop.

Step 3. Then, read the thought again, but this time imagine the best possible consequences of *not* believing the thought (e.g., "I will see people as they are and be able to accept them with all their human fallibilities. I will be able to love a real person, not a phony cardboard image taken from some Hollywood fable"). Use your imagination and feel free to exaggerate (e.g., "If I accept people and don't reject them as soon as I find a flaw I will have more friends [*picture having them*], more adventures [*picture them*], and more romances" [*picture them*]). Continue in this fashion. When you have thought of the best possible consequences, you can stop.

 So, what can we do to improve our intimate relationships? Maybe it's best to remember what James Cagney said on the occasion of his 50th wedding anniversary. Some of the press had noted that it was unusual for a marriage to last 50 years, particularly in Hollywood, a community not known for long lasting fidelity. When the reporter asked him why his marriage was so successful, he answered simply, "We didn't expect too much."

Taking Out Your Mental Trash

chapter 35

Loonies and Wackos
Belief 3: I Must Be Crazy

Happiness comes of the capacity to feel deeply, to enjoy simply, to think freely, and to risk life, to be needed. MARGARET STORM JAMESON

IN THIS CHAPTER
• Understanding mental health
• A scale for emotionality

When some people feel a strong emotion, they cut off their feeling by thinking, "I must be crazy to feel so strongly." They view strong emotions as signs of an unpleasant, scary, condition they call "sick," or "mentally ill." Because they use these words, they are more likely to display the emotions and behaviors that the "sick" label elicits. They think of themselves as emotionally crippled, unbalanced, diseased, or in some way deranged for feeling so strongly. And then they start to play the part, acting out the role of a victim by being passive, feeling helpless, and expecting some kind of doctor to cure them.

Applying the "sick" label where it does not belong has damaging effects and can cause all kinds of problems. This thought should be one of the first ones you throw into the trash.

EXAMPLE

THE STORY OF BETH

Beth was an attractive, intelligent, woman in her 30s who was successful in business. Unfortunately, she was also very suggestible and imagined having all kinds of problems that in truth she did not have. She had been in analysis for 6 years, three times a week. Originally, she had entered therapy to work out her grief and anger over the early loss of her parents. After their deaths, she had been sent as an adolescent to live with her aunt and uncle, whom she described as unemotional, rigid, and rejecting. She believed that the analysis had helped her cope with her grief and anger, but was puzzled when after four years of treatment, her anxiety attacks began. During her final two years of analysis, they had become progressively worse.

Later on, she found out what had happened. A belief she learned in her analysis had triggered her anxiety attacks. During a session with her analyst, she had misunderstood what he had said about the "id," which in turn caused her to think that deep down inside her unconscious she was a very sick and potentially crazy person. She described the fear as, "It's like an evil force inside of me could take me over at any time. I have to constantly guard against these unconscious impulses erupting and making me go crazy."

This thought would occur whenever she felt spontaneous emotions like anger, fear, or sadness. She would immediately label these feelings as sick and dangerous, and then she became afraid of losing control. Her anxiety continued for two years.

In most cases, her emotions were perfectly normal and could be understood in the context in which they had occurred. However, she had to work very hard to see that her emotions weren't the problem, but rather her labeling them as a sign of mental illness. Only when Beth learned and accepted that she wasn't crazy, did her anxiety leave.

We can rightly ask, what makes a person mentally ill, and what makes a person mentally healthy? Apparently, many people think they know. In a survey, a sample of people were asked to describe the characteristics of mental health. Overwhelmingly they mentioned traits such as: composed, serene, self-controlled, unruffled, even-tempered, unemotional, and logical. They thought mentally healthy people are always cool, calm, and collected.

Is this true? Is being mentally healthy a matter of feeling calm, relaxed, and serene? It may be useful to find out. But first, before we discuss mental health, you may wish to take the following survey and see what kind of score you get. Afterwards we can talk about what it means.

Homework

EXERCISE

35.1 Am I Sick?

In the last month, have you . . .

- spontaneously expressed feelings like, anger, joy, fear, grief, or caring, without thinking about it?
- changed your view on an important issue when you heard new evidence?
- brought some inexpensive item you wanted just on impulse?
- done something no one expected you to do?
- listened long enough to hear a religious, political, or personal viewpoint with which you disagreed?
- allowed your imagination to run freely on a fantasy trip?
- soaked in a warm bath just relaxing for a half hour?
- sat on a beach, by a stream, or on a mountain meadow without trying to accomplish anything?
- done what you wanted to do, instead of what you thought you "should" do?
- made a decision on the spur of the moment without having everything planned out ahead of time?
- expressed an unpopular opinion in the face of majority opposition?
- helped someone without his or her knowledge?
- allowed yourself to laugh, shout for joy, or cry out loud?
- admitted you were wrong?
- risked sharing your personal feelings with someone you didn't know very well?

Are you sick if you answered yes to some of these questions? Absolutely not! Carl Rogers, one of the most prominent psychologists of the last century, developed the therapy behind the checklist (Rogers, 1961). According to him, a growing open, healthy person answers "yes" to many of the questions. He does not give an exact score because his idea of being an open, whole, spontaneous human being is that we can't be dissected and jammed into a statistical box based on some little survey.

He lists more items, but you get the idea.

Mentally healthy people don't strive for emotional blandness. They aren't usually calm, unruffled, and even-tempered. Often, they are a bit of the opposite. They use logic, but are not enslaved by it; they try new experiences and are constantly growing. But most of all, healthy people are emotionally alive and show their feelings openly and spontaneously.

SLOW

Of course there is something called mental illness, and some people are sick. However, being mentally ill is never based on being spontaneous, acting unconventionally, or transparently expressing emotions. Psychotic patients, alcohol and drug dependent clients, and those with medically based brain disorders such as schizophrenia or manic-depression do have a biochemical-induced illness. But these problems can be treated and most of these people can live rich, fulfilling lives.

Mentally healthy people experience all their feelings, aren't afraid of any one emotion, can manage their emotions without repressing them and utilize their emotions to freely and creatively interact with the world around them.

chapter 36

Traumatic Experiences
Belief 4: Traumatic Life Experiences Must Always Dominate Me

The happiness of most people we know is not ruined by great catastrophes or fatal errors, but by the repetition of slowly destructive little things.

ERNEST DIMNET

IN THIS CHAPTER
- Discovering why traumatic experiences are so damaging
- A preliminary exercise

Belief 4 appears to be correct. Mustn't early traumatic life experiences always dominate us? Some people have been through such terrifying experiences that we can't expect them to adjust. Can we?

It is a common problem. At least a third of us have had a horrible life experience that has left a large scar or scars. It may have been living through the sudden death of a loved one, facing our own death, being involved in a serious accident, seeing someone die, being physically or sexually abused, fighting in a war, being a victim of a violent crime, having a life threatening illness, or some other highly traumatic event. These experiences will always affect us, and for some of us they still have the power to dominate our lives.

The experience could have occurred in childhood, as an adolescent, or as an adult. But no matter when it occurred, even if it was years ago, for many of us it is still always on our minds and governs how we see ourselves and look at life.

THE STORY OF ANNA

Anna was a married, 55-year-old woman when she told her story. She had suffered through one of the worst childhood experiences anyone could imagine. Anna was born in a small Russian town before the Second World War. When the Germans invaded her village, they enslaved the townspeople and forced them to work for the Third Reich. But partisans living in the surrounding area kept sabotaging army supply lines, so the Germans decided to make an example of Anna's village.

Early one evening, SS troops rounded up everyone in the town—men, women, and children—and marched them to a gully. Anna and her mother were among them. The Nazi's forced the villagers to huddle in the gully. Then they lined up machine guns on the outer edge and fired. As the people were screaming and trying to climb out, Anna's mother pushed her underneath the falling bodies. The pile of dead and dying shielded Anna from the bullets.

She hid there all night, soaked in blood, with sounds of moaning all around her. After several hours the moaning stopped. Everyone was dead, including her mother. Anna was the only one who survived, yet she felt too terrified to leave.

The next morning, people from a neighboring village arrived to search for relatives among the dead. They heard Anna crying and frantically dug through the bodies until they uncovered her. They carried Anna to the home of one of the villagers and gave her food and comfort. She was the only survivor of her village, so the partisans cared for her, moving her from one town to another, and hiding her from the SS. Finally, they arranged to smuggle her out of Russia through the underground. She eventually settled in the United States, where she lived with some distant relatives.

Anna could never forget what had happened. When young she suffered from nightmares and intrusive memories. But when she became a mature adult she clearly had learned to cope with what had happened.

She couldn't erase the appalling event that had occurred; yet, she had changed the way she looked at not only the event but also life itself. She thought about the broad, sweeping problems all people face. She explored her deeply felt values about philosophical and religious subjects such as life and death, and good and evil.

She would always feel some pain, but Anna had learned to accept what had happened. This was the key. She understood that sometimes horrible things happen to good people for no reason. She agreed that she didn't deserve it, that she had done nothing to cause it, and that there was nothing she could have done to prevent it. But most importantly, she learned to accept that many times the universe isn't the way she would like it to be. It can be horrible and painful, and it has no obligation to be different from what it is. When she could accept living in this kind of world, she was able to move on in her life.

What happened to Anna was powerful. It didn't destroy or dominate her life because of how she perceived what had happened. Terrible childhood experiences are no different from other experiences. They are triggers or stimuli, but they don't control a person. They may cause worlds of pain and incline us to hate, despair, or live in terror, but they don't make us. We make ourselves. Strong predispositions created by early traumas can often be offset or mitigated by what we conclude about the event, the world, or our selves.

 Anna's story teaches us a great truth. Human beings have an amazing ability to adapt. No matter how bad, traumatic, or horrible our experience may have been, we can rise above it and free ourselves.

For you readers who have experienced a horrible, traumatic event, there are a number of powerful exercises and techniques that can help you cope with what happened. They have helped hundreds of thousands of other people. But they must be done carefully by a trained therapist, who is sitting across from you listening to your personal story and who can monitor and shape your exercises. If you are now in counseling, you have the help available now.

 But some of you reading this book may not be in counseling. This Guide is intended to help people clear out some of their cognitive trash, not to dig into their past uninvited and try to remove the effects of a great trauma. In no way can this Guide substitute for therapy.

Digging up an old wound may be necessary, but it will cause some pain; it is manageable pain, but it is pain nevertheless. Living through great trauma is a human experience, and you need another real live human being listening to you and caring for you to help you cope with what you went through. You need the warmth of human contact. For now, all I want to do is offer you the following exercise to give you hope and to encourage you to get help if you need it.

Homework

EXERCISE

36.1 Counterthoughts

Use Worksheet 36.1, "Counters to My Thoughts"

Look over the worksheet and read the example on pages 236–237 before you begin the exercise.

Step 1. Read over the list of beliefs in column 1. People who have gone through very traumatic experiences frequently mention these thoughts as causing the most problems. Of course, some of these beliefs only apply to certain types of traumas and not to others.

Step 2. In column 2, write the best counterargument you can think of that disputes and challenges the belief.

Step 3. Read over the counters that I give you in the example section. You may discover that the ones you wrote are superior to my examples. So much the better.

WORKSHEET

36.1 Counters to My Thoughts

Belief	Counter

I should have done something to prevent it.

_____

I'll never be the same.

_____

Because it happened once, it is more likely
to happen again.

_____

I feel ashamed at myself because it occurred.

_____

I shouldn't tell anyone what happened.

_____

The only way to protect myself is to be very
concerned and dwell on the possibility
that it might occur again.

_____

Most people who know me, think about the
fact that it happened to me.

_____

I was stupid, I should have known better.

_____

It is unfair and unjust that it occurred.

_____

It has made me emotionally unstable.

_____

The only way to feel better emotionally is if
someone is punished.

_____

Add your own

_____

EXAMPLE

Counters to My Thoughts

I am providing you with some counterarguments. Some you will like, some you won't. Correct those you don't. Remember, counters must fit the person doing the countering.

Belief	*Counter*
I should have done something to prevent it.	Who am I, God?
I'll never be the same.	The experience never touched me. I mean it never touched who I really am, and what I am really worth. It never could. A thousand traumas never could. It changed the way I felt and the way I thought about my world, and myself, but this I learned and this I can unlearn. The "I" in "I" is untouched; it is sole and unique.
Because it happened once, it is more likely to happen again.	It is less likely. Before, I didn't know the world had such events stirring around in it. Of course, I knew intellectually, but I had no personal feeling for the knowledge. Now, I know. I have learned. I have been warned.
I feel ashamed at myself because it occurred.	I am mostly ashamed at being human with all that entails. I find it difficult to accept that I am part of a bungled and botched species—striving to be like the angels but missing the mark badly. At times, we are close to our animal, savage roots.
I shouldn't tell anyone what happened.	It is private knowledge not meant to be shared with everyone. But it is helpful to find a band of brothers or sisters who have shared my experiences and could understand what I feel.
The only way to protect myself is to be very concerned and dwell on the possibility that it might occur again.	Look at the cost of the protection! I may protect my life so much that I give up living the life that I mean to protect.

Most people who know me, think about the fact that it happened to me.	Other people are not that different from me. They think mostly of themselves, not of me.
I was stupid, I should have known better.	If we knew ahead of time what was going to happen to us, what's the point of living? Everything laid out in front of us? No struggles, no challenges, no purpose to life whatsoever.
It is unfair and unjust that it occurred.	Certainly! But who promised me otherwise. Only humans seek fairness and justice. Nature cares nothing about such matters.
It has made me emotionally unstable.	It doesn't have the power. It happened. It's gone. It exists in the past and nothing in the past can influence the present unless I bring it into the present. I do this by my beliefs; and I can change these beliefs.
The only way to feel better emotionally is if someone is punished.	There is not enough punishment in the world to make things equal again. Living well today is the best revenge.

 If you have gone through a horrible trauma and feel you need help, let me encourage you. You can get it. I have seen remarkable changes with hundreds of people who have experienced terrible events. See someone. Pick a professional who knows the techniques, is trustworthy, and who will lend you an empathetic ear.

chapter 37

Coveting Thy Neighbor
Belief 5: The Grass Is Always Greener on the Other Side of the Fence

If we knew how little those we envy take pleasure in what they have, we wouldn't be envious. WAYNE UP

IN THIS CHAPTER
• Examining the cause of envy
• Understanding the cost of fame

Most of us would probably understand this belief to mean that people get envious of things that others have. The grass could in fact be greener on the other side of the fence, but even if it isn't, we humans have the uncanny ability to make it appear to be. All we have to do is use our imaginations. If we picture that somebody else has a better life (greener grass), then, presto, our life fades into insignificance (our grass looks dull and drab).

Idolizing others can cause mountains of problems for our society in general and chronic distress for each of us in particular. We misunderstand others by making their lives appear better than they are, and we dishonor our own life by making it appear worse.

The reason we make this mistake is that we are only looking at other people in the abstract, at a distance—necessarily, since we are living are own lives, not theirs. We see only their glitter and their shining moments. But because we are removed from their life and only see a small snippet of what their day is like, we have a distorted vantage point. We notice only a thousandth part of what they experience in a day, and we only observe those aspects that trigger our envy. But we see ourselves in closeup, and encounter all the monotonous, drab smudges all people experience in life. Our envy is usually triggered by the type of experience demonstrated in the following case.

Red/Green-Eye Flight

EXAMPLE Imagine you want to visit your aged mother on the opposite coast, but you can only afford a coach ticket on a red-eye, transcontinental flight. You arrive late because you have to wait for a second airport shuttle because the first one is full. You stand in a long line and when you get to the counter, the only seat left is a middle seat in a five seat row near the back of the plane. For two hours there is a baby crying in the row behind you; the man on your left has a cold and has been sneezing in your face; the obese man on your right has taken your portion of the armrest; and your legs are tucked up under your chin because the person in front has his seat pushed all the way back. And you are only halfway through the flight.

You start thinking about the movie star who was interviewed in the in-flight magazine you are reading. He is part of the tinsel culture of Hollywood, 30, single, tall, slim, well built, and extremely handsome. He has three mansions, one in Hollywood, one in midtown New York, and one in Aspen. He has a private jet, with a fully equipped bar, a bath, a movie viewing area, and a large plush bed. He arrives at the airport, at a time of his own choosing, in a stretch limo, accompanied by a beautiful young starlet. His multiple pieces of luggage are totally taken care of by his three personal attendants. Upon boarding, he immediately sits down in his massive easy chair to receive a complete lunch prepared for him by his gourmet, catered kitchen. Your reverie is broken when the obese man on your right starts snoring in your ear.

It is understandable that in such circumstances many of us venerate the rich, the beautiful, the powerful, yearn to escape from what we view as our mediocre lives, and fantasize trading places with the rich and famous. No wonder at times we are envious.

Although it is understandable, our view is myopic. We see things in this way because we are temporarily frustrated and annoyed, and imagine a movie star's world where our temporary frustration would magically disappear. We do not focus on the permanent payment we would have to make to gain such relief from our temporary displeasure. The next exercise should help broaden your view so that you can discover the hidden costs.

Homework

EXERCISE

37.1 So, You Want to Be a Star?

Step 1. Most people consider the following abilities or attributes as worthwhile, but the tinsel culture rarely mentions them. Look at each one individually and decide how many you possess in at least some degree. Mark the column "Me."

Step 2. Pick a person or a group of people you are envious about and mark how many of these abilities or attributes they possess in the column "Them."

Abilities or Attributes	Me	Them
Autonomy: freedom to go where we want to without constantly being harassed by fans, paparazzi, or the curious		
Intimacy: being able to develop successful, close, long lasting, relationships with a spouse and a family		
Authenticity: being able to be genuine, open, candid, and straightforward in expressing our self to the public.		
Tranquility: peaceful and tranquil, not being constantly bothered and interrupted by others		
Genuine acceptance: feeling liked, loved, or respected by others because of who we are not because of our image		
Anonymity: the ability to blend into crowds so that our every action is not under constant scrutiny, observed, commented on, and criticized by the press and the public		
Succor: being able to provide genuine love and affection to others		
Sense of personal worth: feeling that we have accomplished something for humanity whether we are recognized for it or not		

Step 3. Compare the two lists of answers. What do you conclude? Do you have a reason to be envious?

Most people who did the exercise answered no, they concluded that things usually equaled out. While certain people have special privileges and advantages, they must pay for them by giving up certain valuable abilities and freedoms that the rest of us take for granted. Envy means we are rejecting our own freedoms and substituting them for the canned, socially approved, prefabricated values of the superstar that are hyped only by the tinsel culture. We forget that we all must pay for whatever we get in life and that the payment is usually equal to what we gain.

Remember the rich and powerful man who had no influence over his sons who were kicked out of school because they were heavily into drugs. Or the beautiful model who had five divorces because men were only attracted to her appearance and never bothered to know who was there behind the beauty? Or the famous scientist who spent every Christmas alone because he had never had the time to have a family? Or the movie star who hid in his mansion because he was afraid to go to a grocery store where he would be bombarded by herds of paparazzi and autograph hounds?

 We may envy people who have something that we don't have; but we forget how much they had to pay for it. Paradoxically, many of those we envy dream of having what we have and envy us. It may, indeed, all equal out.

chapter 38

Inventing Problems
Belief 6: Where There's Smoke There's Fire

Reporter: Where there's smoke there's fire.
President: No. Where there's smoke there's a smoke-making machine.
JOHN F. KENNEDY

IN THIS CHAPTER
• Creating phony crises

The saying implies that if there are warning signs of a problem there must be a real problem behind it. When the attitude applies to individuals, it means that if we feel upset about something, there must be some real thing out there causing our distress. We accept that it may be a small thing. We know we could be making a mountain out of a molehill, exaggerating it, catastrophizing it, but we still believe there must be at least a molehill. We can't be making everything up, can we?

It may surprise some readers, but yes, we can. Sometimes this is exactly what some people do. They make the whole thing up out of thin air. Not intentionally, not to fool others, but they create a problem that wouldn't exist otherwise.

Our brains can be the smoke-making machine without needing any fire as the following example shows.

THE GREAT SCHNOZZOLA EFFECT

Leona was a 25-year-old single woman known for her beauty. She was tall and thin, had a beautiful figure, long auburn hair, long silky eyelashes, and large "Betty Davis" eyes. But most ideal was her nose. It was so cute and petite, the kind of nose everybody wants; the kind that women go to plastic surgeons and say, "Give me one like hers."

Everything was going fine for Leona, until one day she was sitting in her hairdresser's waiting room and she noticed an old copy of *National Geographic*. She paged through it until she came across an article about the Kup tribe, a Stone Age culture that lives in the highland forest of New Guinea (Gilliard, 1953). She noticed that the women there were beautiful, but they all had large noses. The Kup people considered large, broad grand noses as a sign of beauty, sexuality, and virility. The women go out of their way to make their noses grander by putting shells, feathers, bark, and reeds in them to make them look bigger. In a wedding ceremony, the chief and his bride put flowers and bark in their noses to make them look large and beautiful, and have an elaborate ritual of rubbing their noses together as part of the marriage ceremony.

Later that night, before Leona went to bed, she looked in the mirror and saw her nose. Of course, she had seen her nose thousands of times before, but this time it looked different. "You know," she thought, "It probably could be a little bit bigger. It would make it sexier." The next morning when she looked in the mirror again she thought, "Yes, it definitely could be bigger."

During the days and weeks that followed, Leona thought more and more about her nose. She even asked others what they thought. When they all answered, "It's perfect just the way it is," she rejected their opinion thinking they were just trying to be nice. She soon became convinced that her nose was puny and ugly. She envied those with larger noses wishing, "If only I could have one like them." At night she would dream of broad, big noses, and have nightmares of her nose shrinking smaller and smaller. It became almost impossible to put the image of her nose out of her mind. She tried not to think about it, but the more she tried, the more the picture of her nose appeared to her.

After months, Leona finally gave up fighting her impulse and went to a plastic surgeon to have her nose enlarged. He stared at her in amazement. "Your nose is perfect," he said. She pleaded with him, but he refused to do the operation and gave her the name of a psychologist. She went to other plastic surgeons who said the same thing and refused to do the operation until she met one who said, "I'll do it, but first you have to bring me a letter from a therapist." Finally, out of desperation, she saw a psychologist.

The psychologist refused to write a letter until they had several therapy meetings to discuss the matter. It was during these sessions that Leona discovered the cause of her problem. It took several more sessions, and much work, and more practice, but in the end, Leona stopped dreaming of big noses and was able to accept her nose as it was. Leona finally realized and understood what had happened—her imagination had made the whole thing up.

Leona's case is an extreme one, but we all have the same tendency (albeit to a smaller degree). We human beings have a propensity to make up things that don't exist and then bother ourselves about them. The novelist Kurt Vonnegut offers an intriguing reason for this. He suggests that human beings have brains that are *too* big. He notes that our brains are constantly beguiled by possibilities and incapable of restraint or idleness, forever demanding increasingly mental challenges (1985, pp. 3, 270). The result is that we are not only a highly suggestible animal, but are uniquely autosuggestible. We indoctrinate ourselves with all kinds of arrant trash and continue believing in the nonsense by actively and energetically reindoctrinating ourselves.

We may fantasize that our thighs are too large, our breasts too small, our penises too short, our hair too thin, our ears too big, our rears too flat. We may demand that we should be more aggressive but less hostile; more accepting but less gullible; more relaxed but not dull; loving but not vulnerable; smarter but not egotistical. We create these demands out of nothing, with no basis in fact, and then criticize ourselves unmercifully for not living up to them. Since we all have this tendency, we had best be on our guard. The following exercise may help.

Homework

EXERCISE

38.1 Counterfeit Catastrophes

Step 1. Think of some of the phony catastrophes you have created in the past. For example, remember a time when you were unduly concerned about your appearance, or when you thought you had a terrible medical problem that you didn't have, or when you worried about becoming broke, or when you lost sleep over some terrible thing happening to a loved one. Be sure to pick only those situations where nothing bad happened.

Step 2. What do you think caused you to make up these phony crises?

Step 3. When and how did you discover they were a sham?

Step 4. What do you believe now?

 Almost everyone who did this exercise could find multiple examples of problems they created with their runaway imaginations. Almost everybody concluded that they had enough real problems in their lives so that they didn't have to go out of their way to make up phony ones.

chapter**39**

The Power of the Mind
Belief 7: Our Minds Are All-powerful

There are people so addicted to exaggeration that they can't tell the truth without lying.
JOSH BILLINGS

IN THIS CHAPTER
• Facing our humanity

Believing we have great strength is an encouraging, empowering thought, but it can lead us into problems.

One problem is an unfortunate trait of being a human being. Some people tend to take a good idea, a sound, solid idea, and twist and stretch it into some bizarre exaggeration—this idea is an important premise of this book. Put most simply, the premise is: *we are disturbed by our thoughts about things, not by things themselves.* Our beliefs, attitudes, and values are crucially important to our happiness, and if we wish to remove our mental trash, we had best look first at our beliefs.

Now, this is hardly a new idea. It is at the heart of Albert Ellis's philosophy (Ellis, 2004b) and more than 2,000 years ago, the Greek philosopher Epictetus discovered the same thing (1952). Unfortunately, let us see what has happened to this good, ancient idea.

From a TV ad we notice: "Unlock the secrets of your mind. Learn how to control your brain and gain incredible, personal power."

It seems the cost of unlocking one's mind is quite high. You must buy a series of 10 cassettes that cost $350. The tapes display a watered down version of the 2,000-year-old discovery but lack certain useful elements such as practicing, identifying the correct thoughts, accepting that there is a reality existing outside our brains, little things like these. The person who produced the tapes didn't understand the discovery and apparently contrived everything just to make a buck.

A newspaper advertisement announces a free public lecture from a visiting doctor. It reads:

> Attend Dr. _____'s free lecture. Dr. _____ is the international expert on subconscious thoughts. He will teach you the secrets of how to tap the strength of your hidden power. Wealth and love will be easily within your grasp.

It didn't say what kind of doctor he was, but he turned out to have a degree in business administration, which figures. The lecture was free, but it was a promo for a one-week workshop that would cost $1,000. The hidden secrets promised were a warmed over, sanitized, inaccurate, distorted, botched version of the 2,000-year-old discovery. A good idea, exaggerated, can do more than just take our money; it can hurt us. Consider the case of Johnny.

Johnny's Story

EXAMPLE

Johnny was a typical 16-year-old boy. He was a good, energetic, bright kid, but like many adolescents he felt unsure of himself, was naive, and highly impressionable. He dreamed of being a hero, rescuing women in distress. He fantasized about impressing his parents with his masculinity, showing the entire community that he was special and not just another pimple-faced kid (Hollywood has made a fortune churning out movies that appeal to this fantasy). In fact, a young man's yearning for fame is equaled only by his passion for sex. Often, in a boy's mind, the two are inextricably tied together; and for most boys equally scarce).

He craved his corner of fame by trying to excel in sports. It's the adolescent boy's royal road to respect. But like most boys, he wasn't an exceptional athlete. He wasn't bad, merely average, right smack in the middle. Unfortunately, for an adolescent, being average is the same as being invisible. The one thing he didn't want to be was average. He searched and searched for something to excel in, but he couldn't find anything. Like many other adolescent boys, he felt weak, inferior, and unmasculine.

One day a friend invited him to join a group of other young men and women that met on Sunday to discuss various topics. Since he felt lonely and had few other friends, he decided to join. After several meetings, he found out that it was a quasi-religious cult that taught only one principle: "You can control anything with your mind."

The elders of the cult told him he could acquire everything he wanted if he learned to control his thoughts. He could gain fame, power, great wealth, change the world, stop wars, cure injuries, stop his acne, anything at all. All he needed was to have faith and believe that he could.

Johnny spent a year testing the principle by trying to stop his acne from exploding or by striving to make himself famous, rich, and powerful. But, of course, he didn't succeed. So, he went back to the elders suggesting that maybe they were wrong. They shook their heads and said he hadn't enough faith. They insisted, "You must have absolutely no doubt whatsoever. If you doubt even a little, this uncertainty will obliterate your power." They also expressed their disappointment that he was not turning out to be the type of novitiate they had hoped for.

So, Johnny went out and tried some more, this time even harder. But no fame or power appeared, and he became poorer rather than richer because of all his required donations to the cult.

For two years Johnny tried to find enough faith to make his thoughts powerful enough, but he never succeeded. To him this was just another failure, so he felt even worse about himself.

Because he felt guilty for failing, he sought help from an older man who was not part of the cult but who was aware of its teachings. After some guidance, he realized that the elders' ideas were absurd fiddle-faddle. Thoughts are indeed powerful, but not that powerful. He finally learned that the elders had twisted the 2,000-year-old discovery beyond all recognition. They made it into a mutant, a monster that consumed everything before it. See if you agree with the philosophy presented to Johnny. Do the following exercise.

Homework

 EXERCISE **39.1 Two Worlds**

Step 1. Read the following essay:

Every human being lives in two worlds, the inside and the outside. What happens in one sphere cannot influence the other unless we build a bridge connecting the two. Our thoughts are in the inside sphere, inside our body, that is. Things like our beliefs and attitudes can influence anything that is also occurring inside our body. Since our spinal cord connects our brain to various bodily systems, thoughts can be very powerful. Our thoughts can produce changes in our digestive system (causing stomach problems), our respiratory system (producing asthma or hyperventilation), our cardiovascular system (accelerating our heart or blood pressure), our endocrine system (secreting hormones that can produce panic, or rage, or despair), our defense and lymphatic system (reducing our ability to withstand disease and infections), our muscular system (causing migraine headaches or low back pain), or our reproductive system (making us aroused or impotent).

But our brains are not connected to ham sandwiches, the stock market, unlimited bank accounts, weather systems, or the combined military–industrial complex of nations. These things are in the second sphere (outside us) and all the thinking or wishing (inside us) won't change this sphere one wit.

If we want to change the outside sphere and make a difference on this planet, we had best build a bridge—between the inside and the outside. We already have one: it's called behavior and it means action. It may take the form of physical energy, speaking, or writing, but this is how we change the world. It's not dramatic, or exciting, or quick like the "power of the mind" drivel, but it does accomplish results. To get power we have to be willing to put away mind games and get down to some hard, concrete work.

Step 2. What items in your life would you put in each sphere? Consider where you would put such items as emotions, beliefs, intimate relationships, wealth, success, fame, knowledge, health, appearance, and love.

Step 3. How do you plan to build a bridge from one sphere to the other? For instance, if you decide that intimate relationships are in both spheres (your feeling of love is inside of you, while how you act toward others is outside), how would you behave toward your lover to show him or her what you are feeling on the inside?

 Most people who took some care in doing the exercise and thought about the matter, concluded that we are creatures, not gods. That while we are the most powerful species on Earth, it is still a small planet and the universe is far bigger than we are. Therefore, we have a limited ability to change everything that we wish to. They further concluded that it is probably best if we spend our time controlling those things we can control, while letting go of those things we can't.

Part VI

Specific Problems

chapter 40

Run to the Roar
Problems with Fear

Courage is being scared to death, but saddling up anyway.   JOHN WAYNE

IN THIS CHAPTER
- Handling fear and anxiety
- A risk-taking scale
- When fear is useful

We all have a key instinctual reaction to danger. It is the command our body shouts at us. Our body screams, "Run away from the danger!" We are hot-wired to react to threats instantaneously, without bothering to sit down and try to decipher everything out logically. If we waited in a dangerous situation, we could be killed, so our body quickens our heartbeat, tenses our muscles, and amplifies our breathing, all to help us run away from the danger as fast as we can. Throughout history, the fear–flight connection has been helpful; had it not been, fear wouldn't have been humanity's constant companion throughout our 3-million-year-old journey. But times have changed. We are no longer faced with hairy mammoths, gigantic cave bears, or saber-tooth tigers. Today, running away can create more problems then it solves.

The best illustration of the problem is the following story from T. Bakker (1982). I have been informed it is quite true.

THE OLD LIONS

EXAMPLE

The daughter of a missionary lived on the Serengeti plains in Africa. She grew up around lion prides and noticed they acted differently from other species. While other animals let there elderly members die when they could no longer catch their own game, the lion prides made use of the old lions. First, a pride would trap antelope and other animals in a ravine. Then the young lions would line up on one side and the old clawless, toothless lions would line up on the other. The old lions would roar as loudly as they could. The animals in the ravine would hear the roar, go in the opposite direction, and run straight into the waiting group of young lions.

The lesson for the antelope was clear, although few were left to benefit from it. Had they run to the roar, they would have been safe, but they were too afraid. While running away from the sound of danger, they ran into the very danger itself.

Anxious people run from what they fear; they are constantly looking for a calm, safe place to hide on the planet. If they are afraid of planes they avoid flying; if they fear crowds they stay home by themselves; if they are scared of water they avoid swimming in lakes and oceans. Their fears never lessen; they only increase. The more they run, the more afraid they become.

Depressed people also run from something. They refuse to accept that they are like others and think they should be better than the average person. Depressed people, arrogant? Isn't it just the opposite? Don't depressed people feel inferior to others? They do. But beneath the depression, some of these people harbor a curious expectation that they are supposed to be superior to others, and when they find out they aren't, they get depressed. These people run away too. They run from the reality that they are fallible human beings like everyone else, instead of the demigods they think they should be.

Alcoholics and drug addicts run away at a feverish speed, refusing to accept that they are addicted. They keep fighting the truth and hoping to get away with using. Alcoholics notice that other people drink in moderation and think they can too. Addicts' pride keeps them from admitting that they can't handle drugs. They refuse to accept that they are biochemically different from others. Alcoholics and addicts can lose everything: their families, jobs, and health, yet they still keep pretending that they can use drugs or alcohol safely.

 The solution to these problems is the moral of the story—*run to the roar*! If we turn around to face our problems, most of them can be solved. If the man who is afraid of water can approach the water, put his feet in the surf, paddle around in the shallow end of swimming pools, and force himself to sit in rowboats, he can conquer his fear. Had the depressed woman categorically accepted that she was a fallible human being like everyone else, she would not have become depressed when she goofed up again. Similarly, if the addicted person could have completely accepted that his chemical dependency was a physical problem that led him to be inextricably hooked, he could have figured out that he must find a way to quit.

To understand the meaning and the importance of the principle run to the roar, do this exercise. The results may surprise you.

Homework

EXERCISE **40.1 Losses and Gains**

Use Worksheet 40.1, "Losses and Gains"

Step 1. Look at the worksheet and list in the first column the most important things in your life that you have chosen to avoid or to run away from. They can be any type of activity: opportunities not taken (applying for the higher paying job), relationships avoided (asking him or her out), experiences forfeited (taking the harder but more interesting college courses), adventures abandoned (working in another country). List each time where you ran *away* from the roar.

Step 2. Now make a parallel list, but this time record in the second column the most important decisions where you ran *toward* the roar, toward what you perceived as dangerous. If you had no choice, and couldn't run away, you can still include these types of situations in the list because voluntarily or not, you still faced your fears.

Step 3. Review each list. Looking back from the perspective of time and distance make a decision about each item. Do you approve of the decision you made or do you regret it. Make a decision now and write down an "A" for approve or a "R" for regret in the narrow column. If you can't decide either way, leave it blank (it is best to complete the lists first before you rate your choices).

Step 4. Look at both lists and sum your results. Which actions do you regret the most, the times you ran away, or the times you ran toward what you feared?

40.1 Losses and Gains

Those risks you chose *not* to take (Ran away from the roar)	A/R	Those risks you chose *to* take (Ran to the roar)	A/R
1.		1.	
2.		2.	
3.		3.	
4.		4.	
5.		5.	
6.		6.	
7.		7.	
8.		8.	
9.		9.	
10.		10.	

Which decisions do you regret the most: the risks you took or the risks you avoided?

Most people who did the exercise, report they regret running away far more than trying, even if they failed. What did you find?

 This exercise is a good illustration of the problem with maxims and other advice you find in books like this, they are never 100% true. No doubt there are situations in your life where you probably thought, "Thank God I ran away, avoided, or escaped from that one!"

When Fear Is Useful

 The difficulty, of course, is how to tell if we should run toward, or away from danger. In general, running away is appropriate if all the following conditions are true.

- Fear is useful if there is a real danger to us and real damage could occur. On the other hand, it is not useful to be afraid of monsters under the bed because they do not exist, and something that does not exist cannot hurt us (e.g., some people are afraid of sorcerers and witches).

- Fear is useful if the level of fear is equal to the level of possible damage. However, it is inappropriate to feel terrified about getting a small splinter in a foot, since the fear would be far greater than the potential damage (e.g., many people are terrified of making minor social indiscretions in public).

- Fear is useful if the fear is appropriate to the probability of the danger occurring. But if we are afraid of being hit by a meteor, the fear is not helpful because of the low probability of it happening (e.g., many people are remarkably fearful about low-probability dangers such as plane crashes, while oblivious to much higher probabilities such as automobile accidents).

- Fear is useful if the danger can be controlled. Fear of the sun turning into a supernova would not be useful because the event is beyond human manipulation (e.g., some people are afraid of having some kind of hidden hereditary disease).

- Fear is useful if it keeps us more alert to an avoidable danger (e.g., being alert about having a "nervous breakdown" does not in any way reduce the probability of having one).

- Fear is useful if the damage of running away is significantly less than the damage of facing the fear. This is where most of our fears fail to be reasonable. We recognize the damage we could encounter by running toward danger, in fact the risks are often obsessively clear and potent in our minds. But we fail to recognize the damage of spending our whole life avoiding risks, running away from problems, and playing everything safe. If we put the two types of dangers on a balance scale, many people conclude that the best course is to run to the roar.

To handle fear, we had best catch the emotion early when it first starts to bud. It is at this point that we should immediately decide whether our fear is valid and useful. If the fear is both, then we have three choices:

- We can try to change the situation to reduce the danger.
- If we can't change the danger, then we can try to run away from it.
- And if we can neither change it nor run away from it, then we are left with only one final decision—*to accept it.*

Most people don't analyze their fears at any point; they just experience them. They keep focusing on the worst possible things that could happen to them in a given situation, which naturally terrifies them even more.

If you are one of these people who has a runaway imagination and catastrophize your fear, consider this. Consider stopping, turning around, and facing your fear. You may find out that the danger you have been running from is really just an old, clawless pussycat.

chapter 41

A Gaggle of Humans
Problems with Groups

It is in our nature to conform; it is a force which not many can successfully resist. What is its seat? The inborn requirement of self-approval.   MARK TWAIN

IN THIS CHAPTER
- Looking at group dynamics
- Understanding conformity

We often rely more on what our group believes rather than what we think. Groups powerfully influence our behavior often because we believe in one core thought, "I need everybody in my group to like me." This belief may cause the difference between how we act when we are alone versus how we behave in a group.

You may have found that people as individuals are generally kind and fair, demonstrating good common sense. But you may have also noticed that when these same individuals form together into a group, everything changes. There seems to be something about groups that removes some people's basic good sense. Observe a person individually and he or she may act sensitively and reasonably, but put him or her in a small group and kindness and fairness fly out the window and conformity becomes epidemic.

SMALL GROUP PROCESS

EXAMPLE

Group behavior is often difficult to fathom. You may have been a part of a small group of six to eight people formed for some specific purpose—a volunteer community group, a business subcommittee, a neighborhood planning committee. If you joined in the beginning, you had an opportunity to observe the small group grow through its adolescence to its maturity. For a while, everything seemed to go smoothly; people responded well, the group looked as though it would reach its goals smoothly and quickly. But then, all of a sudden, it veered off in a new direction contrary to its plan. You didn't know why it went in that direction; you saw no cause, or trigger, but away it went anyway. You coped with the change because you understood that people aren't totally predictable machines; they have there own free will. So, after awhile you were adjusted to the new direction and as a loyal group member you tried to facilitate the change. Then suddenly the group shifted again; and off it went with you holding on for dear life, trying to catch up with whatever direction the group had decided to take. You told yourself, "Well, people are very unpredictable," so you went along with the change as best you could. Finally, just as the group seemed about to complete its business, it took a 180-degree turn and doubled back on itself. You had to dive out of the way to keep from being run over by the group process.

After the group has made a hundred turns, spins, side tracks, and flip flops you may have given up trying to understand what was going on, and resolved not to get involved in this kind of group again.

So far, we have been talking about only small groups, tiny, puny groups consisting of six or eight people, a gaggle of humans. But when several gaggles combine, you get a swarm, and then the real trouble begins. The society must ride these swarms like great ocean swells. The currents and undertows are enormous, and where the swarm is headed is unknown to mortal minds. Swarms can empty theaters in panic, turn on their own members and kill them in mob rage, or put such pressure on fairness and compassion that these delicate sensitivities are washed away in the cruel tide of the mob. In a swarm, individuals can act in ways that they would never consider doing alone, and if they ever did, it would horrify them. The group pressure to act in a certain way can become so strong that only a martyr would dare resist it.

Swarms of people working together in an institution are called—a corporation. Because of the group dynamics of institutionalized swarms, some corporations have made terrible decisions despite almost all the individuals in the company realizing the plans wouldn't work. They knew this as individuals, based on their own separate judgments, but in the swarm, they gave up their individual opinions and conformed to the groupthink. The power of group pressure can sabotage any endeavor—as the following example demonstrates.

CORPORATE SWARMS

EXAMPLE
There was once this dog food company. Because of slumping sales, the CEOs decided to develop a completely new product. They hired the best nutritionist to make the healthiest dog food that would provide a completely balance diet. They ordered a new, lightweight biodegradable can to appease the environmentalists. They developed new sales distribution procedures so that every little grocery store in the country could immediately put the product on its shelves. They created a new computer program so that they could keep track of every can, every retail outlet, every delayed payment, and every damaged can. They then conducted a two-year study of the best way to advertise the dog food. They analyzed which markets were best; what price would make the product most marketable while providing the best profit. What color on the label would be most appealing? What celebrity would best advertise it, etc.

So, they did everything they could think of, and then after millions of dollars in TV and magazine ads they released their new product to the public. Every supermarket chain, every mom and pop grocery store in the country got the product in a week.

In six months the product was dead on the shelves. The company almost went broke. The CEO's were fired. What happened?

The dogs didn't like it![1]

Individually, we may have known that the dogs might not like it, but we did not tell the group. When there's a conflict between our individual beliefs and the group's attitudes, we often give up our own good judgments and yield to the group pressure. The pressure doesn't even need to be explicit; the group doesn't have to threaten or intimidate us. The pressure may be only our thought that we need the group to like us. Therefore, the mere existence of a group judgment that is different from our own may cause us to conform.

Being liked by our group is a primitive and fierce desire. It is the primeval fear of being rejected by the tribe. In the dawn of humanity, being kicked out of the tribe was equivalent to receiving a death sentence. We would have

---

[1] This story comes from Dr. William Truax, one of my graduate school instructors from many years ago. The moral of the story is as true today as it was when he first told it. All groups of any size must first and foremost serve the customer, whether the customer is a dog, a client, a patient, a community, a nation, or humanity in general. No group should ever exist for itself.

done anything not to be left alone. But the world has changed. Humanity is no longer on the edge of extinction. We are not huddling in caves hearing the roar of ancient predators, nor are we competing with other humanoids for the meager scraps available in an African savanna. We are now the dominant species on the planet and the survival of our earth is dependent on us.

 Today too much conformity is not a virtue but a vice. Going along with the group is far less important today than making the right decisions about what we should do and how we should act. If humanity makes a mistake now, we could destroy everything. Therefore, today it is crucial that we hear all viewpoints from everyone. We may not like what we hear, but we need to hear them. In the final analysis, we do not know which viewpoint or which judgment may be correct. We need to hear them all, so that we can then select the best one.

The power of group pressure is dramatically revealed in a number of experiments. The following exercise asks you to place yourself in a small group that is pressuring you to agree. Imagine the situation as clearly as you can and be as honest with yourself as possible.

Homework

EXERCISE 41.1 What Would Make You Most Likely to Conform?

Step 1. Imagine that you are in a small group that meets regularly. One day your group needs to come to a decision about an important matter. The leader decides to canvas the room and asks each member individually what he or she believes. You are the last person to be asked. To your great surprise, each member before you has expressed a judgment that is completely opposite to what you believe. Your turn now comes; the leader asks you what you think; everyone turns to look at you in anticipation of your answer. What do you say?

Step 2. Under which of the following circumstances would you be most likely to conform to the group attitude and tell them what they want to hear? When would you express your contrary opinion openly, just as you believe it? Circle the appropriate circumstances.

Overall likelihood of you conforming to the group	low	medium	high

MOST RELEVANT FACTORS

Size of group	1 or 2 other people	3 to 9 others	10+ others
Makeup of group	family	business colleagues	strangers
Strength of your judgment	weak	medium	strong
Strength of the group's judgment	weak	medium	strong
Status of others in the group in comparison to your status	I have lower status	about the same	I have higher status
Importance of the group decision	fairly unimportant	moderate	very important
Likely group response to your opposition	ignores you	silent reproach	critical attack
How much do you like the people in the group	like	neutral	dislike

Most people report that they are more likely to yield to the majority in a medium size group (about 4 to 9 people). The opinions of a smaller group would be less persuasive, while a group of 10 or more wouldn't significantly increase the pressure to conform.

People said they could disagree with strangers better than family or business colleagues because the consequences of not going along with the group would be less. They could disagree more easily if they were sure of their judgment, if they thought the decision was very important, and if they disliked the other group members. They would be more likely to yield if the group was more certain of its opinion and if the group attacked members who disagreed.

Possibly, the most interesting response was the answer to the first question—"What is the likelihood that you would conform to the group?" The vast majority of people thought they would not give in to the group no matter what the pressure.

They may have overrated their ability to be independent. In some famous studies, researchers found that anywhere from 37 to 50% ignored their own judgment and gave into to the group's opinion (Asch, 1955; Crutchfield, 1955). They explained that they wanted to feel part of the group. They were concerned that they might appear strange and absurd to the majority. One subject said: "Despite everything, there was a lurking fear that in some way I did not understand, I might be wrong; I feared exposing myself as inferior in some way" (Asch, 1955).

 There is great pressure in society to publicly say that we are all independent thinkers, but then to give in to the group privately when push comes to shove. As Mark Twain said, "It is by the goodness of God that in our country we have those three unspeakably precious things: freedom of speech, freedom of conscience, and the prudence never to practice either of them (1897, p. 195).

Active Listening
Problems Understanding People

When we talk about understanding, surely it takes place only when the mind listens completely—the mind being your heart, your nerves, your ears—when you give your whole attention to it.   J. KRISHNAMUTRI

IN THIS CHAPTER
- Grasping another's point of view
- Practicing active listening

If we want to understand people better, there is one step we need to take before any other—we need to learn to listen. Most people hear, but don't listen. They want others to think they are listening, even though they aren't. Look at two examples.

WHAT DID THEY SAY?

When you observe a group of people talking to each other, you may have noticed how little people actually listened to what the other people were saying. It appeared that they would focus on a small point the speaker was making and then not listen to the rest of the talk because they were thinking of a counterreply. You may have heard one person introduce one issue, and then a second person follow with a different issue, and then a third person switched to a very contrary subject. Nobody appeared to be listening to anybody else, nobody seemed on the same page. Without listening, they couldn't understand and therefore didn't communicate with each other.

There can be no real communication unless someone listens to somebody else. Apparently being able to listen carefully is a very difficult skill for many of us. We are often thinking about what we are going to say in reply, rather than carefully attending to what the person is trying to tell us.

The problem occurs with all kinds of communications. Consider the following everyday conversation.

QUALITY TIME

She says: You come home from work, plop in your chair, stare at the TV for three hours, and then go to bed.

He says: I've had a long day at the office.

She says: Well, I've had a long day too. I had to pick up the kids from school, drive them to ballet class, go to soccer practice, clean the kitchen, go to the supermarket, and . . .

He says: Well, I had to handle a problem in the Mitchell account, try to get the copier fixed, put out a personnel problem in the Toledo office, and . . .

Neither person was actively listening to the other. They focused on the content of what the other was saying, not on the underlying feeling being expressed. As a result, the conversation deteriorated into a battle of cataloging what each had done during the day. The mistake was made because they each supposed that listening simply means being quiet while the other person was talking. Their passivity caused the failure in their communication. It may have been perceived as a lack of interest or involvement and may have been experienced by the other as indifference or rejection.

But if both people were actively listening, they might have heard what the other person was really communicating. They would have been able to read between the lines and pick up the fundamental meaning, the subtle feelings that were being expressed.

He might have heard, "I'm lonely and I miss you. I spend all day with the children and I need an adult to talk to. I want to know you value me more than just as a baby sitter, cook, and chauffer." While she may have heard: "I get weary and tired at work. I have so many fires to put out all the time and all these people are watching me trying to catch me make a mistake. I never get any rest. My only escape is when I get home, where I can get a moment of peace until I have to go back into the battle."

If we are going to understand people, the necessary first step is to hear the person's deep, felt feelings. The exercise can help you do this. It will show you how to listen in a way that you may not have listened before.

Taking Out Your Mental Trash

Homework

EXERCISE **42.1 Active Listening**

Step 1. Pick two or three people you would like to understand better. Pick those with whom you have an ongoing relationship. They can be a spouse or lover, relatives, colleagues, or friends with whom you have frequent interactions.

Step 2. Next time you talk to these people, try something different. Instead of just being quiet while they are talking, sense, so far as you are able, the private world of the people as if it were your own. Try to understand not only the content of what they are saying, but also the mood and the tone of voice they use to convey their feelings. Try to perceive their world as they perceive it. Lay aside all observations from your own internal frame of reference while doing so. Actively try to experience what they mean and what they feel. Try to get inside of them instead of just observing them from the outside, and try to catch every nuance of their words, tone, attitudes, and feelings. Absorb yourself as completely as you can into their emotions. Experience their frustrations, hopes, and fears.

Step 3. Because you are another individual and not the person you are listening to, you cannot empathize completely. Look at your task as a goal that you can never fully reach, but it is a goal you can get close to at times.

Most importantly, realize this procedure is not just a technique, it is a philosophy that you must create, a philosophy of caring enough for the other so that you are willing to set your own needs aside for a moment and as you to become the other person. As such, it is something you can't (and probably shouldn't) do all the time. But when you really need to hear and really need to understand, you had best do active listening.

People who have done this exercise report that there is nothing magical about the approach. It is totally based on concentration, and the more they concentrate the better they get.

It is not easy. We are all so locked into our own private worlds that it difficult to put our own point of view away for a few moments and tentatively adopt another's world. No one can do it immediately. It takes at least 10 to 20 minutes for most of us to begin to see inside the other's world. When we do, though, it seems almost magical. Our brain clicks over and we suddenly start seeing what others perceive and feel. We have an "ah ha" type of experience.

The Art of Persuasion
Problems Influencing People

If you would win a man to your cause, first convince him that you are his sincere friend.
ABRAHAM LINCOLN

IN THIS CHAPTER
• Understanding the art of persuasion
• Developing core belief bridges

Most of us probably accept that it is very difficult to change another person's opinion. No matter what we do, we will usually fail. Most of the time, people don't change what they strongly believe. How many times were you able to change another person's belief to yours in an argument? Could you even imagine a political debate where one candidate said, "You know, John, now that you have explained your reasons, I think you are right and I am wrong, so I'm going to change my opinion to your point of view." Most of us could never imagine such a thing happening.

But in another way, the concept is not true. Although we can't argue someone into believing in our position, at times we are able to persuade others, and we have been able to do this at various times throughout our life.

We may have noticed that some people are more persuasive in their arguments than others. We may have admired their ability to influence others without really understanding how they did it. We may have wondered how their arguments were so potent and produced such dramatic changes. Intuitively, we knew their influence was powerful, yet exactly why? Why do some comments immediately change a person's total out-

look? Why can certain words transform what we feel and lead to a radically different attitudes?

Here are two examples.

BOY ON A BIKE

EXAMPLE

A young boy was riding his bike across a busy street and didn't notice a car in front of him. He ran head first into the car. With his bike a mangled mess, he collapsed unconscious on the street. The other cars on the street pulled off and several people got out to see if they could help. The police and an ambulance were called. The boy turned out to have only a mild concussion, and except for a headache for a few days, he was fine. But at the time, he didn't look fine. Somebody had called his mother who was close by and she came running as fast as she could to the accident. When she saw her son lying unconscious on the street, she started to scream. She screamed as loudly as she could and flailed her arms back and forth, as she kept running toward him. Witnesses had never heard anyone scream so loudly and intensely. She screamed so much that her face turned bright red, and she started to pound the street with her fist. The onlookers started to worry more about the mother than the son because he was beginning to come around.

She kept screaming anyway. So, the onlookers tried to calm her down; they tried to talk to her for several minutes. They said the ambulance had been called, and it looked as if her son wasn't seriously hurt, and she would find it useful to relax her breathing, things like this. But she looked as if she hadn't heard a word they said and kept on screaming.

Just at this time, an auto mechanic from a nearby gas station came running up. He looked at the boy, turned to the mother, and said in a quiet soft voice,

"Your screaming is hurting your son. He needs your help now, not your yelling. Go and comfort him!"

She looked at her son; looked at the mechanic; and then back at her son. All of a sudden, instantaneously, she stopped. She cut off her yelling in mid-scream. She had no residual whimpers or sobs. It was as if she had cut her emotions off with a knife. She then calmly bent down and stroked her son's forehead, whispering to him until the ambulance arrived.

While the boy was not seriously injured, what is striking is the power of the mechanic's statement. He had said exactly the right thing, in exactly the right way, at exactly the right time.

A Little Old Woman

I was watching some well-known people on a talk show discussing the causes of poverty. They were college professors, economists, political scientists, agronomists, sociologist, engineers, and the like. They all had Ph.D.s and were preeminent in their fields. They discussed the causes of poverty in areas like Bangladesh, India, and Ethiopia. The professors disagreed with each other about the causes. The engineer said poverty was a lack of industrialization; the political scientist suggested political conflicts were the culprit; the sociologists discussed class stratification; the economist talked about supply and demand. They all argued about the problem in minute detail. They were well informed, lucid, and certainly seemed to know what they were talking about. The intricacies of their arguments were impressive, but the studio audience had difficulty deciding which of these complex theories were correct.

That evening I saw a public television station presenting a documentary about Mother Teresa. The program didn't interview her; it mostly showed her traveling in the poverty areas of India, Peru, and Lebanon and other countries, helping the poor and sick. One short scene showed her climbing some steps with her fellow sisters into a building in Calcutta. A newspaper reporter kept on shouting questions at her, but she ignored him. Finally, the reporter asked, "Why are there so many poor people in the world?" She kept on walking, but at the top of the stairs she turned around, looked him in the eye, and said, "Because people don't share." She turned around and went into the building.

The documentary didn't dwell on this moment or consider her comment remarkable but quickly moved on to other events in Mother Teresa's life. But her statement was shocking. It first appeared to be a facile thing to say about such a complex problem. However, after her comment has a chance to sink in, and the more we think about it, the more we may realize she was exactly right. Her short sentence cut through all the erudite comments of the professors and captured the core of the matter. It changes our view of poverty immediately and completely. What a powerful thing to say!

Over the years people from diverse backgrounds have shown the ability to persuade: statesmen or used car salesmen, poets or Army sergeants, auto mechanics or tiny old ladies dedicated to helping the poor. Their exceptional skills all have something in common. They all seem to be able to reach inside our brains, find a core principle, and give it a twist.

People who have learned the art of making these types of statements are able to know which core principle to grab, and how to twist it. The mechanic knew. He realized that the mother's major concern was the welfare of her son; she was screaming hysterically because she thought her son was in great danger. The mechanic's statement grabbed the mother's core feelings of loving her son and threw it against her own screaming. When she saw this, when she perceived her crying could be hurting her son, she stopped instantaneously.

Mother Teresa also understood. She knew the world well enough to realize there are enough resources on the planet to feed the poor; but she also knew humanity well enough to recognize that some of us are too selfish. Her comment cut through all our objective rationalizations and grabbed us by our core selfishness to show how we cause other people to be hungry.

 Being able to persuade people is an art, not a science. It's not a matter of learning a few persuasive tricks. It's a matter of us understanding and accepting other people, how they feel, and how they think. It requires focusing on what people deeply believe.

To be truly persuasive we have to give up our old attitudes about how to convince people. We must shift our focus away from trying to win arguments or conquer adversaries, instead we must focus on how to help other human beings see something that they aren't seeing. We must try to guide others to a deeper understanding of their own profound feelings and their own core beliefs. The following exercise can help guide us in the right direction.

Homework

EXERCISE 43.1 How to Persuade

Use Worksheet 43.1, "Persuasive Bridging"

Step 1. Old belief. Pick an old belief or attitude you want to change. It can be another person's belief or one of your own. For example,

Old Belief: "People are no good; they are mean and spiteful."

Step 2. New belief. Make up a new, more useful replacement belief.

New Belief: "People are human beings. They act the way nature planned. Sometimes we like what they do, sometimes we don't."

Step 3. Bridge belief. To help change from the old belief to the new, you need to make a bridge. Using Steps 4 and 5 below, search for a belief that is already accepted by the other person (or by you) that could serve. Create a bridge that has the most personal meaning and that is emotionally powerful.

Step 4. Key components. Find the core components that underlie the beliefs. To do this, look at both the old and new belief. Break down the concepts inside each attitude into their core beliefs. For example, if you analyze the old belief, "People are no good; they are mean and spiteful," you may notice that there are two components—the subject "people" and the core belief that "they are mean and spiteful." The new belief, "People are people. They act the way nature planned. Sometimes we like what they do, sometimes we don't." has the same subject, "people," and it too acknowledges that human behavior can be disappointing, but it interprets that reality as a fact of "nature."

Graphically this relationship can be shown as:

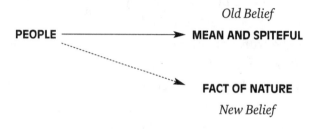

Figure 43.1 Old and new beliefs

Step 5. Find the bridge. To find a bridge between the old and new belief, you need to find a core belief that includes "people," but is connected with "a fact of nature," rather than "mean and spiteful." There are many possibilities, but one appears powerful: babies. Most people like babies, very few of us would consider them "mean and spiteful" for throwing tantrums, wetting their pants, or spitting up food. Most of us would think, "That's silly. They're just doing these things naturally."

To make the bridge work, all we need to point out is that people who yell at us because they have a cold or who withdraw when they are scared, are acting out of much the same motivation as babies—naturally. If we can accept and even like babies, perhaps we can accept such adults as well. "Babies" is the bridge that carries the emotion from one attitude to another.

Expressed in graphic terms it looks like this:

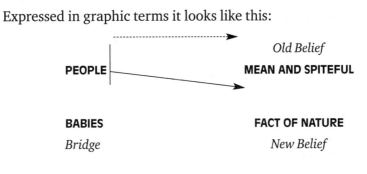

Figure 43.2 Bridges between old and new beliefs

Step 6. Practice. Once the bridge has been made, we have to practice shifting from the old belief to the new (e.g., every time we think of people as mean and spiteful, think of a baby). A good imaging technique is to picture the person you are thinking about as a very large baby in diapers. Practice the image until the new attitude replaces the old.

Look at the two examples on pages 275–276 for further help.

43.1 Persuasive Bridging

WORKSHEET

1. Old Belief: _____

_____

_____

2. New Belief: _____

_____

_____

3. & 4. Subject ⟶ Old Core Belief

⤍ New Core Belief

5. Bridge Belief: _____

_____

_____

_____

_____

A Neighbor

Old Belief

A close neighbor who is a friend of yours tells you she is afraid of riding a ski chairlift. She says, "If I get anxious on the chair I won't be able to escape for 10 minutes, and I could get too scared and embarrass myself."

New Belief

A chairlift is an opportunity to relax, look at the beautiful winter scenery, anticipate the downhill run, and talk with a fellow skier.

Bridge Belief

As a friend you could offer her the following philosophy as a core belief bridge.

> You can look at all the enjoyable, pleasurable, or beautiful things in life in a negative fashion. While you relax on an ocean beach, you could imagine that a tidal wave could engulf you or a great white shark could gobble you up. You could be bitten by a black mamba snake while lying on soft grass next to a gentle country stream. While sailing under a silver moon on a Caribbean lagoon, you could hit a coral reef and drown. A sparrow in an English meadow could suddenly attack you à la Hitchcock. You could break your eardrums while listening to Mozart's Jupiter symphony, or your stereo system could electrocute you. While making love, you could have a heart attack or catch a disease. Even if you watch one of your favorite plays by George Bernard Shaw, the theater could catch on fire. You could also worry about playing with young children because some adult could accuse you of molesting them, or you could choke to death eating a tender, juicy drumstick from your mother's Thanksgiving turkey.
>
> You could try to protect yourself by avoiding all the enjoyable and pleasurable things of life. You could retreat to your house and worry about being trapped in an earthquake or the room catching on fire. But once you throw away the bright and beautiful, what worthwhile aspects of life do you have left to protect?

Your Ten-Year-Old Son

Old Belief

Your son complains to you and says: "You prefer my older brother. You give him everything, and I get what is left over."

New Belief

We love you both, but we treat you differently because you are different people. We celebrate your individuality and wouldn't want you to be a clone of your brother. We give you what we think you need, and we give your brother what we think he needs.

Bridge Belief

Remember those two kittens you took care of when you were young? One was warm, fuzzy, and always wanted to be petted; he loved to cuddle next to you while you slept. The other was frisky and adventuresome; he was always chasing mice, climbing trees, and getting into our potted plants. If the kittens could speak, one could have accused you of giving more freedom to his brother, the other of not giving him enough love. But you loved them both and didn't prefer one to the other. You gave both what they needed. We are treating you the same way.

Some people have the skill to shake us up and start earthquakes inside us. Sometimes, we don't like their comments; we wish they wouldn't bother us so; we prefer them to keep quiet about such things, but we desperately need them to show us what we really believe.

Bridging helps us move from our old beliefs to new-more useful attitudes. It does this by tapping our core beliefs, those already in our repertoire. All the bridge does is to show us what we already know.

 It takes a lot of time and practice to find the right bridge. If we can find it, our old belief will change dramatically. But we don't just make up bridges out of nothing. We need to have a deep understanding of and care for the person we are considering. If we don't care, we won't listen patiently to the person's inner attitudes, core beliefs, and feelings. If we are unwilling to listen (see previous chapter) we won't know where to find the bridge that has the strongest personal meaning, and we won't be able to persuade the person.

chapter 44

All that Glitters Is Not Gold
Problems Being Genuine

The world is governed more by appearances than realities, so that it is fully as necessary to seem to know something as to know it.   DANIEL WEBSTER

IN THIS CHAPTER
- Presenting ourselves to others
- Assessing our genuineness

Almost everyone would deny believing that appearance is more important than essence. Most would reject that how we appear is more important than how we are; and most would decry this as a shameful attitude. Yet, if we look at human beings by what they do rather than what they say they do, this thought would hold an honored place in many peoples' social religions. Must it?

The importance of images in today's world cannot be overemphasized. The more politicians, talk show hosts, TV personalities, actors, professionals, and corporate CEOs we see, the more convinced we become that the present art of living on this planet is to create the correct appearance. Whether there is any substance, any truth behind this appearance seems to be becoming less and less relevant.

HOITY-TOITY

EXAMPLE

In the old days, the people most concerned about image were often the upper classes, particularly in European countries. Nowadays, a part of our society seems to be going back to powdered wig times. More people are spending more of their time and energy trying to create the correct image.

Politicians and CEOs attend special video training sessions to appear more competent when interviewed on television. Some physicians and lawyers start a private practice by first finding an office with the appropriate status that is more impressive than their colleagues' offices. Medical and legal practice can deteriorate into the battle among interior decorators. Some, doctors, lawyers, and businesspeople who own the most expensive pin striped suits, wear designer dresses, or who drive the most expensive cars are often considered the most successful in their fields.

The trouble with all the facade building is that it has a great cost. We can spend all our time and money creating a good impression, or we can spend it solving problems, helping others, learning or creating something new. We really don't have the time to do both. The result of all this image building is that we now have millions of people enhancing their images but reducing their knowledge and their skill. We are producing better appearing people, but possibly at the expense of better skilled ones.

It is a choice for all of us to make.

SHALLOW KIM

EXAMPLE

Kim was a 40-something, balding, Boston lawyer who chose image. In law school he wasn't a very good student. He didn't know the precedents, statutes, or case law, and he just barely passed some of his exams. By flattering his law professors he got special privileges just to keep up with his fellow students. It's not that he was stupid or lazy; it's just that he spent all his time building his image rather than studying law.

When he graduated, he had to take his bar exam many times before he passed. Through finagling, he was able to get a job at a decent law firm. The first thing he did was to get on the right side of the firm's senior partner. He brought the same type of clothes the partner wore—Armani pinstriped suits with Gucci ties. He joined the same country club and learned to play golf so he could play with the senior partner. Instead of reading the appropriate articles for his cases, he looked in the law review to find all the articles the senior partner had written. During their weekly golf game, he would ask flattering questions about the articles.

But worst of all was the way he served his clients in court. He chose law only because he thought he could make a great deal of money; accordingly, he never studied court precedents carefully enough to use them effectively. His clients were getting less and less help, but he always had an explanation as to why the case went badly and how another associate had caused the mess-up. Meanwhile, he spent his time impressing the senior partner at staff meetings until one day he was made a partner himself and given a swank corner office on the top floor. He probably flourishes to this day.

 We all have to make a choice. Are we going to go for image or essence, or some combination of the two? We are free to choose what we wish. But even if we choose to fool others, it is important that we don't fool ourselves. We should know what we are doing, why we are doing it, and accept the consequences of our choice.

If you are not sure what you have chosen, the following exercise is designed to help you find out. It shows you how to analyze how much of a facade you are presenting to others.

Homework

 44.1 Facilitative Genuineness

Step 1. Imagine six typical situations where you present yourself to the public. Pick three where you present yourself formally such as when you are giving a presentation at a conference, speaking to the press—radio/TV—or giving a formal talk at work.

Step 2. Pick three more scenes where you are talking at an informal situation, a gathering after work, speaking at a social club, or at a party with neighbors at home.

Step 3. Visualize each scene separately. Use all your senses until you can imagine and feel that you are actually in the situation, speaking. Picture giving your whole talk.

Step 4. While imagining being there, judge how genuinely and transparently you are behaving. Use the following scales to rate yourself (Rogers, 1961). Which stage would you pick?

> *Stage 1.* What you are presenting to the public is clearly unrelated to what you are feeling or what you believe. There is a considerable disconnect between your inner feeling and what you are expressing either verbally or nonverbally.

Example: You are giving a talk to a group of 20 people at a small conference. The talk has a well-rehearsed quality to it. You demonstrate in the content of what you say, your voice quality, and your mannerisms, that you are trying to appear to be more of an expert, more knowledgeable, or more confident than you really feel you are. Your answers to questions from the audience are defensive and aimed at trying to protect your image.

Stage 2. There are no disconnects between what you say and what you believe, but you make sure you are always socially appropriate and politically correct. You volunteer nothing about your inner feelings or your deeply held values.

Example: You are sitting around your living room with a group of 10 neighbors, most of whom you don't know very well. You are talking about many subjects, current news, and politics, what's going on in the neighborhood. You comment about what you think about the various subjects, but edit out any strong feelings or positions that you think would be controversial. You share nothing personal of yourself.

Stage 3. You openly reveal what you are feeling and thinking. You are spontaneous in your statements and are clearly being yourself by employing your own genuine feelings in your comments. You censor almost nothing and are transparent.

Example: You are in a small conference room at work presenting a project to some administrators in the company. Though you are prepared and have a PowerPoint presentation, you speak freely and non-defensively in your interaction with the group. You mention your positive and negative feelings about the project transparently, and respond to the group's positive and negative comments spontaneously based on what you truly believe and feel.

If you rated yourself close to Stage 1. in the scenes, it means you have chosen, either consciously or unconsciously, to enhance your appearance or image. Scores at Stage 3 mean you are more congruent and transparent in how you present yourself to others.

The majority of people who did the exercise rated themselves somewhere in between. They pointed out, quite correctly, that their behavior varied considerably; depending on who they were talking to and why. We all act differently when talking to the chairman of the board of directors than when we are at home talking to a close friend. But people who were most concerned about their image had a stronger facade and kept it up in both types of situations, while those who acted more genuinely, had an overall weaker facade and were far more likely to drop it in informal situations.

Ultimately, most people discover that spending one's life just to create an image is a mistake. Politicians, media personnel, business executives, professionals, or any of us who spend years on creating the correct facades, are often eventually dissatisfied with what we have created. Images and facades are not substantial. They are illusions, mirages, and shadows that give no real sense of accomplishment, no real feeling of completion inside. Facades are not as reinforcing as the real thing. Few of us can find meaning in life by always playing a game.

chapter **45**

How Tight Is Your String?
Problems with Stress

The cure for boredom is curiosity. There is no cure for curiosity. ELLEN PARR

IN THIS CHAPTER
- Appreciating that stress has a positive and negative side
- Understanding one aspect of depression
- Feeding our curiosity drive

In recent years, we have been flooded with the thought that stress kills! Newspapers, magazine articles, TV documentaries, and many self-help books have been written to help the modern man and woman reduce stress. There are antistress diets, counterstress exercises, relaxation tapes, and vitamin pills to combat stress. Some social scientists work full time for various organizations for the sole purpose of reducing corporate stress.

Stress has been linked to many kinds of maladies: heart disease, cancer, fatal accidents, aging, marital problems, impotence, failure in school, criminal behavior, alcohol and drug addiction, obesity, and depression.

The supposed causes of stress are even more numerous than the supposed effects, ranging from broken homes, working mothers, mothers who aren't working, parents who were too indulgent, parents who were too severe, bad potty training, urban glut, environmental pollution, the ozone layer, junk food, too much TV, poor schools, lack of vitamin E, or global warming. Most problems that humans have had, are having now, or might conceivably have in the future are imagined to be either the cause of stress, or the result. Thus, stress has become the devil of modern times, the new evil spirit that possesses the human race. It underlies many of our present social ills, or so it is said.

The word stress comes from the Latin- "strictus," which means to draw tight, like a bow or a violin string. The root of the word makes sense. When we feel stress, we feel taut like an overtightened string.

Obviously, some people's strings can be drawn too tightly, and it's clear that these people would be a lot happier if they reduced their stress, but therein lies the problem. What's the best way to help people loosen their strings?

Many people have become alarmed because well-meaning physicians, teachers, employers, and talk show hosts have told them, "Watch out! Stress kills! If you don't reduce it, you will have a heart attack, a nervous break-down, or some horrible disease." There is probably no better way to make people anxious then to tell them that stress will kill them. The person will concentrate and pay attention to every little internal twinge which may be a precursor to stress. They will then worry about missing these twinges and obsessively scrutinize them. Wait a little bit and this worry will turn into panic. A few months of this type of treatment and the person will be monu-mentally stressed.

All this may be true, but isn't it also true that chronic stress can be damaging?

Yes, of course. But not having any stress can be equally damaging and can cause depression. Not enough stress means our string is too slack, not a good thing either. As the American Institute of Stress (which is dedicated to reducing stress) states:

> Stress is not always necessarily harmful. Winning a race or election can be just as stressful as losing, or more so, but may trigger very different biological responses. Increased stress results in increased productivity—up to a point. However, this level differs for each of us. It's very much like the stress on a violin string. Not enough produces a dull, raspy sound. Too much tension makes a shrill, annoying noise or snaps the string. However, just the right degree can create a magnificent tone. Similarly, we all need to find the proper level of stress that allows us to perform optimally and make melodious music as we go through life (http://www.stress.org).

 One reason that too little tension may be damaging and cause depression is that we have two conflicting core drives. The first drive is to be safe, secure, and protected. But the second may even be stronger, possibly the most powerful force that motivates us—curiosity. More than anything else, our species seeks the odd, the rare, the exotic, anything novel and peculiar. The real terror for us may not be the lack of safety but the fear of boredom. Boredom is the first step of depression, and we will do anything, anything at all, to keep from being bored. Consider the evidence.

CURIOUS SPECIES

If you leave a baby alone and then place some novel object in the crib, the baby will drop everything and explore it. The baby will grab the object, touch it, smell it, lick it, or suck it until it is totally sensed and absorbed into consciousness. After a while, the baby will feel bored and search for a new object. Many of us spend our lives like infants exploring one curiosity after another. We become desperate if we run out of things to explore.

Our movies, TV, and newspapers exploit our curiosity drive. They present portraits of the aberrant and the weird. A show about ordinary people living their ordinary lives would be so monumentally boring that no one would watch it.

For example, consider cops and robbers shows. Imagine watching a movie about the life of a *real* police officer? The first hour he sits in the station hearing about new department rules; next he directs traffic at Fourth and Main for a couple of hours; then he rescues Mrs. O'Leary's cat out of the tree, again—which takes another hour. He tickets Irving Swartz for not making a full stop at a stop sign. The movie ends with him throwing Melvin in the drunk tank for the third time this month. No one would ever go to see the movie.

Or, imagine a TV series, *The Young Lawyers*, where each week all the lawyers of a large law firm spend most of their time sitting in law libraries reviewing legal precedents or preparing business contracts. The series builds to a climax at the season finale, when somebody actually shows up in a courtroom—one of the lawyers attends a hearing to get Irving Swartz out of his traffic ticket! Such a show would be remarkable only because it would pull in the lowest Nielsen ratings in the history of television.

Newspapers try to tickle our curiosity drive. They parade in front of us every zealot, fanatic, or strange person that reporters have been able to dig up. Extraordinary, offbeat happenings are most likely to appear in print— "News" means "new."

One of the unfortunate side effects of this phenomenon is that people who don't live in a community get a much-distorted view of what the place is like. For example, some Australians think that most Americans are walking around their cities dodging bullets, suing their mothers, and sleeping with everybody they brush against. After all, that's what they've seen on TV. Similarly, many Americans believe that Australians spend all their time wrestling crocodile, eating witchetty grubs on a bush walk in the outback, and fondling Koalas, for so they have seen in the movies.

The truth is that many Americans, Australians, and almost everybody else for that matter, do much the same thing every day. They get up, go to work, come home and eat dinner, watch some television, and then go to bed. For some of us, that's about it, life on the blue planet. With such monotony, it's easy to understand why many rely on movies, television, and newspapers to take them to the extraordinary.

Trying to meet our curiosity drive by watching TV will not nourish us. We need the real thing, not vicarious adventures or counterfeit excitement. It is crucial for all of us, that no matter what else we do in life, we keep feeding our curiosity drive. It is OK to strive for safety, tranquility, and peace of mind. But we will never really be happy with these alone. To be truly content, our species must keep growing, keep learning, and keep expanding our horizons. When we find ourselves overwhelmed with the boredom of life, it is time we took some risks. If we ever stop being curious, we stop living.

The following short quiz may give you a quick idea of how close to the vest you have been playing life.

Homework

EXERCISE 45.1 Have You Been Feeding Your Curiosity Drive?

In the last month, have you . . .	Yes	No
Read a book on subject you knew little about?		
Been to a place you've never been before?		
Tried a new ethnic food or a new restaurant?		
Been positively excited by something?		
Driven home from work by taking a new route?		

Talked to some people you hadn't met before?

Listened to a point of view different from your own?

Engaged in a physical activity, exercise, or sport you hadn't tried before?

Made love in a new room of the house, at a new time, or in a different way?

Done something just for the fun of it?

Tried something where you had less than a 50% chance of succeeding?

If you didn't say "yes" to any of these items, you may wish to create more challenges and take some more risks. Most importantly, consider either tightening up or loosening your strings a bit more to play music that is more melodic.

It Takes Two to Tango
Problems in the Family

If you cannot get rid of the family skeleton, you may as well make it dance.
GEORGE BERNARD SHAW

IN THIS CHAPTER
• Understanding the dynamics of families
• Learning how to improve the dance

A family is far more complex than some of us may think. To accurately understand the dynamics of our families, we need to take a close look of how family members relate to each other. The following story may be instructive.

THE DANCING CRANES

EXAMPLE An elderly couple who had been married for 35 years were referred to a family counselor by their grown children. They had been having these huge arguments so loud and noisy that the police had been called several times. They never physically attacked each other; the fighting was all verbal, but verbal at an ear-splitting level. They had been arguing this way for years and years, but they never thought of getting a divorce. They just stayed together and fought. Finally, their children forced them into therapy because of all the years of arguing, and they very reluctantly agreed to see a family counselor.

During the first counseling session, the couple didn't behave as expected. They were nice, polite, and friendly; they even seemed to like each other. They acted quite differently from their children's description. The counselor smelled a rat and suspected they were faking. She was right. They had decided they would put on their Sunday best, probably just to keep an outsider from pushing her nose into the family's business. But the counselor had to get to the roots of the problem, so she asked them to argue in front of her just so she could see why the children were so upset. They didn't do it immediately, but she kept stirring them up until she got them to fight. It worked.

Once they got into it, the fight was loud and noisy. They punctuated their attacks with wild gestures and absurd exaggerations. For instance, she said things like, "You constipated old man. You are a worthless, wrinkled up prune. I could have done better in a zoo."

And he would say, "You fat old cow. I've had to put up with your bitching, griping and whimpering for 30 years. Nothing works in your body anymore except your tongue."

They talked that way. Certainly, they were not candidates for "couple of the year." But despite it all, their attacks seemed to lack the vile hatred heard from some other couples. True, they used the right words, but they lacked the tune. All the while they were shouting nasty things, they seemed to show a kind of caring for each other—a freakish type of love. Whenever they were interrupted by the counselor and instructed to calm down, they vehemently objected to her interference and came up with some new more creative invectives.

Watching them argue, reminded one of a National Geographic special which showed these African cranes going through this elaborate, 12-hour ritual tangolike dance before they mated. These birds would peck at each other; flourish their tail feathers; bob their necks up and down; make mock attacking strides; prance and strut and screech. They made a terrible fracas all with the most ostentatious posturing and swaggering.

One could imagine this couple flaunting their plumes and tail feathers jumping up and down, and cawing. But they had not been doing the tango for just 12 hours; they had been doing it for over 30 years.

The image of the cranes captured the essence of their fighting. They were dancing a tango and didn't want to stop. Despite their children's objections, they wanted to continue, and they did. After the tango was explained to the family, the children learned to accept their dance.

Everyone Is Doing the Tango

EXAMPLE

We can see the tango most easily with young couples in love. He yells at her. She pretends to be hurt and cries. He tries to comfort her, but she walks away in a huff. He sulks. Then after a brief time, he runs after her asking for forgiveness. She refuses initially until he reiterates his undying love, and they end up in an embrace.

Men and women have many types of dances. The jealousy rumba—she feels ignored by him at a party, so she flirts with another man. He gets jealous, pulls her away from the party, and drags her home. They make up in bed.

Or there is always the sex versus marriage cha-cha. He hints at commitment to get sex; she hints at sex to get commitment.

Families do a folk dance in which everybody does a slightly different step, but all steps are synchronized with each other. Father plays the heavy, and does a meringue like—"Why are kids so irresponsible today. When I was a kid I didn't have a car until I was 25." Mom counters with a Virginia reel, "Leave the kids alone, all their friends are allowed to use the car, so why can't they." The son does a jive step, "I'm old enough to own my own car." And daughter tries a salsa by dancing into her bedroom crying, "Nobody understands me around here."

One of the most intricate dances is the alcoholic waltz. The whole family plays. Dad leads off by drinking each night. He loses four jobs in a year, gets picked up for three DUIs, and ends up in a detox unit. The rest of the family responds with carefully choreographed countersteps. Mom cleans up Dad's messes, keeps bailing him out of jail, and calls his boss saying he is sick again. Daughter blames Mom for being a rotten wife and applies for the job herself. The son feels ignored and tries to get attention by going out and scoring a line of cocaine, blaming both Mom and Dad for being such rotten parents. Even though the dance is destructive, it's hard to break up.

People can't stop doing the tango. They wouldn't even if they could. One reason there are other people on this earth is to give us someone to tango with. How else would we fill in our time as we wander around the planet? It's no fun to tango alone.

The following exercise will help you discern what type of tango you and the other people around you have been doing.

Homework

EXERCISE

46.1 Let's Dance

Use Worksheet 46.1, "My Family Dance"

Step 1. Discover your family tango and learn the steps people around you are doing. First, identify the people in your dancing troupe (spouse, kids, mom, dad, in-laws, aunts, uncles, cousins, or even people who aren't even alive if they still influence the family's steps (grandparents, famous ancestors, infamous relatives).

Step 2. Consider each member of your troupe and how they have danced with you. Who took the first step? What was the initial counterstep? The following steps? À la Arthur Murray imagine all the footsteps drawn on the floor that show everybody's part in the dance. Try to hear what music is playing in the background—cha-cha, hip-hop, tango, rap, minuet, waltz, rock and roll, Virginia reel, etc

Step 3. Do the members keep doing the same dance, or do they change steps at times and dance to a different rhythm?

Step 4. If you are unhappy with the family dance, before you consider changing partners, you can try to learn some new steps and teach them to your dance troupe. Simple steps are best in the beginning; then you can get more complex. Promise everyone that they will be far happier, more confident, and the life of the party if they learn this new dance. They may not like the old dance with the same old steps, so it's not impossible.

Step 5. If you can't teach your troupe the new steps, you can always change your response to the old leads. This will break up the old pattern because it takes two to tango.

SLOW Remember, however, your troupe may hate you for changing the steps. They will feel uncomfortable in the beginning as with learning any new dance, but if you all practice hard, the new steps will become as familiar as the old. And if the steps are stylish, the dance will be a lot more fun, and you won't get your foot stepped on so often.

46.1 My Family Dance

1. Members of my family:

_____   _____   _____

_____   _____   _____

_____   _____   _____

2. & 3. How do they dance with me? (Who took the first step? Countersteps? What is the dance and music?). Visualize the footprints on the floor.

_____

_____

_____

_____

_____

_____

_____

_____

_____

_____

_____

4. & 5. If you are unhappy with the dance, what steps or countersteps would you like to change?

_____

_____

_____

_____

 We can look at all relationships as a tango. Everybody is doing the tango with everybody else. Sometimes the tango is pleasant, sometimes not. But if we look closely, we can hear the music and follow the steps.

chapter 47

A New View of Love
Problems with Our Intimate Relationships

(At Eve's grave) *Adam: Wheresoever she was,* there *was Eden.*   MARK TWAIN

IN THIS CHAPTER
- Examining the concept of love
- Discovering what we love about our lover

Talk show hosts and TV pundits like to expose government corruption. They enjoy having their audiences express anger and disgust after discovering that the government spent $650 for a toilet seat or $10 for a pencil. One show in particular stands out. The announcer was all excited because he had uncovered a story that the government had spent $500,000 to study love. "Can you imagine that," the announcer said, "All that money just to study what we all know about anyway. Some things should be left unstudied."

Most of the time we the public don't have any direct knowledge of what pundits tell us so we assume that what they say is true. But in this case, many people were familiar with the study. It was the most massive, objective research analysis on love and romance that had yet been undertaken. Many people knew that the study was important and eagerly waited for the results, and because they knew about it, they also knew that the announcer was wrong. It wasn't a frivolous misuse of taxpayer's money; it was a crucial and important study that would have wide ramifications for our society (Fisher, 2004). Just because the pundit didn't know anything about the research, didn't mean that the study was useless.

The study of love is important and the subject of love is so crucial because there is probably no more consequential matter for peoples' emotional health. A large number of murders, suicides, and acts of violence can be ultimately traced to love problems. A gunman in Killeen, Texas killed 22 people and wounded at least 19 more in a shooting rampage inside a restaurant; he was a jilted lover, recently divorced. Love or the lack of it is the crucial factor behind most of the suicide attempts of young men and women and of the elderly. Many people enter therapy complaining of phobias, depression, or feelings of inferiority. But when you dig beneath these symptoms, you find many of them are suffering from a lack of companionship. And for those people who later find a good relationship, it is amazing how quickly many of their psychological problems disappear.

So, love is crucial to both the mental health of an individual and to the emotional health of a society. What is surprising is that such an important topic had not been thoroughly studied before. Scientists were reluctant to do so in part because of the reaction of the media. But they are now beginning to study the process, and they are discovering some interesting facts.

Two Kinds of Love

Not the least interesting, is that there are two kinds of love. The feelings we have in each are quite a bit different. We call the first kind romantic or passionate love. It's what we think of when we picture love. It is hormonally influenced and what most movies celebrate. In romantic love, we obsess about our lover; we can't concentrate on anything else; we can't tolerate being separated from them. Our passion and sexual feelings dominate our consciousness. We picture our lover as perfect. We see no faults, only a few cute little idiosyncrasies such as the masculine way he puts his fists through the wall when he gets angry, or the cute little feminine way she complains for hours about his clothes. This type of love thrives on insecurity, not knowing our lover very well, and not being sure he or she loves us.

Now, there is one overwhelming fact about romantic love: it almost never lasts. Nine months is usually the limit. Lack of familiarity feeds it. The better we know our lover, the less likely we are to have overpowering romantic feelings. The reason is simple: Romantic love is an illusion. We are not in love with a real person; we love our hormonal fantasy of them. Years of living together usually remove many of our hormone-induced illusions and thus destroy much passion. Of course, a few couples manage to sustain romance for years, but only with special help—such as the relationship ended before the romantic stage was completed—one partner left, or died, or fell in love with someone else. If couples don't finish the romantic stage, they may hold on to their passion for the rest of their lives.

For many of us that's all love means, the romantic kind. We become very disillusioned after the nine months and our feelings fade. We think something went wrong. As a result, we may conclude that we have picked the wrong partner, so we go trudging off looking for someone more suitable, someone with whom we may keep this romantic feeling permanently. We often find someone else; fall in romantic love again; but in nine months this too burns out and then we go off again looking for another. On and on we search. Some of us can go through five or more of these relationships still looking for permanent love. We never discover what is wrong. We keep concluding that we picked the wrong partner. We never guess that we were searching for the wrong type of love.

The second stage of love is rarely written about. It's undramatic, not very emotional and, therefore, is often ignored. It's called companionable love. Even the term doesn't sound exciting. It doesn't stir up the passions or produce the emotional mountains and valleys of the romantic stage. It feels like a quiet, soft contentment. It's peaceful and calm rather than heated and inflamed. As opposed to romance that dominates our life so that we can think of little else, most people who have companionable love don't even know they have it. If someone asked, "Do you love him," the answer may be, "Yes, of course, but I really just kind of like being around him."

We become aware of companionable love only when it's gone. If our lover leaves on a trip for a few weeks, we begin to notice a rather empty feeling gatering over us. While this loneliness builds gradually, it builds to an overwhelming power. We may develop all kinds of neurotic symptoms during this time without a clue as to the cause. At the peak of our loss, the grief of missing our companion seems far more shattering than the loss of a romantic lover. Loss of a romantic partner is a searing, piercing kind of pain, but loss of a companion is like an earthquake. The whole ground of our being feels as if it has been taken away from us.

Although companionable love is less celebrated, it is deeper. Romantic love lasts several months, but companionable love can last a lifetime. Romance builds passion, but companionship builds families and shared lives.

The simple fact that there are two kinds of love should be taught in all secondary schools, it would save many people much pain. Psychologists can't count the number of clients who ruined their lives because they mistook one for the other. We have observed a parade of middle-aged men in their midlife crises who threw away companionable love for a chance at the romantic. They left their wives and families for their 22-year-old secretary's body. They thought their romantic passion for their secretary was more important than their companionable love for their wife.

We tell such men that they can have romantic feelings toward a multitude of women, but companionable love for only one person at a time. But such men rarely listen. Instead they come back a year or so later, after the fire for the secretary has burned out. They want their wife back, but usually it is too late. The well is poisoned; there has been too much pain, and the wife is ready to move on to other things. Only at this point do the men finally realize the monumental nature of their mistake.

I say men because males have a predilection for making this kind of error. Women can make it too, but usually only when they are young and inexperienced in love. Men may make this mistake all their lives, and may be untrainable in this regard. Many men seem to have no clue that there are two kinds of love. Women appear smarter about the whole thing or at least wiser. I have found women are experts about relationships, while men are experts about objects and confuse the two types of love.

Another Look at Love

Many people complain that their love relationships are bungled and botched. Most grumble about their partners. Married women lament that their husbands don't listen. Husbands say their wives are boring. Even single people complain that they can't find Mr. Right or that all the good women are taken. So it doesn't matter who they are, almost everybody gripes about their intimate relationships.

After hearing many people complain, we may well wonder if any relationships work at all. It seemed surprising that anybody stays together anymore. Why don't most people just disregard the whole thing and go through life alone? But few of us do. Most of us get involved and stay involved with someone despite all the problems, annoyances, and frustrations. Some people will cling to horrible marriages just so they won't be alone. And almost all of us go through intense grieving when even these terrible relationships finally end.

What is it about our love intimacies that keep us all throwing ourselves back into them even after we've been hurt repeatedly? Many psychological theories don't answer the question usefully. Love has been described as: (1) sexual reinforcement conditioned to a love object; (2) egocentric feelings of emotional gratification; (3) transference of childlike attachments for our parents displaced onto our lovers; (4) just the secretion of enzymes and hormones in postpubescent organisms; (5) only a biological instinct for reproduction.

These explanations are not helpful; certainly, they are not romantic. They all seem grossly incomplete and appear to miss the mark. Love is one of the most powerful emotions we can have. We will give up other things, self-respect, wealth, or even life itself just for the opportunity to be loved. Surely there is something more to love than these intellectual theories.

To find out what may underlie your intimate relationship, do the following exercise first and then compare your answers to others.

Homework

EXERCISE

47.1 I Love . . . ?

Step 1. Take a few moments and think of exactly what you love about your spouse or sweetheart. If you do not have a partner at the moment, ask yourself, "What do I think I would love about a future partner?"

_____

_____

_____

_____

_____

Step 2. When you finish thinking about your partner, look at the example, and see what other people said they loved.

Taking Out Your Mental Trash

WHAT LOVERS PICKED

EXAMPLE
Many of us would expect the people who did this exercise to pick the same kinds of traits. We would think they would pick those socially approved, Hollywood advertised reasons for loving a man or a woman, "He is so big, tall, strong, and handsome," or "She is so sexy, pretty, soft, thin, and kind." But such answers were rare. Only adolescents said these things; most other people rarely mention them.

Instead, mature people listed different features that often didn't go along with the Hollywood stereotype of what an ideal man or ideal woman should be. They would pick some facet of their lover and say they loved him or her for this or that trait. But the features they picked often contradicted each other. One woman said she loved her husband because he was slender, while another loved hers because he was stocky. One man said his wife's gentleness and kindness attracted him while another delighted in his wife's energy and assertiveness.

It seemed clear these people didn't love just the traits; they loved something else. They seemed to pick traits arbitrarily just to answer the question. They loved first, and searched for the reason for their love, second. So, if it is not the traits we love, what is it?

A possible answer is that we may love the gender. We may love the contrast between the way males and females see the world. Many women perceive the world in terms of relationships among things, not only between men and women but also between parent and child, the environment and humanity, animals and people. Life to many women is the relationship among creatures. To many the universe is a story of creation, living beings, love, bonding, caring, and nurturing. They celebrate life and growth.

Many Western men at least don't see the world in this way. Males often perceive the universe as a realm of objects. The cosmos is like a gigantic machine, an eternal clock made up of billions of parts that all clink together in some kind of order. Men's purpose in life seems to be to understand how the parts fit together and when necessary to try to repair the clock.

To many men the world is an understandable place, but it lacks spirit and warmth. When a man is alone without love, he wanders through life tinkering with the cold lifeless clock. But when he is loved, he is able to see, at least in part, through a woman's eyes. He gets an inkling of another aspect of the universe. Being with his woman makes the world alive for him. She helps him perceive the billions of relationships going on throughout the universe. So, at least for a time, his cosmic mechanical clock disappears and is replaced with a world brimming with emotions, interrelationships, and feelings. Men need women to see this aspect of the cosmos for few men can see it alone. Women provide men with the eyes to see.

And women, what do they receive from men? They may learn the male perspective. Loving a man may enable them to see something of the masculine view of life. Together both the male and female perspectives merge to form a more complete picture.

Maybe the most eloquent commentary about what each gender gains from the other, comes from the book, *The Diaries of Adam and Eve* by Mark Twain. He wrote this soon after the death of his beloved wife, Livy.

In the book, Eve reminisces about why she loves Adam. This soliloquy occurs near the end of their life together after they have lost Paradise. She says:

Eve's Soliloquy

EXAMPLE

When I look back, the Garden is a dream to me. It was beautiful, surpassingly beautiful, and enchantingly beautiful; and now it is lost, and I shall not see it any more.

The Garden is lost, but I have found him, and am content. He loves me as well as he can; I love him with all the strength of my passionate nature, and this, I think, is proper to my youth and sex. If I ask myself why I love him, I find I do not know, and do not really much care to know; so, I suppose that this kind of love is not a product of reasoning and statistics. . . .

It is not on account of his brightness that I love him—no, it is not that. He is not to blame for his brightness, such as it is, for he did not make it himself; he is as God made him, and that is sufficient . . . .

It is not on account of his gracious and considerate ways and his delicacy that I love him. No, he has lacks in these regards, but he is well enough just so, and is improving.

It is not on account of his industry that I love him—no, it is not that. I think he has it in him, and I do not know why he conceals it from me. . . .

It is not on account of his chivalry that I love him—no, it is not that. He told on me, but I do not blame him; it is a peculiarity of sex, I think, and he did not make his sex. . . .

He is strong and handsome, and I love him for that, and I admire him and am proud of him, but I could love him without those qualities. If he were plain, I should love him; if he were a wreck, I should love him; and I would work for him, and slave over him, and pray for him, and watch by his bedside until I died.

Yes, I think I love him merely because he is mine and is masculine. There is no other reason, I suppose. And so I think it is as I first said: that this kind of love is not a product of reasoning and statistics. It just comes—none knows whence—and cannot explain itself. And doesn't need to (Twain, 1996/1906, pp. 95–103).

 We may not just be in love with the other person, but more especially, we may be in love with the other gender. A woman loves a man's masculinity; a man loves a woman's femininity. Masculinity and femininity come in many shades, varieties, and nuances, so we can love many different traits. They all represent maleness or femaleness.

We may pick our partners not because they are our one true love and better than everyone else. We may pick one person because she or he opens the best doorway to make known the other gender. Loving one woman opens the door for a man to experience the feminine wisdom of life. Loving one man gives the woman access to experience masculinity itself.

 I believe Mark Twain is right. Traits of the other sex such as beauty, strength, intelligence, or whatever are irrelevant. What counts is our ability to experience the essence of the other gender. Through our lover, we complete our picture of the universe.

chapter **48**

Sanctuary
There's No Place Like Home

Not merely an absence of noise, real silence begins when a reasonable being withdraws from the noise in order to find peace and order in his inner sanctuary.
PETER MINARD

IN THIS CHAPTER
• Finding a safe mental home

Too often, we live in the middle of a heap of mental trash we have collected over the years, and we become very weary of all the clutter and confusion around us. Sometimes we need to clear a silent space for ourselves where we can sit still and feel protected, a place of refuge, a sanctuary. We need a respite from the hazards of the world. Some of us try to physically remove ourselves by taking vacations and going on holidays, but as many of us have learned, a holiday, with all its itineraries, timetables and unexpected turns, may become more harrowing then staying at home. Some of us listen to relaxation tapes, our favorite music, or the sound of nature while imagining lying on a tropical beach or resting in a mountain meadow. These aids can be helpful, but they are made commercially by others and are not our own. The most powerful sanctuaries are usually those we create for ourselves from our own deep-rooted memories of an earlier time.

CHILDHOOD HOMES

EXAMPLE

Those of us who had happy childhoods often use the memory of our childhood home as our sanctuary. The first house we lived in may forever be our definition of what a home should be. A man who grew up in a three-story house made of stone never feels quite comfortable in brick houses or ranch-style wood structures. Many people search desperately in Wyoming for colonial style houses or look for adobe haciendas in Maine. Some Australians quietly yearn for a house like one near the Murray River, as one of their folk songs describes:

> Give me a home among the gum trees,
> With lots of plum trees,
> A sheep or two or a kangaroo,
> A clothesline out the back
> Verandah out the front,
> And an old, rocking chair.

If they are searching outside Australia, their hope is forlorn. But for them and for some of the rest of us, our first sanctuary is our first house, the only real house, and everything else we consider inferior substitutes.

The family we grew up in can also be our sanctuary. Our idea of family is often a snapshot of the way our family looked. The true definition of a man is often our father, the definition of a woman, our mother. A real marriage is what they had with each other, even if it was bad.

We tuck these family memories away in a secret place in our brain where we feel relaxed and calm, safe and secure, immune from present day troubles. We honor these early experiences as sacred heirlooms of our most innocent encounters with life. Even though we have long since grown up, we carry this little part of childhood inside us and return to the sanctuary of our memories of early family life during times of worry and strife.

Those of us who had unhappy childhoods find a different sanctuary. Often we pick that childhood place we used as a retreat when the troubles at home became overwhelming. A man who grew up in Pennsylvania fantasized his place of refuge. He pictured himself leaning against a big apple tree which overhung a babbling brook meandering through a clearing in a forest. The forest was thick with ferns, and the grass was heavy and soft. There were sunflowers and dandelions covering the clearing; scores of robins were flying from tree to tree, and gray-brown squirrels were scampering up branches carrying acorns.

A man from northern Florida imagined a swamp, with willow trees overloaded with moss. The swamp was steamy and moist, and he heard the sound of alligators in the background. Another man from Kansas pictured a prairie pond surrounded by rushes and the sound of loons. A woman from Oregon imagined lying on a thick mat of pine needles in the twilight sun of an evergreen forest. A Pacific Islander visualized floating in a lava pool, looking at hundreds of multicolored fish swimming in and out of the coral. An Australian pictured a billabong while hearing the cry of kookaburras and cockatoos.

These sanctuaries came from where they grew up. As a child, the man from Pennsylvania loved to play in the woods whenever he needed a respite from the ordeal of growing up. The woods are long since gone, a huge housing development covers them. But it still exists in his mind as a special place. As an adult he has visited many places that were objectively more beautiful, but they never produced the same feelings, the same sense of serenity as his woods.

 And so it is with all of us. Our mental sanctuaries come from those places where we have experienced the peacefulness of life, our earliest feelings of calmness, serenity, and respite from the awareness that we live in a trouble-sewn world. We value these early sanctuaries more than our later places. Search as we might and imagine as many different places as we will, we never feel quite as comfortable, quite as peaceful as when we mentally return to our early places of refuge.

Sanctuaries can be many things other than physical places. We all seem to have a variety of experiences and memories that form the core mental base that we use as a standard in later life. These shelters appear across many different spheres.

SAFE PLACES

One such base is our first mentor, the first teacher who cared for us and taught us some meaningful principle of life. We may have learned from many other teachers since then, but we give a hallowed place in our psyche to our first. We remember them as unique people.

Our first beliefs are also important—Santa Claus, the Easter Bunny, the Tooth Fairy, all make us feel warm inside. Our first religious belief seems like the only true religion. We may have long since become agnostic or rejected the old theology, but in times of confusion, we feel drawn back to our earliest faith.

Another example of a sanctuary from our early experiences is our pride in our first achievement or accomplishment. The time we won the blue ribbon for the three-legged-race or scored the winning basket will take precedence over later and greater accomplishments.

Taking Out Your Mental Trash

The first time we traveled to a distant culture will make this culture and these people forever special. One man remembered his first trip to South America, when he flew from Miami to Lima, Peru. The flight seemed to take forever, but when he arrived and walked around the Plaza de Armas, he was enchanted by the people with multicolored costumes and the buildings dating back to the conquistadors. Since that time, whenever he sees pictures of Lima or reads an article about Peru, he feel strangely invigorated.

We often consider a substantial job as the first one that gave us solid satisfaction, and we may view other endeavors, even those that are far more profitable, as little more than lucrative hobbies. Of course, our definition of true love is often our earliest romance, even though it may have been short-lived or (objectively) a poor match. We hold it in a special place in our memory, which later, more important relationships rarely assail.

These early sanctuaries take on such importance because they are fresh and new. We enter them with few frameworks to guide us, so our initial encounter becomes our first look, the model by which we judge all that comes later. When our early experiences are positive they give us a gentle reference point, a soft reminder of home. We have a sanctuary from which to accept our own fallibility and gently view the world.

It is often useful to remember your sanctuary in very specific ways so that you can go to it when you need to. The following focusing exercise (based on Gendlin, 1996) may help you. If you don't want to be disturbed by reading the steps, you can speak the instructions on a tape recorder and then listen.

Homework

 EXERCISE **48.1 Find Your Sanctuary**

Step 1. Go to a darkened room where you won't be disturbed and lie down. Relax briefly to ease any tautness in your muscles. Close your eyes if you wish. Try to clear your mind and focus inward.

Step 2. Look inside yourself for the place where you feel things, where you feel happy, sad, scared, or relaxed. Look inside this place right now and try to find the feeling of tranquility. Find the spot of calmness and safety that you have felt at some time in your life. Even if it has been a rare feeling and you don't have it right now, try to find the feeling in your memory. Allow all the chatter your brain is throwing at you to fade into the background. This is like looking through a dark cloud trying to find a pinpoint of soft light in the distance.

Step 3. You can't make the spot of calmness appear; you have to wait until it emerges. Keep focusing on that spot of still tranquility until you can feel the memory of it. Take all the time you need until you feel it, even if it's just a tiny speck of calmness. Once you notice something, keep focusing on it.

Step 4. Let yourself experience the calm spot, but let it enlarge and expand until it becomes an overall feeling. Be silent with yourself and let the calm feeling cover and envelop you. Do this silently for at least one minute.

Step 5. Keep focusing on the overall feeling silently, but this time notice different aspects of it—the quietness, the feeling of being protected, the feeling of immunity, the shelter from the storms and lightening of the outside world. Keep focusing on these aspects until they become clear in your mind.

Step 6. Keep focusing on the feeling, but this time notice what's around you. Where are you now? What place are you in? Allow this place to emerge and become distinct. Is it a place you used to go as a child? Is it a mental rather than physical home?

This is your sanctuary.

 If you didn't find your sanctuary this time, don't worry. Sometimes the honks, screeches, and roars of everyday life shield us from feeling the calm spot. Try later when you feel more relaxed. You will find it.

Or sometimes our safe places don't feel quite so safe as they once did. If you are one of these people, don't worry. It simply means that your old sanctuary had some negative feeling associated with it. Get some help from an empathetic ear if you need to; he or she can help you create a *new* sanctuary.

We all need a place to rest, a moment of peace, and an escape from which to look out on the world. We all need a sanctuary.

Take rest; a field that has rested gives a bountiful crop. (Ovid)

appendix **A**

About the Author

As a psychologist, I have spent my professional career doing therapy full-time with clients. This is a bit unusual for authors of psychology books because many writers are professors at universities who see clients on a part-time basis only. Although I have been associated with various institutions, I have maintained a full clinical practice and worked as a clinician in a variety of settings. After receiving my Ph.D. and becoming a licensed psychologist, I did therapy as assistant director of a college-counseling center in Pennsylvania. I was then a senior clinical psychologist for a large urban mental health center in Colorado. It was here that a colleague, Bill Casey, and I created our brand of Cognitive Restructuring Therapy—a type of psychotherapy that is used in mental health centers, hospitals, and counseling agencies throughout the world.

I founded and directed the Counseling Research Institute in Denver, Colorado for 10 years, a company engaged in basic research to discover new treatment methods for people not helped by other approaches. I now run the same institute in Hawaii. I was deputy chief psychologist for a large urban hospital in Sydney, Australia. I was part of the department of psychology at a state psychiatric hospital for 10 years, and have had private counseling practices in Colorado, Australia, Washington State, and Hawaii.

The thousands of people I have counseled over three decades have come from all economic levels, from all age groups, and have ranged from growth clients to those with more severe difficulties. They presented problems such as adjustment reactions, relationship difficulties, phobias, anxieties, depression, panic reactions, obsessions, posttraumatic stress disorder, drug and alcohol dependence, severe chronic psychotic symptoms, and many others.

As one of the originators of Cognitive Restructuring Therapy, I have published 10 books on CRT, four of which are listed in this book's references.

I have also presented at many conferences and conducted hundreds of workshops, seminars, and symposia on counseling and psychotherapy for undergraduate and graduate students, professional therapists at universities, hospitals, government agencies, schools, mental health centers, and private treatment agencies in several countries. I have supervised hundreds of therapists, including psychologists, psychiatrists, social workers, school psychologists, psychiatric nurses, and students from the mental health professions.

At present, I practice clinical psychology in Hawaii. I counsel clients, consult with area mental health agencies, supervise other mental health professionals, and continue my research and writing.

To the Professional Therapist

Why I Wrote a Consumer's Guide

This is the client's guide to accompany my book for professionals, *The New Handbook of Cognitive Therapy Techniques* (2000), as well as my other professional works.

I wrote it for two reasons.

First, there is no present consumer's guide or client manual for Cognitive Restructuring Therapy (CRT). The *New Handbook* cannot be used as one because it is written for therapists and most definitely not for the layperson. It includes technical language, academic citations, instructions to therapists, sequelae of certain treatment interventions, and refers to the substantial body of knowledge and therapeutic experiences possessed only by professionals. However, it is clear that a client guide is needed, and in actual practice, CRT clients are always given extensive homework materials so that they can achieve maximum benefit from their individual or group sessions. The active therapeutic element of CRT is experiential, not didactic. Clients benefit by performing the exercises, not by listening to the therapist. I discovered many years ago that the average client understands and remembers less than 30% of what the therapist says in a counseling session. But, when a client is given an accompanying guide or manual, which reviews the key points of a session and repeats the exercises in a step-by-step fashion, the client's understanding and retention increases to over 70%. In the past we would simply type up some materials for our clients and hand them out after sessions. However, this was an informal process subject to many gaps and omissions. The present book corrects these gaps. It has 48 separate chapters that cover the key areas of CRT. Each chapter discusses a concept in informal, nonacademic language, avoiding extensive footnotes and keeping APA citations to an absolute minimum. Important points in chapters are highlighted with icons, concepts are explained with personal examples and picture-forming stories, and the exercises are presented in a systematic fashion using accompanying worksheets and examples.

The second reason I wrote this book is that it may also be helpful to therapists new to CRT. My books for professionals have both an advantage and a disadvantage. They are very comprehensive, explaining more than 300 distinct therapeutic interventions. Many of them are delineated for specific DSM diagnoses or specialized populations; some are advanced procedures that should be used only by a trained therapist and only after a client has successfully completed exercises that are more basic. Based on some correspondence and a few reviews of my books, I concluded that professionals inexperienced in CRT are not sure which interventions they should try first, with which exercises, and in what order. This guide should help clear up any confusion. It presents only 48 out of 300+ techniques (less than 16%) discussed in my professional works; however, they are the basic techniques and the key exercises that are used with almost all CRT clients. Most importantly, the techniques are presented in the exact order that we offer them to our clients, with the accompanying descriptions, examples, homework exercises, and worksheets. Therefore, even if you are an experienced cognitive therapist, you may find it helpful to peruse the guide to get a clearer understanding of how CRT therapists actually conduct their sessions.

Typical Therapeutic Hour

Usually a CRT counseling session consists of discussing the client's week (20%), reviewing homework (20%), presenting the session's content (50%), and preparing next week's homework assignment (10%). Of course, these are just averages. Therapy is not done by numbers, and client concerns and crises are handled as they appear. Nevertheless, the underlying structure is always kept in mind. Experience has taught me that if you keep jumping around indiscriminately from one topic to another, the effectiveness of therapy rapidly decreases. This consumer's guide should significantly help to keep therapy on track.

Similarities and Differences

I tried to make this book parallel to the *Handbooks* wherever possible. I rewrote and simplified my writing for the layperson and endeavored to use the same or similar stories, examples, descriptions, and exercises so that both you and your client are familiar with the same material. However, there are some important differences between this guide and my professional *Handbooks*. First, I picked the concepts, stories, and exercises that I thought were most compelling and most powerful, even if they were not in the *Handbooks*. Some I took from my earlier professional writings, or I wrote them for this book (60% of the exercises in this guide are new). Second, I also include new chapters that are not in the *Handbooks*. The reason for this is that the guide is aimed at the lay public and I needed to describe in far greater detail certain principles and techniques that are second nature to practicing therapists. For instance, therapists can distinguish the difference between environmental events (stimuli, S^ds, external triggers) and cognitive (schemas, beliefs, attitudes, values, perceptions) or emotional (activation of sympathetic or parasympathetic systems) events, but many clients can not do so. And almost all clients have difficulty finding the core beliefs that are tied to their problems, even when they are obvious to their therapist or to others around them. Therefore, the additional chapters and exercises are included to explain some rudimentary concepts in more detail.

How to Use the Guide with Your Clients

The guide is divided into six parts and 48 chapters. Some of the chapters should be read by all clients, others you can assign on an individual basis. In general, it is best to present all the concepts and exercises first in your therapeutic sessions and then assign the appropriate chapters for review afterwards. Later in the sequence of therapeutic sessions, your clients can read the chapters and do the exercises on their own. To this end, I have written the chapters so they can be understood without your instructions. I have found, however, that many people misunderstand or reject some aspect of what they read, or believe a concept is simple because it was presented simply and are unaware of its complexities, so it is always important that you review your client's work later.

Part I: ABCs

The first seven chapters give the foundations of CRT. Your clients should read all of them. You can decide which chapters you want to discuss in your sessions in more detail. Clients will need your help in understanding the difference between thoughts, feelings, and situations (Chapter 2, "The ABCs of Cognitive Restructuring Therapy"); they many disagree that their beliefs are so important (Chapter 3, "Our Mighty Thoughts"); and they will probably have difficulty finding the core beliefs underlying the critical events that have occurred in their lives (Chapter 5, "Critical Life Events" and Chapter 7, "Core Beliefs").

Part II: Types of Mistaken Beliefs

I list 11 common beliefs that cause many people problems. Have your client read the beliefs that you think may apply to them.

Part III: Analyzing Your Beliefs

Some cognitive therapists do not pay special attention to this section of counseling, but CRT therapists do. If you look at CRT as a three-step process (i.e., finding the core cognitions, deciding which beliefs are useless or invalid, and changing damaging beliefs), then this section concerns the second step. After people have identified their key beliefs, values, and attitudes, this section helps people to make a decision about which beliefs are damaging and had best be thrown into the trash, and which ones are useful and helpful and had best be kept.

Part III gives people six basic tools to help them make a decision. All clients should read the first and last chapters in this section (Chapter 19, "Analyzing Beliefs" and 24, "Our Cosmic Dance"). You can assign the other chapters based on what you think would be most helpful for a particular client. Chapter 20, "Gut Feelings," is for those clients who are too enamored with their own intuition; Chapter 21, "Who Says So?," is for those who are overly dependent on authority; Chapter 22, "Finding the Good Reason," is for those who rationalize extensively; and Chapter 23, "The Law of Parsimony," is for your more sophisticated clients who want a more involved exploration of personal epistemology.

Part IV: Changing Beliefs

At the heart of cognitive therapy is changing dysfunctional beliefs. This is where the art and science of being a therapist comes into play. You can select from any of the hundreds of techniques offered in the *Handbooks* or you can choose your own from the substantial body of knowledge underlying all cognitive therapies. In this guide I only provide eight elementary techniques to give your client a basic understanding of what is required to change a thought. I discuss countering thoughts, looking for alternative beliefs, removing past perceptions, shifting the way we perceive, and living up to our own values. It would probably be best if all your clients read Chapter 25, "Countering," and Chapter 30, "Quantum Leaps."

For the remaining chapters, you can assign them according to need: Chapter 26, "Alternative Beliefs," is for those who only need to follow a simple technique to change some of their mistaken past beliefs; Chapter 27, "Changing the Past," is for clients who would benefit from a slightly more involved technique; Chapter 28, "Making Choices" and Chapter 29, "Breaking Through the Dam," are for those who are stuck in ruts and need to break loose. The last two, Chapter 31, "Living by Our Core Values" and Chapter 32, "Beyond Payoffs," have been helpful to many. You can choose any chapters that you feel are most appropriate. These chapters should provide a good foundation for the more advanced techniques that only you, as their therapist, can offer.

Part V: Seven Beliefs to Be Trashed

In this section, I provide some basic arguments and counterarguments against seven specific beliefs that have caused trouble for many people. Assign only those chapters that are relevant to your client. The subtitles of these chapters identify what specific beliefs are addressed.

Part VI: Specific Problems

Since most people are more aware of their problems than their causes, in this section I focus on some common problems people have, such as anxiety, getting along with others, depression, and intimate relationships. Of course, these are huge topics that I do not even attempt to cover completely. Clients will need your therapy to sufficiently address these areas. All I am attempting to do in this section is to plant a small idea, a cognitive "seed," which may give people a new angle to consider when they work on the problem. If you believe that your client would benefit from having this cognitive seed planted, assign them the appropriate chapters.

Your Suggestions

CRT has developed and matured primarily because of the many thousands of therapists who have used it. Over the last 30 years I have received hundreds of comments, letters, and emails from full-time therapists who have read one of my books or articles, attended one of my workshops, or listened to one of my seminars. They reported on their successes and failures, presented process or outcome research data from their clients, offered advice, or gave suggestions to improve CRT. From their feedback, CRT has grown immensely.

I wish to continue this process. I can be reached by email: rian@hgea.net. Of course, emails can change quite frequently, so you can always get in touch with me by contacting my publisher: W. W. Norton & Company, Inc., 500 Fifth Avenue, New York, New York, 10110.

References

The primary sources for the material in this book are my books written for professionals, especially, *The New Handbook of Cognitive Therapy Techniques* (McMullin, 2000). In the *New Handbook*, I list over 1,000 citations. Anyone interested in the documentation or support of my ideas should refer to this and my other professional works. The references included here are only those works specifically referred to in *this* text.

Asch, S.E., (1955). Opinions and social pressure. *Scientific America, 193,* 31–35.

Bakker, T. (1982). *Run to the roar.* Harrison, AR: New Leaf Press.

Block, H. R. & Yuker, H. E. (1989). The Mediterranean Sea. In *Can You Believe Your Eyes* (p. 38). NY: Garner Press.

Crutchfield, R. A. (1955). Conformity and character. *American Psychologist, 10,* 191–198.

Dallenbach, K. (1951). A puzzle-picture with a new principle of concealment. *American Journal of Psychology, 64,* 431–433.

Ellis, A. (2004a). *Rational emotive behavior therapy: It works for me—it can work for you.* Amherst, NY: Prometheus Books.

———. (2004b). *The road to tolerance: The philosophy of rational emotive behavior therapy.* Amherst, NY: Prometheus Books.

Epictetus. (1952). *The discourses of Epictetus* (G. Long, Trans.). Chicago: University of Chicago/Encyclopedia Britannica.

Fisher, H. V. (2004). *Why we love: The nature and chemistry of romantic love.* NY: Henry Holt.

Gendlin, E. T. (1996). *Focusing-oriented psychotherapy: A manual of the experiential method.* NY: Guilford Press.

Gilliard, T. E. (1953). New Guinea's rare birds and stone age men. *National Geographic 102*(4), 421–488.

Hill, W. W. (1915). *Puck.* November 6.

Lakoff, George. (1987). *Women, fire and dangerous things: What categories reveal about the mind.* Chicago: University of Chicago Press.

Maultsby, M. C. (1984). *Rational behavior therapy.* Englewood Cliffs, NJ: Prentice-Hall.

McMullin, R. E. (1986). *Handbook of cognitive therapy techniques.* NY: W. W. Norton & Company.

———. (2000). *The new handbook of cognitive therapy techniques.* NY: W. W. Norton & Company.

McMullin, R. E. & Gehlhaar, P. (2004). *Bogus beliefs: An exposé of the core attitudes that keep chemically addicted people from recovering.* Kaneohe, Hawaii: Sauria Press.

McMullin, R. E. & Giles, T. R. (1981). *Cognitive-behavior therapy: A restructuring approach.* NY: Grune & Stratton.

Milgram, S. (1983). *Obedience to authority.* New York: Perennial.

———. (1992). *The individual in a social world: Essays and experiments.* (2nd ed.). J. Sabinir & M. Silver, Eds. NY: McGraw-Hill.

Quine, W. V. & Ullian, J. S. (1978). *The web of belief* (2nd ed.). NY: Random House.

Rogers, C. R. (1961). *On becoming a person: A therapist's view of psychotherapy.* Boston: Houghton Mifflin.

Solomon, M. (1995). *Mozart: A life.* NY: Harper Collins.

Twain, M. (1962). Letter to the earth. In B. DeVoto (Ed.), *Mark Twain: Letters from the earth* (pp. 103–107). NY: Crest. (Original work published 1887.)

———. (1996). *The diaries of Adam and Eve.* NY: Oxford University Press. (Original work published 1906.)

Twain, M. (1897). *Following the equator: A journey around the world.* Hartford, CT: Edition.

Vonnegut, K. (1985). *Galapagos: Where life is just a state of mind.* NY: Dell.

Index